MELODRAMA

MELODRAMA

GUEST EDITOR
DANIEL GEROULD

JEANINE PARISIER PLOTTEL, General Editor

CHAMPLAIN COLLEGE

NEW YORK LITERARY FORUM

NEW YORK • 1980

Library of Congress Cataloging in Publication Data

Main entry under title:

Melodrama

    (New York literary forum; 7 ISSN 0149-1040)
    Bibliography: p.
    Includes index.
    1. Melodrama. I. Gerould, Daniel Charles, 1928–
II. Series: New York literary forum; v. 7.
PN1912.M4   809'.91   79-52615
ISBN 0-931196-06-X

A good melodrama is a more difficult thing to write than all this clever-clever comedy: one must go straight to the core of humanity to get it, and if it is only good enough, why, there you have Lear or Macbeth.

Bernard Shaw, letter to Ellen Terry, 1896

I'm still interested in melodrama. I don't see why there shouldn't be a little bit of melodrama. It's a play, you see, the theatre's make-believe.

Sean O'Casey, on The Bishop's Bonfire, *1955*
(from E. Mikhail, The Sting and the Twinkle: Conversations with O'Casey)

Melodrama is perennial and . . . the craving for it is perennial and must be satisified. . . . So long as novels are written, the possibilities of melodrama must from time to time be re-explored. . . . You cannot define Drama and Melodrama so that they shall be reciprocally exclusive; great drama has something melodramatic in it, and the best melodrama partakes of the greatness of drama.

T. S. Eliot, "Wilkie Collins and Dickens," 1927

CONTENTS

Preface

Illegitimate and semiliterate offspring of Gothic romance and heroic pantomime, castout grandchild of the *drame bourgeois* and sentimental novel, melodrama is an upstart genre not yet two hundred years old, but this guttersnipe of dramatic forms has proved so tenacious and full of crude strength that it was able to impart vigor and color to a languid nineteenth-century theater and even found a temporary home in the higher class fictional worlds of Balzac and Dickens, Dostoevsky and James. More recently, this once despised orphan has been adopted by the avant-garde, first in the Soviet Union immediately after the revolution and then in the United States during the disruptive 1960s and 1970s. Ever-present in our popular literature, film, and television, melodrama is now so deeply embedded in our sensibility and consciousness that the word is always on the tongue as a term of critical abuse or praise and—more rarely—as an analytical device.

This issue of *New York Literary Forum* is devoted to melodrama, its standard formulas and surprising innovations, its paranoiac vision, its polarities of innocence adrift in a dark night of urban crime and depravity, its fascination with murder, blood lust, and vindictiveness, and its spectacular and naively ingenious effects designed to scare us, shock us, and make us laugh and cry. Michael Kirby strikes the keynote in his "Melodrama Manifesto of Structuralism," asserting that, for all its casual familiarity, melodrama, like no other genre, is available for whatever use—serious or frivolous—we wish to make of it. The rest of the issue is an extended exploration of this truth, long known to writers and artists who find themselves drawn to melodrama for the primitive force, theatricality, and intensities and perversities that can be extracted from it.

In Part 1 eminent practitioners of the genre look at Sweeney Todd, the Demon Barber of Fleet Street—one of the three great nineteenth-century melodramatic colossi (the other two, *Tour de Nesle* and *Two Orphans* receive special scrutiny in later sections). Many years before Zola and naturalism, the melodramatists, exploiting the scenic delights of exactly reproduced milieu, showed men and women on the job—in cottages, mines, and factories—and one of the beauties of the tale of Sweeney Todd, the barber, is that the hero's place of work and the tools of his trade cease to be background and become the murderous agents of the plot. And the cannibalism of Mrs. Lovett's meat pies clearly announces that in the slums of London man eats his fellow man.

Stephen Sondheim, in "Larger than Life: Reflections on Melodrama and Sweeney Todd," declares melodrama (along with its obverse side farce) to be the heart of the theatrical experience and his favorite among the genres but cautions that it must be played seriously and approached as high art. Only on these conditions could the Demon Barber of Fleet Street become a tragic figure worthy of operatic treatment. Christopher Bond's "The Theater of Pyramids: (and a Camel)" is the eloquent plea by an actor, director, and playwright for exciting visual theater, rather than boring verbal drama. In the quest for what will amaze and astound our eyes, Bond suggests that there is much to be learned from nineteenth-century melodrama, the last truly populist theater. In "Further Adventures of Sweeney Todd Alias Bertolli," part of an ongoing collage serial by Cozette de Charmoy, the infamous barber undergoes further metamorphoses into a Faustian hero of the Industrial Revolution and protean romantic figure, who even meets his counterpart Lenin in Zurich. By means of precise shapes and unexpected images, Cozette de Charmoy projects Sweeney Todd into the world of our dreams. The music-hall ballad, "Sweeney Todd the Barber" by Robert Weston (as sung by Stanley Holloway) transforms the grim exploits into a macabre example of cockney humor and wordplay. A concise Toddography by Daniel Gerould traces a century and a half of the Demon Barber in the arts from the lowest Victorian pennydreadfuls and bloodbath theaters to John Cranko's choreography at the Royal Ballet Company and Sondheim's innovative musical thriller.

Part 2 of the volume considers the position of melodrama in the theatrical life of several different cultures where it has been specially prized. The melodramatic tableau, coming at act and scene endings, is a special trademark of the genre, commented upon by most writers on the subject. In "Speaking Pictures," Martin Meisel finds the origins of pictorial stagecraft in Diderot's theories and late eighteenth-century practice, judges the integration of player and scene a true theatrical revolution, and discovers an analogue for the dramatic tableau in the popular Victorian parlor game of *tableau vivant*. Mel Gordon's "Yiddish Theater in New York, 1900" delves into the rich lore about melodramatic actors and acting on the lower East Side at the turn of the century and explains why melodrama became a central moment in the lives of poor emigrants from Eastern Europe. A few years later in communist Russia the old genre made a startling comeback. During the great decade of Soviet theater immediately following the revolution, the outstanding directors and theorists of theater, such as Stanislavsky, Meyerhold, and Tairov, went back to melodrama, not as a fossilized and absurd form, but as a paradigm of theatrical vitality, and they discussed at length how it should be performed. In "Melodrama on the Soviet Stage, 1917–1928," Daniel Gerould and Julia Przyboś trace the rise and fall of melodrama on the Bolshevik stage, documenting the strong impact of American cinema and urbanism. Alma H. Law's "*Two Orphans* in Revolutionary Disguise" explores a significant instance of melodramatic cross-fertilization among film, drama, and literature in Soviet theater, providing a translation of the orgy scene from the Moscow Art Theater's *The Sisters Gerard*—a Marxist recasting of W. D. Griffith's *Orphans of the Storm* (itself a conflation of Dennery and Cormon's *Two Orphans* and Dicken's *Tale of Two Cities*).

From *Uncle Tom's Cabin* to Eugene O'Neill, American drama has shown a fondness for the excesses and overstatements of melodrama. In "Old Forms Enter the New American Theater: Shepard, Forman, Kirby, Ludlam," James Leverett describes how the current American avant-garde, rejecting the realistic tradition of the 1940s and 1950s, has looked over its shoulder at melodrama with feelings of nostalgia for its childishly exuberant theatricality. By stripping the genre of its sharply delineated framework of good and evil and fragmenting its rigid conventions, Shepard, Forman, Kirby, and Ludlam—Leverett argues—have released melodrama's primal theatrical energy of aggression, anxiety, and eroticism and let them float freely in the abstract.

Popular melodrama can also be a weapon for social criticism. It was not in the multireel feature film, but in the multivolume *roman feuilleton*, that the genre reached its highest level of complexity as a picture of reality, no matter how hyperbolic, feverish, or distored the melodramatic imagination might be. Part 3 considers two of the vast social fictions of nineteenth-century melodrama as well as an ironic coda to the tradition that refashions the genre. Peter Brooks and Daniel Burt penetrate into the *mysteries*—the sordid underside of affluent society—of two great melodramatic cities, Paris and London, in works by Eugène Sue and G. W. M. Reynolds. In "The Mark of the Beast: Prostitution, Melodrama, an Narrative," Brooks shows how Sue in the process of writing *Les Mystères de Paris* began to imitate his fictive hero and became involved probing in the real world the social sores presented in the novel. Brooks's study of melodrama as a vehicle for changing the world leads him to an exploration of the place of prostitution in the nineteenth-century life and literature and from there to speculation about the nature of narrative. Burt's "A Victorian Gothic: G. W. M. Reynolds's *The Mysteries of London*" plunges into the horrific core of the most popular British "penny blood" of the century. The sensational crimes and horrors of city life depicted in Reynolds's twelve-volume thriller have their parallels in other literature of the period: Henry Mayhew's *London Labour and the London Poor*, London street ballads, and Dickens's novels. Zdzisław Najder in "Joseph Conrad's *The Secret Agent*" argues that Conrad by combining incompatibles—irony and melodrama—creates a new departure for the genre in the interest of unusual esthetic effects and a specific intellectual message about the nature of reality.

Film and melodrama, the subject of Part 4, provide the natural focus for much twentieth-century investigation of the genre. More than any other medium, the moving pictures satisified melodrama's boundless hunger for the visually spectacular and quickly superseded the stage as the sources of thrilling action and simplistic morality for masss audiences. Albert Bermel and Stanley Kauffmann both direct attention to the mutual attraction between melodrama and farce, that curious pair at opposite ends of the generic spectrum which Sondheim finds quintessentially theatrical. Reminding us that genre distinctions are slippery, Bermel in "Where Melodrama Meets Farce" signals the interplay and oscillation between the two forms at high points of tension in films such as Buster Keaton's *Our Hospitality*, where, during a rescue sequence, audience gasps and laughs grow almost indistinguishable. Stanley Kauffmann's "Melodrama and Farce: A Note on a Fusion in Film" demonstrates how the very nature of slapstick comedy was modified because of a change in film length; when the film clowns moved into six-reel feature films, they chose melodrama as their armature. Commenting on the kinships between the two genres, both built on fear and threat of violence, Kauffmann points out that parodies of melodrama—performed as afterpieces—go back to the mid-nineteenth century and were written for, and enjoyed by, the same audiences who minutes before had shuddered and wept at the terrible dangers menacing the heroine. The sequence: melodrama-farce is a psychologically sound one.

Wylie Sypher's "Romeo and Juliet Are Dead: Melodrama of the Clinical" is concerned with what is unhealthy in a melodrama of disaster when it grows subjective and claustrophobic. Comparing and contrasting *Romeo and Juliet* and *The Last Tango in Paris* as studies in erotic automation, Sypher finds melodrama's binary coding—as opposed to tragedy's bifocal system—responsible for the film's disturbing clinical pathology. In "Melodrama, the Movies, and Genre," John Fell applies techniques of cinema genre study to melodramatic conventions using *The Invasion of the Body Snatchers*, *The Adventures of Sherlock Holmes*, and the early sound films of Hitchcock to produce an analytic schema for science fiction, adventure, and detective movies. In "The Moral Ecology of Melodrama: The Family Plot and *Magnificent Obsession*," Noël Carroll sees the recent resurgence of melodrama extolling the reconstituted family, in films such as *International Velvet* and *Uncle Joe Shannon*, as a reaffirmation of traditional values and traces back the ancestry of these works to Douglas Dirk's *Magnificent Obsession*, where morality is treated as part of the basic structure of the universe. A revival of old-fashioned melodramatic plots and conventions—with lost and recovered parents and children—can serve to support moral order and equilibrium in human affairs.

Part 5 assembles a number of texts and documents that illuminate the history and development of nineteenth-century melodrama but have not before been available for modern readers. *The Forest of Bondy, or The Dog of Montargis* is a full-length play by René Charles Guilbert de Pixérécourt, the father of melodrama. With its falsely accused but congenitally speechless young lover saved by the canine hero, Dragon, equally incapable of speech (except for occasional, expressive barking), Pixérécourt's famous play celebrates the theatrical value of muteness and the ethical value of loyalty, sometimes stronger in animal than in man, and became the model in the theater for numerous "dumb beast" melodramas, including a *Hamlet* in which the Prince delivered the soliloquies to his dog, and on the screen for such stars as Rin-Tin-Tin and Lassie. In the French original, the villain kills Dragon offstage in the second act. In the anonymous English version (appearing in this issue of *New York Literary Forum*), which was used for London and New York productions in 1816 and captures the period flavor of the work, not only is Dragon allowed to live, but he pursues the villain to his death in the final scene—the only denouement possible for a dog-loving Anglo-Saxon audience. In the "Historical Note" that served as a preface to the melodrama, *The Forest of Bondy*, Pixérécourt substantiates the historicity of the Renaissance dog who carried out God's judgment and brought his master's murderer to justice; the father of melodrama even supplies a learned bibliography that might have puzzled the public at a performance of his play, since he himself had declared, "I write for those who cannot read."

By applying formalist poetics to Dumas père's *La Tour de Nesle*, the erudite Russian playwright and theoretician of drama Vladimir Vol'kenshtein reveals the elegant structural patterning that lies behind the immense theatrical tensions of the work. In selections from his *Memoirs* Dumas reveals himself to be a self-conscious artist and craftsman, cleverly contriving thrilling and terrifying effects and not hesitating to find analogues in Sophocles and Shakespeare. In his essay "Fear in Literature," the grand master of the Grand Guignol André de Lorde explores the psychological basis of the eternal human longing to be terrified. (In fact, during World War I, special performances of the Grand Guignol were organized for wounded soldiers and troops home from the front on leave.) Citing Poe as his teacher, de Lorde argues for precision and realism in horror and describes the new areas for the tale of terror opened up by science in the twentieth century.

As an afterpiece, the documents section closes with a parodistic sketch, "The Orphan's Dowry"—which we can regard as the heritage of melodrama—viewed by the French humorist Cami with a loving eye for the absurdities of the genre.

Finally, the present state of scholarship in melodrama is reflected in Forum Reviews of contemporary books on the subject, while the full bibliography and index serve as an invaluable tool for the serious scholar.

This melodrama issue of *New York Literary Forum* is a unique mixture of critical, creative, and scholarly work. It brings together in a single volume a wide range of opinions and approaches by American, British, French, Polish, and Russian authors (among whom a composer-lyricist, actor-director-playwright, and graphic artist), all celebrating the vitality and importance of this most popular of genres. The twenty-four contributions include manifesto, song, collage, memoir, drama, and parody, as well as essay, history, and analysis. Like a good melodrama, the volume has the variety and breadth of appeal capable of attracting not only the serious student of the genre but also the amateur who simply enjoys the high spirits, thrills, laughter, and tears of melodrama.

MELODRAMA MANIFESTO OF STRUCTURALISM

Michael Kirby

Melodrama has been scorned and rejected. It is laughed at behind its back—and to its face. "Melodramatic," which means "like melodrama," is used as a pejorative term.

Melodrama is thought to be obvious, exaggerated, and trite. Its characters are considered one-dimensional, its plots contrived. It is a form for the unintellectual, the easily mystified, the depressed, and the escapist.

Melodrama is compared to real life and is found wanting in every respect. That is not the way people behave; things do not happen like that. Melodrama is deprecated because it is not a realistic copy of the empirical world.

Melodrama is attended and defended by some so that they may make fun of it. It is self-parody, it is cute, it is childlike, it is quaint and charming burlesque. To laugh at what the common person enjoys makes these people feel superior; the intellectual gloats over the simplicity of others.

Melodrama is performed by some who, to their secret shame, are attracted to it. It becomes hidden in ridicule, its traits exaggerated, its tone completely changed. The condescending and patronizing attitude of the intellectuals dominates the performance; melodrama devours itself.

Structuralism may use any materials, melodrama among them, to achieve its goals. In melodrama, Structuralism finds clear, dynamic structures that repeat themselves in limited variations and versions. The code of these archetypal structures may be deciphered, simplified, magnified, emphasized to make the structure of the Structuralist play the most important element.

Structuralism is not involved with ethics or metaphysics, with visions of goodness or truth; it contains no moral or message and does not preach or teach. Thus, melodrama may be used by Structuralism to the extent that the traditional form is unreal and does not refer to the real world. Structuralism accepts the artificiality of melodrama.

Structuralism refers to art—at times to the form of art known as melodrama—rather than to the external mundane realities. It sees in melodrama the model of theatrical reality believed and accepted by most of the people and treats this reality in a real fashion. In borrowing the stage language of the majority, Structuralism stands against style for its own sake, against elegance and chic, against the arty and the artsy.

Structuralism knows that melodrama is neither good nor bad, engrossing nor laughable, profound or superficial. Melodrama is material available to everyone, its devices, characters and situations instantly known, implanted by the culture in the psyche of each of its members. This material may easily be aroused, activiated, used.

Structuralism recognizes in melodrama psychic traps—snares laid in childhood and adolescence—that are waiting to be sprung. The triggers of these traps are not in extended exposition, explanation, and preparation. Instantaneous, direct, and powerful, they are released by indications, hints, individual traits and characteristics, details that suggest and call up a multitude of immediate associations—and there is no defense against them, even for the intelligent and the informed.

PART 1

SWEENEY TODD: THE DEMON BARBER OF FLEET STREET

Larger than Life: Reflections on Melodrama and Sweeney Todd

STEPHEN SONDHEIM

The Nature of Melodrama

I have the feeling that melodrama has its own meaning for different people. Some think of melodrama as villains twirling mustaches and lashing young virgins to railroad tracks, in other words, something that is to be spoofed or is funny. I think that's always implicit when someone says, "Oh, stop being so melodramatic about it."

There are others—and I am one of them—who think of melodrama simply as being high theater, theater in whatever form you care to think of theater—what I am talking about is the kind of theater that takes place in an auditorium with a proscenium arch. Thus, for me, melodrama is theater that is larger than life—in emotion, in subject, and in complication of plot. I do not believe that a melodrama has to be bloody, although many people associate melodrama with blood. Actually, there is a great deal of high drama that I consider to be melodrama. In spite of its simplicity of plot, *Oedipus Rex*, in my opinion, is very close to melodrama. It is a mystery with a stunning surprise solution (surprising for the hero, that is), and

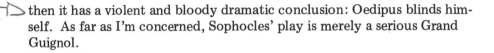

then it has a violent and bloody dramatic conclusion: Oedipus blinds himself. As far as I'm concerned, Sophocles' play is merely a serious Grand Guignol.

Melodrama and Grand Guignol

I saw some Grand Guignol in Paris in the 1960s, although by then it was no longer what it once had been. I went because I wanted to see what Grand Guignol was like. There were three extremely bloody one-act plays. Each had a plot at least as simple as *Oedipus*, only far less interesting, and each had one climactic bloody, gory effect, exactly like *Oedipus*. Actually, to be precise, that was true of two of the plays; the third had about seventy-five gory effects—it was nothing more than a series of disembowelments carried out on various people who simply happened to wander in. The three plays were extremely boring because, bloody as the effects were, if you were squeamish, you hardened yourself, and if you weren't squeamish, it was just red tomato sauce and a lot of people in terrible make-up overacting. Melodrama, for me, has to be a great deal purer than that, and it has to be at least as interesting as other drama.

Melodrama and Farce

Another aspect of melodrama that interests me is that it is the obverse side of farce, which is another favorite form of mine. We find the same qualities in both. Complications of plot, larger-that-life characters, grand gestures, and nonnaturalistic acting are common to both melodrama and farce. The only difference is that in melodrama what we could call tragic events occur, events with truly unpleasant consequences. In farce annoying events happen with comic and generally happy consequences, although there are a number of farces that could be viewed as unpleasant, particularly in the twentieth century when writers started to create black farces, as, for example, Joe Orton did.

The point is that melodrama and farce are essentially the same form, and they represent for me the heart of the theatrical experience. They offer what I do not find in other narrative media. I suppose that one might sometimes find it in novels, if one's imagination is large enough. But not in the movies—movies are a reportorial form—and two-dimensional at that—and there is no direct communication with the audience: the film is a presented object. Television is perhaps even one step further removed and, at the same time, one step closer to the spectator. It is a small, cozy form, and anyone attempting to do anything larger than life on television makes an absolute fool of himself.

The theater is the one place where you can create larger than life, and melodrama and farce represent the two forms best suited to that kind of circusy quality that I love in the theater.

Earlier Sweeney Todd Plays and Bond's Modern Version

Now I had never seen a good Grand Guignol melodrama, and Sweeney
Todd, I must stress, is a special kind of melodrama: Grand Guignol (originally a character in the French puppet theater), which is always associated
with lots of blood and outlandishness. All the Sweeney Todds that existed before Christopher Bond's version were indeed bloody, although nowhere near as bloody as those one-act horror plays I saw in Paris. In fact,
all these earlier Sweeney Todd plays were very boring and essentially over-
written one-act dramas with one or two central incidents and a great deal
of padding. In the nineteenth century I imagine there was also liberal use
of thunder sheet effects and lots of emoting, as opposed to acting. All the
interest and suspense had to do with the scenic effects and with wonder-
ing whether or not somebody was going to get killed in the chair. Todd
was merely a villain, and Mrs. Lovett was merely an accomplice—and a
secondary one at that. There was no attitude or tone. It was simply a
matter of seeing the villain get caught in the end.

Christopher Bond humanized all the characters and gave the story
motivation which had never existed before in the earlier versions of
Sweeney Todd. Yet while enlarging the human dimensions of the play,
Bond remained true to the melodramatic tradition. Everyone in Bond's
version is larger than life; the characters are not real people. The events
are extraordinary, melodramatic in the sense that they are larger than life;
in real life there may have been mass murderers and even ones who used
razors—but their stories were not compressed and heightened in this way.
Sweeney Todd is larger than life as a story and larger than life in technique.

Take the matter of language. Hugh Wheeler, who adapted Bond's
play and prepared the libretto, pointed out to me that Bond had written
half of his play in blank verse, but that the lines were not typed out as
blank verse. All the speeches of the judge, Todd, and the two young lovers are written in iambic meter, and the lower-class characters are given
nonmetered dialogue. This produces a very subtle effect when you read
the play. Beyond the formality of the diction, there is a kind of stateli-
ness in some of the characters that creates an odd juxtaposition with the
rag-tag rhythms in the lower-class figures.

Attention to details of this sort gives Bond's *Sweeney Todd* greater
depth than the usual melodrama, which is quite shallow. It is exactly this
added dimension that we wanted in our musical version, and when Hugh
and I first sat down to work on the piece, we were interested in retaining
the same spirit that had attracted me to the play.

On Taking Melodrama Seriously

Since I hadn't wanted to do the piece alone, I asked Hugh Wheeler—with
whom I'd had two lovely collaborations, three actually, or one and two

halves. Hugh was also a mystery story writer and British born and therefore he understood the whole tradition. He was perhaps the only person in the United States to whom I could say, "Sweeney Todd" and who wouldn't say, "Who's that?"

Hugh and I talked about it and wondered whether we could get away with doing the only thing that would be fun: treating Sweeney Todd seriously. Otherwise it would not be worth undertaking. I do not enjoy camp, spoof melodrama, like *Dracula*, for example. It's not that *Dracula* is not well done; it is simply not a form that I enjoy. I like my melodrama straight. I am a fan of one or two Hammer films; the best Dracula I ever saw is *Horror of Dracula* (the first Hammer film on the subject), which I think is the finest horror film ever made. The reason, once again, is that it takes its melodrama seriously and humanizes the story. For example, it leaves out the whole legend of Dracula turning into a bat so that right away you can believe what is happening because everything is vaguely within the realm of human possibility, even though it's all exaggerated, even though it's all melodramatized and larger than life.

We wanted to take Sweeney Todd just as seriously as that. I wanted to make a melodrama but with a twentieth-century sensibility. Perhaps in a hundred years, or even in fifty years, audiences would hiss the villain and make fun of the play. I wouldn't mind if it acquired that patina, but I wanted it taken seriously by an audience today, the way the original Sweeney Todd was taken seriously in the nineteenth century.

Of course, if it were presented today, the only way we could possibly look at the original Sweeney Todd—without being bored to death—would be to giggle at it, but I would like the twentieth-century audience to experience exactly what the nineteenth-century audience did. And if, in the second act of our show, you look at the frozen faces of all the hip people from 1979, who are glued to their seats because characters with grotesque make-up are slitting each other's throats and shedding stage blood, you will see this effect being produced. But if you told these twentieth-century spectators, "Now this is what the Victorian audience felt, and here is a play that affected them just the way you've been affected," and you showed them the old Sweeney Todd melodrama, they simply wouldn't believe it. That is what we set out to accomplish.

I wanted to scare an audience out of its wits but not by suddenly opening doors in the dark, which can always terrify audiences and produce little shrieks of surprise, but that is not the kind of scare I am referring to. The true terror of melodrama comes from its revelations about the frightening power of what is inside human beings. And if you write about kings and queens and are a great poet, you end up with a first-class tragedy; if you write about ordinary people and are an ordinary writer, you end up with a melodrama. That's exactly what this show is.

Shakespeare, who had to write plays that would entertain everybody, created melodrama in the form of *Hamlet* and *Othello* and *Macbeth*—all of which are blood-and-thunder melodramas. And when it is done right, melodrama really does entertain everybody. The only difference is that Shakespeare is Shakespeare. If he had been given the plot of Sweeney Todd, we would have seen what could have been made of it. I say this not out of false modesty but only to indicate that the dividing line between melodrama and tragedy is not necessarily one of intention, which is what they teach you in school. I think it's in the execution. I do not think that there is any difference in intention between Shakespeare's writing *Hamlet* and our writing *Sweeney Todd.* That is not to say that I thought we were writing a tragedy; rather, I think that Shakespeare thought he was writing a melodrama.

We wanted to establish a serious mood from the beginning, and two things that helped were the set and calling the play a musical thriller. One of the miracles of the set is that when the spectators first come into the theater and see it, they know that we're not kidding. Right away there is nothing about that set to suggest that a curtain is going to drop from the flies, plop on the floor, and disclose bats painted on it. Because of the solidity and scruffiness of the set, even if you wanted to do a spoof of melodrama, it would be impossible to get a laugh, except for the kind of laughs we get, which are character laughs. But for the make-fun-of-it laugh, the set is far too brooding a presence.

A Musical Thriller

There were a number of reasons why I wanted to call the show a musical thriller and not a musical melodrama. The purpose of calling a show one thing or another is to give the audience some idea of what they are coming to see. I would not want to call *Sweeney Todd* simply a musical comedy. I remember when we did *West Side Story* that a number of people walked out during the show, resentful that it was not what they had expected. Someone coming to see a lot of girls kicking up their legs (what we call a tired businessman's show) and getting *West Side Story* would have every reason to resent it and want his money back because the play had been misadvertised. The word *musical* means just a musical. But a musical what?

Now if we called *Sweeney Todd* a musical melodrama, it would have unfailingly suggested making fun of the genre, with villains galloping across the stage, the heroine tied to the railroad tracks, and the audience cheering and clapping. Starting with the subtitle, "A Musical Thriller," and going on to the set and the music, we have made sure that by the end of the opening number the audience will know what they are in for.

In the early previews we used to have a few unwelcome giggles, when, for example, both Sweeney and Mrs. Lovett rose out of the grave, as they originally did before we changed it so that just Sweeney appears from out of the earth. When they both did, a couple of people in the audience would occasionally giggle. They thought, "That's a stage elevator bringing two people out of the stage floor; am I supposed to take this seriously, or am I to think that it's a bit tacky?'' It was an honest mistake because no one had clued them in; it was too early in the previews for anyone to know what this new animal was that was opening at the Uris.

By the time we got into our second week of previews and the show was starting to play with more sureness (which happens after the first few performances) and the rapport between the audience and the cast had gained confidence, it was easy for Len Cariou, who by then was rising out of the grave alone, merely by the baleful look in his eye to tell the audience, "Don't laugh at this, it isn't funny.'' He didn't have to open his mouth; all he had to do was to look at them.

There was already some ambience in the theater, and a little word of mouth had gone around that it was what we eventually called a musical thriller. Thriller is one of those words that people take more seriously; it has all the implications of the colorful part of melodrama without any of the comic inferences that contemporary audiences would draw from the word.

Sweeney Todd at the Stratford East

It all came about not because I decided in advance to write a melodrama but because I happened to be in London with *Gypsy* in 1974 when Christopher Bond's *Sweeney Todd* was playing at the Stratford East. I had heard of Sweeney Todd, because I am an Anglophile, but I had never seen or read anything about him. So I thought it would be fun to see the play, and I just had a wonderful time.

Stratford East is a workingman's theater, attached to a pub; you can bring your beer back into the auditorium and during the interval there's lots of group singing and clunking of beer steins and things like that. A totally informal theater, with quite a small stage, where the play was done in an informal way but with professional actors and directed by a professional. I liked it a lot; it had a combination of charm and creepiness. I don't remember being particularly frightened. I think our version is much more frightening, even though the plot, especially in the first half, is almost identical. But it must have scared me somewhat.

I remember thinking on my way home that it would make an opera, and I spoke to John Dexter, one of the directors of the Metropolitan Opera, who at that time was directing in the West End in London. In the course of our conversation I asked him if he thought that Sweeney Todd might make an opera, and he said absolutely and that encouraged me to look into the rights for it. That's how it all started. It was seeing the play at the Stratford East that sparked my desire to write a melodramatic piece—I certainly wasn't thinking about melodrama. I had written melodrama before although I didn't do the music in the case of *West Side Story*; after all, *Romeo and Juliet* is a classic melodrama. So I wasn't

A scene from the Broadway production of *Sweeney Todd: The Demon Barber of Fleet Street* with Joaquin Romaguera and Len Cariou.

looking for a melodrama; it was just there.

A Melodrama of Revenge

As I worked on Sweeney Todd, I realized more what I liked about it. It was quite easy to write, a lot of hard work, but I understood it very well; they were characters I could relate to. And the collaboration with Hugh Wheeler and Hal Prince was comfortable since we had done three shows together before. During the writing of the first few songs, I discovered very clearly what I related to, on certain emotional levels, in the story.

I believe that there's a little of everything in all of us, and most people can understand and identify with any emotion; the writer simply must draw the audience into the feelings of the characters that he has created on the stage. *Sweeney Todd*, which after all is a melodrama about revenge, poses a problem for a lot of people who refuse to admit to themselves that they have a capacity for vengeance, but I think it's a universal trait. I didn't see any reason why we couldn't do what Christopher Bond had done, which is to make Sweeney a tragic hero instead of a villain, because there is something of Sweeney in all of us, I believe.

A couple of the critics who disliked the show brought up the fact that they couldn't relate to anyone like Sweeney or have sympathy for him, since they were totally unvengeful themselves. These critics claimed that at the end of the show when the cast points around the auditorium that we were spreading the message that each of us is Sweeney Todd, which, of course, is not what I said and not what the lyric says but merely what the critics, who cannot stand to face the fact that there is some vengefulness in themselves, jumped to thinking. What I said and what the lyric very clearly states is that Sweeney—the spirit of Sweeney—is all around us, which is not the same thing as saying that each person in the auditorium is a multiple murderer.

Hangover Square and Bernard Herrmann

There is another reason why I personally was attracted to Sweeney. When I was fifteen I saw a movie that I adored; I sat through it twice, and I adored it partly because of the story and partly because of the music. The movie was *Hangover Square* (John Brahm, 20th Century, 1945), and it took place in Edwardian times (I was already a budding Anglophile). It concerned a composer who was way ahead of his time but who had the misfortune to be insane. The whole movie revolves around a piano concerto. The composer goes insane when he hears high notes, becomes schizophrenic, goes out, and murders people. Then, when he comes back and isn't insane, he's the most talented, perfect person in the world.

The reason the composer's music was way ahead of its time was that it was composed by Bernard Herrmann, who in 1945 when the film came out was writing movie music ahead of his time. It's easy to see why I identified with the film; I also thought it was the best story that I'd ever come across. The music—a one-movement piano concerto by Herrmann—knocked me out, and I wrote Herrmann a fan letter and asked him if it was going to be recorded. I got a nice reply. Herrmann said it would be recorded by Wallenstein and the San Francisco Sinfonietta. I waited and waited, but a year later it had never come out.

There was one page of the music shown on the screen. It was on the piano of the composer (played by Laird Cregar), and the first time I saw the movie, I sat through it twice so that I could memorize that piece of music. And I memorized it. Several years later the piano concerto did come out on record. Like most film composing buffs, I am a great fan of Herrmann's, and I've always wanted to write an answer to *Hangover Square*. That's another aspect to Sweeney Todd: the Bernard Herrmann version of the Sweeney Todd legend.

Sweeney Todd as a Melodrama of City Life

The urban setting was largely Hal Prince's invention. To me, Sweeney Todd was a story of personal obsession, and I really did not relate it very much to the milieu. I did a little bit, perhaps, when I referred to the class structure, because Christopher Bond does that. But the sense of the city, which is, in fact, a sense of the industrial revolution, machinery, steel, and all that, is very much Hal's approach to the material.

Hal Prince always likes to relate the work he does firmly and strongly to the society from which the material springs. That is why most of his shows are what I would call political shows. They are certainly social in that they relate powerfully to the environment. All the time I was writing Sweeney, Hal was trying to find a way of relating to the material because the idea of the kernel itself—melodrama—did not appeal to him. He does not like pure farce or pure melodrama very much. What he likes is social context, and therefore he loves social melodrama, social farce, social anything, as long as it is related to the world around it, so that it doesn't feel tiny. Hal would always prefer to err on the epic side—and he's right.

Now Hal firmly believes that Sweeney Todd is a story about how society makes you impotent, and impotence leads to rage, and rage leads to murder—and, in fact, to the breaking down of society. Fine. In order to make the point, he had to show the society in action. When he grew excited about that idea, I started not so much to make reference to it but to soak it into the score. It's more than likely that I got the idea for the title of the song "City on Fire" as a result of all that. And I'm a city boy myself; it's easy for me to relate to.

Comedy and Character in Melodrama

As Alfred Hitchcock made millions of dollars proving, there is a very thin line between melodrama and comedy, between being scared and laughing. An audience is more vulnerable to laughter—as we are in real life, not just in the theater—when it's most tense. If somebody is tense, you can tickle him; if he's relaxed, you can't.

The kind of comedy that is the most effective and valid on the stage is character comedy, and there are many possibilities for such comedy when the characters are as rich, though two-dimensional, as those in melodrama. The characters in *Sweeney Todd* are not complex; I don't think they should be. If you are to use complex characters in a melodrama, you really have to be somebody like Shakespeare to hold it together. The more outlandish things people do, the less likely we are to believe in them as complex human beings.

In *Sweeney*, Mrs. Lovett's venality can be treated in a comic way because that is what she is: a venal character. Certainly there are a few shadows and lights here and there, but primarily Mrs. Lovett is defined by her practicality combined with her greed. Todd is a man bent on revenge, he thinks of nothing else; that is his dimension. The fact that there is some tenderness and some love in the man is part of the shading and nothing more. And, unquestionably, each of the other characters can be described primarily in terms of a single noun or adjective.

When you have characters like that, you can get laughs quite easily. In fact, Shakespeare gets his laughs in *Hamlet* and *Macbeth* by providing us with characters of one or two dimensions, the Fop with a capital *F*, or what I call the drunken porter syndrome. You know when he brings the drunken porter on, it's to give you relief from the relentlessness of the melodrama. Although the Shakespeare scene is a total breakaway and what we try to do is to get laughs within the scenes, the principle is the same. The two colors are so close, melodramatic emotion and comic emotion, that it is fairly easy to skip from one side of the board to the other.

Of course, there is another kind of laughter, the so-called nervous laugh. For example, people laugh a great deal at the beggar woman in the first scene of *Sweeney Todd*. It is not simply the shock of her obscenity; there is something creepy about the beggar woman, and by laughing at somebody or something, we attempt to ward it off. Now it seems to me that this is a kind of laughter you can create only in melodrama where an audience will laugh to protect itself from being scared.

Sweeney Todd is a play about obsession, and when a person is totally obsessed, everything else becomes irrelevant. In this sense, Sweeney is detached; the only interest from which he is not detached is his obsession: his revenge. The only time this detachment is dramatized on stage, although Len Cariou uses it quite often in his acting performance, is in the second-act sequence called Johanna, where a succession of victims comes into the barber shop; Sweeney sings dreamily and in a detached way while

Another scene from the Broadway production of *Sweeney Todd.*

doing the most bloody things with his hands. That kind of schizoid split could be called detachment, and in fact, that is the word I used to describe to the actor how to play the scene.

But most of all, I think of Sweeney Todd as a person so passionate on one subject that he has no energy for anything else. He is hot after one goal, becomes sidetracked because of circumstances and goes crazy until suddenly another lucky chance happens and he is able to proceed along his path, destroying everything along the way. He is a man interested in only one thing, and he is animated only when he is in active pursuit of that goal.

All the characters in the play are boxed in; they have one thing they want. That is characteristic of both melodrama and farce: the characters can be outlined by the one thing they want. In *A Funny Thing Happened on the Way to the Forum*, Pseudolus wants his freedom, the hero wants the girl, the old man wants the young girl, the wife wants the husband, the pimp wants money, the old man wants his children: everyone is motivated entirely by one want.

The same thing is true in *Sweeney Todd.* Everybody is obsessed by one thing: the judge with his lechery, the beadle with his authority, Mrs. Lovett with her greed, Sweeney with his revenge, the boy Tobias with a home, and the lovers with each other. Everybody wants one thing, they all clash, and there is a terrible collision. When the refuse clears, only two of them are left alive—the lovers. That's part of the tradition of popular melodrama. The show must have some feeling of traditional form. You might argue that it would be more realistic to have the girl killed off, but the audience wouldn't be as satisfied and they certainly wouldn't feel for Sweeney. The ending should be formally satisfying.

(The above extemporaneous remarks of Stephen Sondheim were made to, and recorded by, Daniel Gerould on September 5, 1979.)

The Theater of Pyramids: (And a Camel)

CHRISTOPHER BOND

To describe a play as melodrama is to deride it nowadays. It usually implies that the author has aimed at tragedy, missed, and somehow insulted the intelligence of the audience in the process. Perhaps this is because melodrama aims at the gut, and our modern theater seems more interested in the head. Well, by all means, let plays be as intelligent, witty, and thought-provoking as possible, but let them be something else first. Let them at least *try* to blow our heads off by making us laugh, cry, feel outraged, appalled, sexy, furious, and hopeful (preferably all at the same time), and we can think about them afterwards. For if a play asks us to think in a logical and detached fashion about the people and events it portrays while we are watching them, then it seems to me to be discarding the most potent weapon that the theater possesses; the capacity to passionately involve its audience. This is what melodrama seeks to do to an extreme extent and seeks to do it in a form that is immediately accessible to everyone. It's a bit unfortunate, therefore, to find that most of the extant scripts of nineteenth-century melodramas are so carelessly and unimaginatively put together that one begins to suspect that their authors were seeking nothing more than a fast groat. But never mind, one should never let facts stand in the way of a good theory. If Dickens or Zola had written extensively for the stage, I'm sure that's what they would have sought to do and I'm also sure that melodrama wouldn't be so out of fashion today. Certainly Verdi and Puccini will pack any opera house in the world and pack it with pure passion. Just try sitting and watching *Tosca* or *Il Trovatore* in a logical and detached fashion and you will either fail if the performance is any good or be carried out insensible with laughter before the first interval. (If you are carried out, you may very well find your stretcher parked next to one on which Bernard Levin, an English theatrical critic, is frothing at the mouth: don't worry, it's Wagner not rabies; though the symptoms are sometimes distressingly similar.) But I digress.

Melodrama is difficult to define precisely, but most authorities seem to agree that it needs a larger-than-life story line, simply told; sensational and spectacular action; a bit of music (although this doesn't appear to be compulsory); and a stern Christian moral. Well, let's leave out the stern Christian moral which in terms of Victorian hypocrisy usually means something along the lines of, "She was poor but she was honest so everybody shat on her from a great height until she decided to be rich and dishonest and went straight to hell as a result." Funny people, Christians, but that leaves us with an extraordinary story, simply but spectacularly told with optional music. Even a basically nonnaturalistic representation of this is liable to prove costly in an industry already hopelessly expensive in inflationary times because it is so labor-intensive. No matter; there are basically two ways of paying for theater since subsidies, in England at any rate, are nearly always geared to the number of people attending. The first is to find a few latter-day Medicis (oil companies? detergent manufacturers?) who will pay a great deal of money to see performed the plays you want to do and the second, and more satisfying way I would think, is to attract a vastly greater number of paying customers to pay for the pyramids (and a camel); shipwrecks and Houses of Usher that melodrama may wish to destroy by fire, pestilence, and/or sword. Now, there is a strong argument to be made for the comprehensive stylization of such excesses which can be quickly summed up as "2 actors, bare boards, and a passion; if this Trinity is present, nothing else is necessary." I agree, up to a point, except that in practice it usually means that our two passionate actors spend all their time talking about what's happened/happening/going-to-happen before deciding not to do anything about it; and I want more action and less chat in the theater. (As a child I was taken to the theater a lot, and on one occasion went to see a Greek tragedy in which I was appalled to find that everything I wanted to see happened somewhere else. I was so annoyed I even tried to get around to the back of the stage where I imagined all the juicy bits I was missing out on were taking place in front of another audience who'd presumably bought more expensive tickets. I still feel the same, and if some readers infer from this that I am a childish and prurient lowbrow, so be it. "Now God stand up for low-brows!") My other reservation about "2 actors, bare boards, and a passion" is that unless those actors are saints or fanatics, neither of which are much use in the theater in my experience, sooner or later they will start clamoring for a hat or a chair; or a pot of paint for their bare boards: just as someone who has actually *got* "A jug of wine, a loaf of bread, and thou beside me singing in the wilderness," will rapidly seek out some ice for the wine, some butter and jam for the bread, and a piano or a sitar to accompany thee on. This doesn't seem to me to be an entirely cynical attitude since it is this impulse that probably got human beings to the point where we're doing plays at all. And if our passionate actors can clamor for a pot of paint, why not a pyramid? (And a camel.) I'm not saying, however, that all plays are improved by lavish sets and costumes, expensive stage machinery, and all the paraphernalia of a Roman circus. Far from it, but the verbal aspects of our theater seem to dominate the visual ones to a ridiculous extent, and the attitude of mind that wants to amaze and astound our eyes as well as our ears should be capable of being ingenious enough to make its novelties work without totally bankrupting the organization. And maybe we've got to spend money to get money anyway, for it may be that the lack of some of these very ingredients is part of the reason why our theater appeals to such a tiny minority of the population. Certainly the Blood Tubs and Music Halls of the nineteenth century were the last example of a truly populist theater in England on any national scale. Today, our theaters are for the most part middle-class culture troughs that the vast majority of people are far too sensible to waste their time at, for three very good reasons. First, the subject matter does not excite or interest them; second, it is expressed in a form that is boring or incomprehensible or both; and third, they are made to feel rather less welcome than a nose dropping on a weskit at Royal Ascot if they do not ape the dress, manners, and general grotesqueries of the *haute bourgeoisie* at play.

A return to melodrama won't change all this; we need new forms; but let us learn something from melodrama. Let us remember that people once roared their approbation or disapproval of the actions that gripped them, that the dead hand of respectability and moderation did not always lie heavy on our theater, and that vast numbers of people from every walk of life once went to the theater to be excited, moved, and to involve themselves in the passions they were made to feel a part of. The cinema and television do not, and cannot, do this, and we have allowed that vast audience to drift away and have turned our theater into an elephant's graveyard of silence and dry bones because we did not have enough confidence in our own passions. But all is not lost! For where there are bones there are maggots, and in England anyway, the last ten years have seen the growth of an enormous number of small touring companies and groups based in an unlikely assortment of church halls and warehouses. Their standards vary alarmingly, but the best of them are doing what is for my money the best work being done at the moment. The range and scale of what they do are wide, but much of it is informed with a reckless energy and immediacy that makes most conventional theaters look as dead as they undoubtedly are. Perhaps a reformation is under way. Let us hope so.

It would be nice to say in conclusion that I wrote my version of *Sweeney Todd* as a result of these long-winded and tendentious sentiments. Alas, I can't, because I wrote it at top speed to get the theater I was acting in at the time out of a jam. (We'd announced we were doing *Sweeney Todd* and through one balls-up and another didn't get hold of the original 1847 script until a fortnight before we were due to start rehearsing it and then didn't like it when it finally arrived.) So I was asked to have a go at improving it. I kept the chair and Mrs. Lovett's meat pies, a couple of lines of Tobias Ragg, and the name Jonas Fogg which appealed to me, and invented the rest. Or rather I nicked bits and pieces out of some of my favorite stories, mostly *The Count of Monte Cristo* and *The Revenger's Tragedy*, added market patter I heard as a kid, odds and ends from Shakespeare, and bits and pieces off Brenda who kept the shop opposite where we lived. I finished it in nine days and my only sadness was that I don't think Brenda bothered to go and see it. But then it hasn't got any pyramids in it. (Or a camel.)

Further Adventures of Sweeney Todd Alias Bertolli

COZETTE DE CHARMOY

In 1973 my collage novel *The True Life of Sweeney Todd* was published by Stefan and Franciszka Themerson at their Gaberbocchus Press in London. A Canadian edition, using the London sheets, was published at the same time by Oberon Press, Ottawa. In 1977 Da Capo published the New York edition.

The idea of Sweeney Todd had possessed me for some years before I began his biography. I had grown up in London and his was a familiar name—more than that, the story of the Fleet Street barber was a legend, a horror story from the foggy Victorian past of London. Yet when I asked people what they really knew about him I found they knew surprisingly little.

For sure, he was a Fleet Street barber who slit his customers' throats, a trapdoor sending their bodies down to the cellars. There they were made into meat pies, probably pork pies, with the help of some woman—a neighbor or a wife. And he had been found out by a telltale thumbnail. That seemed to be all that people knew. But everybody I asked believed he really had lived. He was quite as real to them as Jack the Ripper, who we are now discovering was probably not one person but several.

These sketchy details were all I had to start with. Of course, the story of a throat-slitting barber is not peculiar to London. It is said that during the Avignon Papacy there was a barber shop near Notre Dame run by two brothers who invited female custom, cut hair and slit throats. One brother sold wigs from this hairdressing shop. It backed onto his brother's pie shop; this other brother sold pâtés and terrines de campagne. The worldly priests of Notre Dame went there daily, the pâtés were well-known, worth a detour, one would say now. However, that is another story.

As I wrote and collaged the *True Life* of my hero I was, as are all biographers, somewhat obsessed by his personality. He was all things: mystic, resourceful inventor, dreamer, murderer; perfect criminal, superb lover, dedicated workman; a symbol, if you need a symbol, of the destructive energy of technology.

A book which could and would be misunderstood . . . some see it only as a comic book, an exercise in black humour and Victorian gravure, perhaps simply a picture book with a bit of text; perhaps a melodrama.

I often illustrate my own books. But in *The True Life of Sweeney Todd* the collages are not illustrations in the conventional sense. The images I collaged, using as raw material copperplate and wood engravings from nineteenth century English and American magazines, particularly from *The Graphic* and *The Illustrated London News*, are part of the story. I was gratified to see that some reviewers did understand this, and some saw the disturbance, the perturbation. They saw that *The True Life* is not an entertainment and not just a comic turn which may frighten the children. It is a sort of moral tract for the times, if you don't mind morality. In his review "Razor and Copperplate. A Mincemeat World" Val Clery of the Toronto *Globe and Mail* said: "[Cozette de Charmoy] has wisely discarded the warning subtitle traditionally used with the original Victorian melodrama, *The Demon Barber of Fleet Street.* And she has rightly emphasized Sweeney as the Industrial Revolutionary Hero, a neo-faustian materialist visionary who, implacable in his belief in progress and human perfectability, pursues it with his razor and ingenious barber's chair and monstrous human pie machine to the ultimate, the economic immortality of man eating man."

Shortly after *The True Life* was published the Victorian melodrama was revived; I realized my Sweeney Todd could be misinterpreted by someone seeing the original Victorian version. My Sweeney is not a Victorian "demon barber" but a romantic hero. And, like other romantic heroes, he has a sort of immortality.

Sweeney Todd, after his disastrous discovery and escape (as I recorded it), required an alias. So Bertolli was born, and Sweeney Todd alias Bertolli is still very much alive and well and passing among us. S. T. Bertolli. Many people orthographically mistake him for a saint.

I can tell you something of him but not as much as I hope to know, for that is to take another book. For the moment I can borrow from other, current, sources, as well as from unpublished material. Apart from *The True Life of Sweeney Todd*, there is *Voyages* (Geneva- Paris: Terra Incognita, 1978) and *Nose*, to be published soon.

Even at moments of intense joy Sweeney heard the voices. *Thumbnails Sweeney. Take care of thumbnails. The machine must be perfect or all will be lost!*

Of course, all was lost—for a time. His grief at the death of Beth, his crippled sister, so overcame him that he neglected his machines. Hence a thumbnail. Betrayal and imprisonment. *The judge retired famous after this case. He had pronounced Sweeney guilty as charged, sentenced him to be taken away and hanged by the neck until dead. And God rest your soul.*

I showed Sweeney fettered, caught; a rare condition for a Sweeney! There is another point of view of that agony. And with such petty people trying to hold such a Sweeney, it is no wonder he escaped.

The authorities could not stop him, so it was said. He defied the police, the troops, the whole network of authority. Off and away to freedom . . .

Coming from poverty, from humble beginnings, think of the heights to which he rose, moved by ambition, by curiosity. True, *his father was an educated man. He had a laboratory in the attic . . . Young Sweeney spent many hours watching, learning.* Often bored in his mother's company, he spent long hours discovering the world around him. Many an otherwise dull afternoon was passed excitingly.

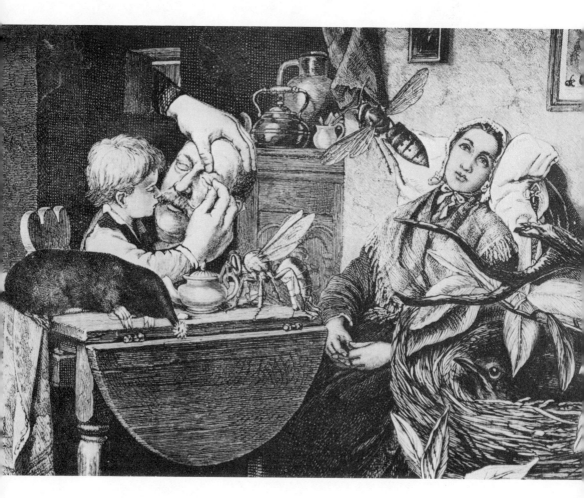

His American aunt, the wife of Professor Sullivan the wealthy embalmer, visited London, took Sweeney about. She bought him expensive clothes, stimulated his curiosity for the world.

Mrs. Sullivan passed as a lover of the arts. She took young Sweeney to avant-garde exhibitions where she allowed herself to be talked to by the critics.

Later, on his first visit to the States, Sweeney worked for awhile with his uncle and developed a great talent for embalming. His need to slit throats was well served by this profession and *it gave him scope for further experiments.* He passed his New York Embalmers' Examinations with honours.

But go back: the well-known scene from *The True Life* displays the death of Sweeney's father. His mother absent-mindedly added some of Sweeney's embalming fluid (he was already making certain experiments) to her husband's bath water. *He swelled rapidly and died*, his hand hanging at the edge of the bath.

Mrs. Todd lost her reason. I remind you that lunacy was also the fate of Rachel, Sweeney's wife. She ended in the London Lunatic Asylum.

I never cared for either of them.

Soon after, his sisters established their brothel. Sweeney *slit the throats of three rich customers.* This was lucrative. More than that, slitting throats fulfilled his secret need. How many of us wish we could gain self-confidence in such a simple fashion! *Slitting a throat is more personal than shooting.* Sweeney was a perfectionist in everything he did and above all in slitting throats.

His many loves were loved intensely, most subtly, though in my *True Life* I dwell only briefly on Sweeney the lover. *Sweeney Inamorato.*

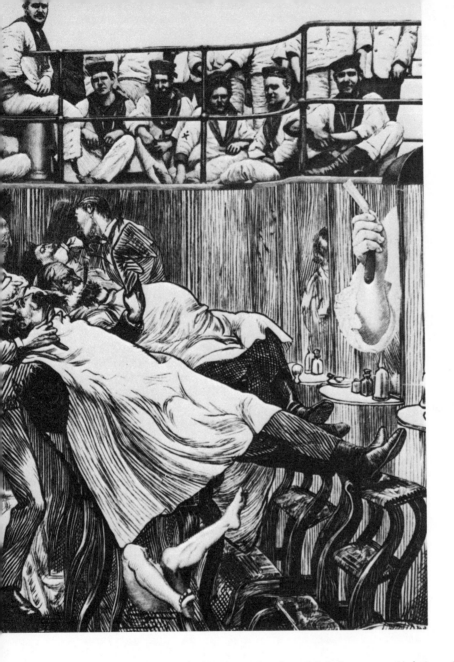

Sweeney Todd did nothing in which he was not interested. He dreaded boredom. During his time as a barber—and that was many years ago—he *discovered insulin and never said a word about it. He had no special interest in diabetics.* You will understand that this was before the official discovery of insulin.

Sweeney Todd, barber, throat-slitter, embalmer, inventor, mischief-maker—and lover. He was rather fond of sailors, perhaps because of his many travels or perhaps that was why he travelled. Whatever the reason, he took great care when they visited his barber shop. They had such beautiful necks, strongly muscled, healthy; and so loving.

Oddly, Sweeney Todd was never heard to sing. He loathed all that was noisy, all that was too obvious. Holy man, mystic, like a medieval man he preferred drastic measures, extreme treatments, excesses. There were so many different ways to experience pleasure.

In *Voyages*, disguised as a fireman, Bertolli is shown rescuing a clan-
destine beauty from the menace of public transport. She melted in his
arms, succumbing to the heat of the first-class compartment and above all
to the ardour and passion of Bertolli, fireman-saviour. He found an empty
compartment. And then an adieu.

When I lived in Switzerland I learned that S. T. had made a private visit to another exile at No. 12, Spiegelgasse, Zurich. He went away disappointed. The man had as great a determination and as much will as S. T. but S. T. worried about his lack of any sense of humour, taking home with him the birth of revolution, but certainly no humour. S. T. was right.

S. T. alias Bertolli is much taken by the work of Denis the Carthusian. He finds inspiration in this extraordinary anatomy of sin and punishment, written by a man so earnest, so lacking in poetry or grace. At breakfast, Bertolli reads extracts from *De Quattuor Hominum Novissimus*. This was the usual reading at mealtimes at the convent of Windesheim. It does nothing for the appetite but thus Bertolli can face the day in better humour. This is a necessity for him because, despite what you might think, as Sweeney Todd he suffered from nightmares. Perhaps they were only the result of his daytime activities. Rachel could never understand his accounts of them.

When breakfast reading fails to restore his sense of humour he resorts to the cleansing element of fire. Fire, ancient of purifiers, magical and powerful as the gods. S. T. Bertolli sets fires carefully, scientifically, studies the results. It never fails.

Sweeney Todd alias Bertolli has travelled a good deal—*Voyages* is
an account of a few of those journeys, physical and metaphysical. When
he is bored with regular modes of travel he finds other ways. Disguised as
bacteria he can pass unnoticed among us. He particularly likes proceeding
underwater. So much that is lost, forgotten, misplaced, can be found
there; history darkly haunting, ominous of resurrection.

Apart from the journeys described in *Voyages* there have been others. Bertolli's voyages have always been eventful. Not for him the calm ship-board romance, the quiet encounter of adjacent deck-chairs. Ships he travelled on were menaced by visions too often misunderstood by sailors. They were distressed, but not Sweeney! His blade ever ready he paced the deck, *saw exotic creatures of the sea and had his way with several of his shipmates.*

It was said he directed one ship on a journey from which neither crew nor ship returned, never seen again. The longest journey of all, seduced by lost tritons, sirens of the deep, the agony of slow death. Only Sweeney escaped.

Sweeney organised a special excursion; people knew it was another last voyage and flocked to join this remarkable company. They clung to him as he urged them on. Crowded on the raft, those who had not felt the swift touch of his blade were swept away to another forgetfulness, the last sleep which follows that last voyage. But Sweeney took off, exhilarated, amused at yet further proof of human frailty. They got what they deserved. Sweeney met their need to be part of history, fulfilled their sense of destiny.

S. T. alias Bertolli was a keen photographer. He turned up where the action was, and if there was none, he caused it. If things were too quiet he created drama, panic. A successful lion-tamer was mauled to death the moment Sweeney focused his camera. But none could prove a connection. No further crime could be pinned on Sweeney. On another occasion he went to a dog show. All was peaceful until he set up his camera. Then madness, and the crowd watched in horror as panic spread, murder in a hot summer afternoon; Sweeney took his photographs and left, laughing.

There is much more, about Sweeney, his elaborate jokes, his experiments. Let me tell you of one more incident. This is one of the more recent reports I have heard of his activities, and I describe it more fully in *Nose.*

Alias Bertolli, S. T. performed clever grafts on bored, rich clients. It had all started with noses; his first rhinoplastic operation caused an international scandal. This was not Bertolli's fault, but the result of unforeseeable complications due to the sexual drive of the donor graft. That happened in London and Bertolli had to move out fast. Safe in New York, he opened a clinic of Biocalisthenics near Times Square. After slitting throats, Biocalisthenics was Bertolli's passion. He was, of course, a success. They flocked to his clinic. Then, without giving up Biocalisthenics, he began surgery again, in secret. He perfected his technique, able at last to satisfy the perverse fancies of his clients, and of himself. Some began to ask for multiple transplants. However, it became much too routine, Bertolli was bored—and he had no time left for throat-slitting. He packed his gear and left town.

No doubt he will turn up again with a new line, a new success. Somewhere out in the world he is at large, slitting a throat or two as the need takes him. Sweeney Todd alias Bertolli—who knows what alias he will use next?

And Bertolli has written a book of instruction for travellers. He tells people *how* to travel with pleasure. His theory is that everything depends on knees: "Remember that millions like you are profiting from the advantage of knees, and for each one there must come a first time!" Then he gives his three tips on how to do it. Then . . . "Go! Take off! Off you go, joyously!"

A Toddography
(Including "Sweeney Todd the Barber" by Robert Weston)

DANIEL GEROULD

Sweeney Todd in Literature and the Performing and Visual Arts

1825 The ur-Sweeney Todd, "A Terrible Story of the Rue de la Harpe"—an English version of the original French account in Fouché's *Archives of the Police* (c. 1820) appears in *The Tell-Tale Magazine*, published by Henry Fisher.

1846 November 21–March 20, 1847. *The String of Pearls, A Romance* by Thomas Peckett Prest is serialized weekly in eighteen issues (31 chapters) in *The People's Periodical and Family Library*, a publication by Edward Lloyd known for his production of cheap, popular fiction.

1847 February 22. George Dibdin Pitt's *The String of Pearls, or the Fiend of Fleet Street* (produced as *Sweeney Todd*) opens at the Britannia Theatre, Hoxton, one of London's minor "blood-bath" theaters famous for its horrifying melodramas. Sweeney
(continued on page 46)

SWEENEY TODD THE BARBER
as sung by Stanley Holloway; words by Robert Weston

In Fleet Street that's in London town,
When King Charlie wore the crown,
There lived a man of great renown,
'Twas Sweeney Todd the Barber.
One shave from him
And you'd want no more.
You'd feel his razor sharp,
Then tumble-wallop through the floor
And wake up playing a harp
And singing:
Sweeney Todd the Barber.
By gum he were better than the play,
Sweeney Todd the Barber.
"I'll polish 'em off," he used to say.
His clients through the floor would slope,
But he had no fear of the hangman's rope.
"Dead men can't talk with their mouths full of soap,"
Said Sweeney Todd the Barber.
Now underneath the shop it's true
Where the bodies tumbled through,
There lived a little widow who
Loved Sweeney Todd the Barber.
She made her living by selling pies.
Her meat pies were a treat,
Chock full of meat and such a size,
'Cause she was getting the meat
From Mister Sweeney Todd the Barber.
By gum he were better than the play,
Sweeney Todd the Barber.
"I'll polish 'em off," he used to say.
And many's the poor young orphan lad
At the first square meal he'd ever had
A hot meat pie made out of his dad
From Sweeney Todd the Barber.
It was Saturday night in old Sweeney Todd's shop,
And his customers sat in a row,
While Sweeney behind a screen shaved some poor mug
And his sweetheart made pies down below.
Though none were aware
It were cut prices there.
They were rolling up in two's and three's,
And his foot was quite sore
Pressing knob on the floor,
And his voice went from saying, "Next please."

First a swell took the chair.
He said, "Ha, ha, my man.
Just a shave and a perfumed shampoo,
For I just got engaged."
Sweeney just pressed the knob
And said, "There! Now it's all fallen through."
Then a bookmaker said,
With his mouth full of soap,
"They're all backing favorites today,
So I'll bet I'll go down."
Sweeney said, "So you will," and he did;
He went down straight away.
But what rotten luck;
The darned trap went and stuck,
For the hinge he'd forgotten to grease,
And a customer there
Started calling out, "Police,"
Just as Sweeney was saying, "Next please."
Yes, he ran to the door,
And he shouted out, "Police."
He called "Police" nine times or ten,
But no policemen arrived,
For the very good reason
The police weren't invented by then,
But up came the brave Bow Street runners,
"Hurrah," and he had to let many a pie burn,
While they dragged him to quod
And next day Sweeney Todd
Was condemned to be switched off at Tyburn.
And there in the gibbet he hangs in his chains,
And they do say a little black crow
Made a sweet little nest in old Sweeney Todd's whiskers,
And sang as he swang to and fro:
Sweeney Todd the Barber.
By gum he were better than the play,
Sweeney Todd the Barber.
They buried him underneath the clay.
And Old Nick calls him from his grave,
Shouting, "Wake up, Sweeney,
I want a shave.
And Mrs. Nick wants a permanent wave."
From Sweeney Todd the Barber.

Reproduced by permission of EMI Music Publishing Ltd., 138-140 Charing Cross Road, London WC2H OLD.

Todd is played by Mark Howard, Mark Ingestrie (the sailor with the valuable string of pearls who is saved from Todd's razor by his faithful sweetheart, Johanna Oakley) by Samuel Sawford, Tobias Ragg by Mrs. Hudson Kirby, and Cecily Maybush by Sara Lane, the manageress of the Britannia.

1861   Alfred Rayner's *The String of Pearls* is given at the Pavillon Theatre, Whitechapel, London, with the manager George Yates as Todd and his wife Harriet Clifton as Mrs. Lovett.

1861   June 6. An anonymous *String of Pearls* opens at the Grecian Theater (formerly the Eagle Saloon) in Shepherdess Walk, London.

1862   July 11. Mrs. Henry Young's *The String of Pearls, or the Life and Death of Sweeney Todd* opens at the Effingham Theatre, Whitechapel, London, a favorite resort of sailors, considered one of the lowest audiences in the city.

1865   July. Fred Hazelton's *Sweeney Todd, the Barber of Fleet Street, or the String of Pearls*, a drama in three acts, plays at the Bower Saloon (jokingly known as the "Sour Balloon"), Stangate. The play appears in Lacy's Acting Edition, volume 102.

1878   An anonymous penny dreadful in forty-eight installments, *Sweeney Todd, the Demon Barber of Fleet Street*, is published by C. Fox, London, no date, 576 pages, issued in four parts, each of twelve numbers, preceded by an illustration.

1892   November 27. C. A. Clarke and H. R. Silva's *String of Pearls* (later called *Sweeney Todd)* opens at the Birkenhead Theatre.

c. 1900   William Latimer's *Sweeney Todd* is produced by the provincial impresario Alfred Denville and toured by his stock companies.

        Todd, Fleet Street, a condensation in seven scenes by Fred G. Brook and Dora Deane, is given as a dramatic sketch in music halls and variety shows.

c. 1925   George Dare plays the role of Sweeney Todd, treating the character seriously as an embodiment of evil.

1927   April 26. Andrew Melville the younger stages and plays his own version of *Sweeney Todd*, including a revival at the Prince of Wales's Theatre as part of a benefit in aid of the Sadler's Wells Restoration Fund.

1928   The role of Sweeney Todd is played by Tod Slaughter at the

Elephant and Castle Theatre, New Kent Road, London, bringing the actor and theater great renown.

The traditional George Dibdin Pitt version of *Sweeney Todd* is published by John Lane (London: G. Howe) with an introduction by Montague Slater. Sweeney Todd's soliloquy at the beginning of act 5, scene 2, after his escape from Newgate, "Straight and swift I ran . . . " is an interpolation from "A Madman's Manuscript" in chapter 11 of Dickens' *The Pickwick Papers*. This version was widely performed by provincial repertory companies; audiences were invited to cheer and boo and make fun of the play.

c. 1930 *Sweeney Todd* is revived by Cambridge undergraduates at the Festival Theatre.

1936 The British film *The Demon Barber of Fleet Street* (66 minutes) by Ambassador Films, directed by George King, scenario by Frederick Hayward and H. F. Maltby, is released, with Tod Slaughter as Sweeney Todd, Stella Rho as Mrs. Lovett, and Eve Lister as Johanna.

1957 "Sweeney Todd the Barber," a music-hall song by Robert Weston, is featured by Stanley Holloway on the record, *'Ere's 'Olloway*, Columbia ML 5162.

1959 December 10. The ballet *Sweeney Todd* (29 minutes), choreographed by John Cranko, with music by Malcolm Arnold, opens the winter season at the Royal Ballet Company, Shakespeare Memorial Theatre, Stratford-on-Avon. Donald Britton dances Sweeney Todd, and Margaret Knoesen, Mrs. Lovett.

1970 April 7. A new version, *Sweeney Todd (The Demon Barber of Fleet Street)* by Christopher Bond, opens at the Victoria Theatre, Stoke-on-Trent (Peter Cheeseman, artistic director), directed by Ron Daniels with costumes and setting by Mary Moore. Sweeney Todd is played by Stanley Dawson, Mrs. Lovett by Susan Tracy, and Tobias Ragg by Christopher Bond. Incorporating elements of Dumas père's *The Count of Monte Cristo* and Cyril Tourneur's *The Revenger's Tragedy*, Bond's play makes Sweeney Todd a victim of injustice and gives motivation for his actions.

1973 March 5. Christopher Bond's *Sweeney Todd*, directed by Maxwell Shaw, setting by Tony Woollard, with Brian Murphy as Sweeney Todd and Avis Bunnage as Mrs. Lovett at the Theatre Workshop, Theatre Royal, Stratford.

The True Life of Sweeney Todd (a college novel) by Cozette de

Charmoy is published by Gaberbocchus Press, London, and the Oberon Press, Ottawa, Canada. It is reprinted by Da Capo Press, New York, in 1977.

1974   Bond's *Sweeney Todd* is published by Samuel French, London. French also has in print two other versions, based closely on George Dibdin Pitt's original: Austin Rosser's *Sweeney Todd, the Demon Barber of Fleet Street* (London), and Brian J. Burton's *Sweeney Todd the Barber* (New York).

1979   March 1. *Sweeney Todd, The Demon Barber of Fleet Street,* "A Musical Thriller," with music and lyrics by Stephen Sondheim, book by Hugh Wheeler, based on Christopher Bond's *Sweeney Todd,* with decor by Eugene Lee, and directed by Harold Prince, opens at the Uris Theater, New York. Sweeney Todd is played by Len Cariou, Anthony Hope by Victor Garber, the Beggar Woman by Merle Louise, Mrs. Lovett by Angela Lansbury, Johanna by Sarah Rice, and Tobias Ragg by Ken Jennings. This version is recorded by RCA on March 12 and 13, 1979 and issued on CBL 2-3379 two-record set. Performances numbered 558.

PART 2

DRAMA:
NINETEENTH-CENTURY
PICTURES,
YIDDISH THEATER,
SOVIET EXPERIMENTS,
NEW AMERICAN FORMS

5

Speaking Pictures

MARTIN MEISEL

Dramaturgy

The revolution in the drama that emerged from the age of revolutions entailed a change in the relation of the subordinate parts to the design of the whole and, indeed, a change in the fundamental building block of the play. In the inherited drama, that building block was transitive and rhetorical. It was a unit of action involving one or more persons in which something had to be said and done, or of passion in which something had to be suffered and expressed. In either case, such a piece of the dramatic whole typically came from somewhere or led somewhere, or both. As between personages, so between units—meaning and the sensation of drama inhered in an articulated succession. It is true that in performance every scene, speech, and action of note may be conceived and experienced as a *turn*, in the music hall sense of the word rather than the Aristotelian. A turn contains its own reason for being and is too full of itself to spare a thought for the whole. Nevertheless (except perhaps in opera), the prevailing model asked that doing and suffering have a justification beyond their intrinsic interest. In this dramaturgy, the idea of the play, however peripatetic its course, however contrastive its juxtaposed units, however divided its plots or contrived for the accommodation of turns, remains an unfolding continuum.

In the new dramaturgy, the unit is intransitive; it is, in fact, an achieved moment of stasis, a picture. The play creates a series of such pictures, many of them offered as a culminating symbolic summary of represented events, while others substitute for action and reaction an arrested situation. Each, dissolving, leads not into consequent activity but to a new infusion and distribution of elements from which a new picture will be assembled or resolved. The form is serial discontinuity like that of the magic lantern or the so-called Dissolving Views.[1]

The best contemporary account of the new dramaturgy is to be found in Edward Mayhew's brief treatise and guide, *Stage Effect: or, The Principles which Command Success in the Theater* (1840). Mayhew discusses the "modern theory . . . that *dramatic success is dependent on situations*'—"situations" which turn out to be, not a single intriguing configuration that governs the play as in a still later drama, but something more plural:

> To theatrical minds the world "situation" suggests some strong point in a play likely to command applause; where the action is wrought to a climax, where the actors strike attitudes, and form what they call "a picture," during the exhibition of which a pause takes place; after which the action is renewed, not continued; and advantage of which is frequently taken to turn the natural current of the interest. In its purposes it bears a strong resemblance to the conclusion of a chapter in a novel.

Mayhew's illustrations, however, come not from melodrama, as one might expect, but from the *School for Scandal* (1777) and the established staging of *Othello*. When the screen is thrown down in Sheridan's play, Charles, Sir Peter, and—according to Mayhew—Joseph cry out, one after the other, varying the epithet, "Lady Teazle, by all that's wonderful . . . horrible . . . damnable." Then "there is a pause; each of the performers remaining statue-like in the attitudes they assumed when the above expressions were uttered; after sufficient space has been allowed for admiration of 'the picture,' Charles turns the interest . . . by bursting into laughter."[2]

Mayhew's illustration from *Othello* shows how the scene of the quarrel on Cyprus (2.3) has been cut to transform an action that is "stirring and continued" into a prepared pictorial effect. In Shakespeare's original scene (as Mayhew gives it), Othello, disturbed by the rumpus, enters with attendants:

> OTHELLO. "What is the matter here?"
> MONTANO. "I bleed still; I am hurt, but not to th' death."
> OTHELLO. Hold for your lives.

IAGO. "Hold ho! Lieutenant, Sir, Montano, Gentleman:
 "Have you forgot all place of sense and duty?
 "Hold. The General speaks to you; hold for shame."
OTHELLO. Why, how now, ho? Whence ariseth this?

"On stage," Mayhew writes, "the passages marked by inverted commas are dispensed with." The scene represents a courtyard with an archway at the center back through which Othello has previously retired. The noise of the brawl increases,

> till Othello appears, and, standing with his sword drawn imme-
> diately under the archway, brings all to a climax by shouting at
> the top of his voice, "Hold for your lives!" at which instant
> Montano receives his hurt and staggers into one corner. Cassio,
> conscience stricken by the sound of his General's voice, occu-
> pies the other. The rest of the performers put themselves into
> attitudes—the stage is grouped—and a picture formed, of which
> the Moor is the centre figure. After this there is a pause; when
> Othello, having looked around him, walks forward, and the half
> exclamation of *Why, how now, ho! whence ariseth this?* be-
> comes an inquiry.[3]

Mayhew complains that not only is Nature as truly expressed in a drunken quarrel affronted here, but the action is injured, and the "conduct of the fable" (narrative development and continuity) "materially deteriorated." Moreover, Iago's artful and officious remonstrance, soon to be echoed by Othello, is lost. But the vivid plunge from sound to silence, from violent activity and disorder to a frozen pictorial order, has made a splendid "effect."

The staging of *Othello* that Mayhew reported seems to have developed in the latter part of the eighteenth century, alongside the drama-
turgy of the *School for Scandal*.[4] Mayhew pays it no heed, but Sheridan himself had something to say about the trend whose onset he illus-
trates. At one point in *The Critic* (1779), Puff, author of *The Spanish Armada*, puts Mayhew's "Principles which Command Dramatic Success" in a nutshell as he tells his rehearsal audience, "Now, gentlemen, this scene goes entirely for what we call *Situation* and *Stage Effect*, by which the greatest applause may be obtained, without the assistance of language, sentiment or character: pray mark!" The premises of Puff's scene are that the two nieces of Sir Christopher Hatton and Sir Walter Raleigh consider their tender feelings for Don Ferolo Whiskerandos to have been slighted. According to the stage directions, they draw their daggers against the of-
fending beloved, whereupon the two uncles catch the arms of their respec-
tive nieces and simultaneously direct their swords at Don Ferolo, who promptly holds his own daggers to the two nieces' bosoms.

PUFF. There's situation for you!—there's an heroic group!—

> You see the ladies can't stab Whiskerandos—he durst not
> strike them for fear of their uncles—the uncles durst not kill
> him, because of their nieces—I have them all at a dead lock!

Sneer concludes they must stand so forever, but Puff manages to turn the interest with "a very fine contrivance," an invocation of the Queen's name.[5]

Historically regarded, the impasse situation of heroic drama, already full-blown in Corneille's *Cid*, has here been materialized as a frozen image, a tableau, whose only function is "effect." Puff's conjunction of the terms *situation* and *stage effect* does not represent a self-evident tautology for us; our own habits of language would not lead us to explain the one by the other, as—sixty years apart—Mayhew and Sheridan do. The mediating term in the equation of the two is "picture." From about 1770 to 1870, situation implied a pictorial effect in drama, and effect was likely to mean a strong situation realized pictorially. Effect had a wider reference and a more essential part to play in shaping and describing aspects of a style. The more inclusive character of effect appears in Mayhew's apparently paradoxical but quite sound account of melodrama, the form that was best able to exploit the new dramaturgy. "A melo-drama," he writes, "is defective in action, possessing too little rather than too much; for it is brought only to a certain point called a situation, and there interrupted. In this view, the fourth act of *'The School for Scandal'* is melo-dramatic. To cover their deficiency of action, melo-dramatists give an undue and irregular importance to the scenes and properties of the theater; and their productions abound in 'effects,' without the aid of which the interest evaporates."[6] A pictorial dramaturgy, then, organizing a play as a series of achieved situations, or effects, created the need for even more effects. These in Mayhew's account are chiefly visual and apparently static; but in fact sound and movement—"real" waves, ships sailing off the stage or sinking through it, forts blowing up and tenements burning down—these too were part of the dramatist's arsenal. Here as elsewhere in drama, sensation in its primitive sense, but sensation charged with wonder over the imitation of a difficult reality or the creation of a marvelous impossibility, was the underlying principle of dramatic effect.

The Critic is a work of practical criticism rather than a program; and while Puff's ideal of the drama is wonderfully clear, he is less than systematic in presenting it, so that even the pictorial character of his "heroic group," his scene of situation and effect secured "without the assistance of language, sentiment or character," must be inferred from the demonstration. The true prophet of nineteenth-century pictorial drama, antedating Puff and urging it as a program, was Denis Diderot. The boldness of Diderot's argument lay in his advancement of spectacle in connection with theatrical forms that were neither ceremonial and celebratory nor musical and balletic but directed toward private life *and* claiming serious literary attention. He also attempted to translate his theory into practice, his program for theater as a whole into a dramaturgy. Accordingly, his play *Le Fils naturel* as published in 1757 came equipped with elaborate directions for pantomime and pose not only as accompaniments to discourse but sometimes taking its place (for example: *"Constance, un coude appuyé sur la table, & la tête penchée sur une de ses mains, demeure dans cette situation pensive"*).[7] In the dialogues on dramatic poetry that accompanied the play, Diderot's spokesman develops a theory of pictorial staging and attacks those contemporary conventions of performance which run counter to it—not looking other actors in the face, always fronting the spectator, holding oneself "en rond, séparés," each at a certain distance from the other and in a symmetrical order. At present, he complains, one almost never sees on the stage a situation that could be made into a tolerable composition in painting. His alternative idea is statable in a striking, if deceptively simple formula: a dramatic work that is well made and well presented should offer the spectator as many "tableaux réels, qu'il y auroit dans l'action de momens favorables au peintre."[8] Diderot further supports such a program in the essay which accompanied *Le Père de famille* (1758), where he defines dramatic pantomime as the tableau that existed in the imagination of the poet as he wrote his play and insists on the necessity for continuously grouping and otherwise manipulating the figures on the stage so as to create "une succession de tableaux tous composés d'une manière grande & vraie."[9] Diderot insists on the essentiality of this spectacular, pictorial dimension in drama; and he envisages pictorial action brought to such perfection as to render words unnecessary.

Diderot's influence is traceable in his own theater and in Germany and through the French and German theaters to England. It is likely that Diderot's own views on pantomime and picture owed something to England in the first place (e.g., to Hogarth and Garrick), just as his program for a "genre serieux" owed something to Lillo and Shakespeare.[10] Nevertheless, it was Diderot, using his dissatisfaction with current practice in the most powerful of eighteenth-century establishment theaters, who shaped these hints into an alternative program with a critical rationale. As program or as prophesy, Diderot's pictorial theater took root in the more popular theatrical forms (helped by a few esoteric and self-conscious experiments) and flourished as the dominant mode for the creation and presentation of plays in the nineteenth century.

Figure and Ground

No revolution is ever neat or complete, and neither was the rise of a pictorial dramaturgy with its underlying assumptions about how to organize audience experience. Nor is it possible to isolate the change in the writing of plays from developments in acting, staging, and scene design, as Diderot's arguments and Mayhew's explanations make abundantly clear.

The course of development in acting can be generalized as progressing from a rhetorical to an illustrative and expressive and then to a fully pictorial style, where composition displaced attitude as the governing visual concern. The second stage, the illustrative and expressive acting which codified itself in the eighteenth century and then handed itself down in nineteenth-century acting manuals, was manifestly not yet the fully pictorial style of the later nineteenth century. Nevertheless, Talma's turn-of-the-century acting (according to a description which is supposed to have greatly affected Goethe's Weimar methods) was "an unbroken chain of pictures," while Edmund Kean's more violently expressive Richard (according to Hazlitt) was, like his Shylock, "a perpetual succession of striking pictures."[11] Such picture-making, however, was not what Irving had in mind in admonishing the actor to learn "that he is a figure *in* a picture, and that the least exaggeration destroys the harmony of the composition."[12]

In the 1760s, Garrick altered the lighting of the stage sufficiently to allow the actor to keep within the picture if he were so minded, and in the 1770s (in Garrick's theater), Philippe Jacques de Loutherbourg converted picturesque and sublime landscape painting to scene and setting and carried the stage a long way toward an illusionistic theater of effect. Nevertheless, much playing continued to take place before or at the proscenium, and there is ample evidence that well into the nineteenth century scenographic art on the one hand and the spectacle of actor and grouping on the other were independent and even mutually interfering effects. For one thing, actors and stage crowds, in motion and in depth, were sure to destroy the scale and perspective of paint. Some such mutual interference lost Alfred Bunn, the patent theater impresario, the services of Clarkson Stanfield, who had the best claim to be the heir of de Loutherbourg. For a grand-slam production at Drury Lane of Isaac Pocock's *King Arthur and the Knights of the Round Table* (1834, based on Scott's *Bridal of Triermain)*, Stanfield prepared a splendid scene representing the "Entry into the City of Carlisle." At the last rehearsal (according to Bunn), Andrew Ducrow, master of equestrian spectacle hired specially for the occasion, "thronged every part of it with *knights, squires, pages, attendants* and all sorts of characters, to give life and animation to the scene. Mr. Stanfield being of opinion that his scene had quite 'life and animation' enough in it, without any of Mr. Ducrow's assistance," demanded that the scene be first discovered "for the audience to gaze on and admire, and the multitude sent on afterwards." Bunn sided with Ducrow, and Stanfield departed.[13] Bunn can be trusted to color his stories; but even reduced to a chaste outline, this one shows how far from complete was the synthesis of the actor and the scene, even in outright spectacle drama, at a time when a pictorial dramaturgy was already full blown.

Charles Kean was certainly not the first to achieve an unqualified union between figure and ground on the picture stage, but he offers a significant landmark. Priorities in the field are vexed, and both Macready and Madame Vestris in management instituted production practices aimed at such integration. But Charles Kean's production of Byron's *Sardanapalus* (1853) illustrates not only an idea of pictorial integration then normative only in some parts of pantomime and extravaganza but also a more abstractly visual and decorative idea of acting than any contemporary formula would envisage. To complement his elaborate scenic resurrection of Nineveh according to the recent archaeological evidence, Kean strove to accommodate "his own attitudes and those of others to the action of the disinterred frescoes." The startled reviewer (who means reliefs rather than frescoes) wonders "whether this literal copying of the angularities arising from the limitations of Assyrian Art, rather than from their probable truth to the living actions of the time represented be desirable"; but he allows that this "adherence to pictorial authorities . . . adds strangely to the remote oriental character of the scene."[14] Probably Kean began with a shrewd preference for an exotic archaeological fact over a commonplace probability in adopting this style of acting and thought himself the greater realist in consequence. But he used his exotic fact to create a visual synthesis that was not only compositional but also atmospheric. Such a synthesis, unifying a rich and varied whole through visual style and atmosphere, would find its fullest flowering in the 1880s and 1890s in Irving's pictorial and atmospheric theater.

It was, surprisingly, not until 1880 that anyone thought to put a picture frame entirely around the stage, and then it had an unexpected atmospheric effect that suggests what the painters called "keeping." In refurbishing the Haymarket, the Bancrofts did away with the forestage entirely and provided "A rich and elaborate gold border, about two feet broad, after the pattern of a picture frame, [which] is continued all round the proscenium, and carried even below the actors' feet." Percy Fitzgerald reports, as the strangest of some singularly agreeable effects, that "the whole has the air of a picture projected on a surface. There is a dreamy softened air about the whole that is very pleasing."[15]

The late achievement of a fully pictorial theater in which actor and crowds were fused with the setting in a sustained atmospheric and compositional unity, may seem out of step with the earlier establishment of a dominant pictorial dramaturgy. (A reviewer, certainly exaggerating, could declare *The Lights o' London* [1885] "the first melodrama in the representation of which the effective disposition of supernumeraries was studied.")[16] The fact is that the dramaturgy of effective situation did not depend upon such keeping but was tied essentially to figural groupings symbolizing relationships and states of feeling and incorporating bodily attitudes that were themselves expressive and symbolic, and these made the picture. "Tableau" in drama meant primarily an arrangement of figures, not a scene and its staffage; and despite the notable successes of a Macready or a Madame Vestris in disciplining and unifying the scene before Irving and the Bancrofts, the actor was not yet so bounded and contained by the picture, so much *within* it, that his "least exaggeration destroys the harmony of the composition." It is rather to the point that the conventions of academic portraiture at least through Lawrence encouraged a similar disjunction between figure and ground, the latter, even as landscape, often suggesting theatrical scenery. The best painters could use the space thereby opened between art and life to say something about both. Even the pre-Raphaelites of the 1850s, however, with their great concern for truthful and effective surroundings on the one hand and symbolically expressive groups on the other, often show a discontinuity between figure and setting, the narrative picture and the natural one.

It should be said that a significant integration of player and scene did not wait for a full unification of solid figure and painted ground in an illusionistic continuum. Where the theater could reconstruct the playing space to conform with real space, built to scale and solidly funished, problems of perspective and even of composition nearly evaporate. Such integration was approached in plays set in domestic interiors, and the evidence for it lies not only in reports of productions but also in dramatic texts and in the character of the dramatic activity. The space between acting and setting dwindles in those melodramas where the interaction of men and things, the players and the "practicable" and active elements of the scene, were the essential drama. It disappears entirely in drawing-room plays like Robertson's *Caste* (1867) and Sardou's *Pattes de mouche* (1860). In the second act of Sardou's play, the crowded and eccentric *"cabinet de Prosper,"* the drama lies in what Diderot called the pantomime; and the approaches and separations, groupings and maneuvers of the actors are wholly integrated with the furniture and its placement, the fireplace, the clutter of bizarre and useful objects, the walls, doors, window, lamp, and the scrap of blue paper that is the prize of the agon. Together and only together they constitute the dramatic action and organize the spectator's interest and response. The "pictorialism" of such a theater, growing up even as the illusionistic theater moved toward a final integration, was not that of the painting but rather that of the stereoscopic photograph.

Tableau and *Tableaux Vivants*

The fullest expression of a pictorial dramaturgy is the tableau, where the actors strike an expressive stance in a legible symbolic configuration that crystallizes a stage of the narrative as a situation or summarizes and punctuates it. For example, in the drama C. H. Hazlewood distilled from Mary Elizabeth Braddon's *Aurora Floyd* (1863), the first act ends with Aurora between her present husband, John, and her blackmailing first husband, the resurrected James, with her virtue under suspicion and her bigamous secret imperiled. The stage direction has her

> *forcing a gay laugh, which suddenly turns into an hysterical one, wild and piercing, so as to express great mental agony—this requires to be done with great force so as to achieve a climax as*

she falls into the arms of JOHN—*at this moment,* MRS. POW-
ELL *from without, pulls back the window curtain, and looks in
exultingly*—STEVE *points exultingly to the certificate he holds in
his hand, regarding* AURORA *with looks of hate as he stands by
door,* R.—JAMES *with his hands in his pockets, and one leg
coolly crossed over the other, looks on with indifference as the
Act drop falls*—*Music.*

End of the First Act

As Aurora's situation defines itself and achieves an emphatic climax, all
the interests and antipathies of the various other members of her world
lock into place.[17]

The dramatic tableau has so strong an association with the act endings in melodrama and the use of the act drop that it is tempting to identify it entirely with this function and technology. Moreover, the curtain
tableau is so useful a solution to the eternal problem of getting "off" that
it is tempting to assume it created a supportive dramaturgy all on its own.
As late as 1888, a handbook for would-be playwrights advised, "Pay great
attention to your curtain. In melodrama it should certainly be upon a situation of some sort—the comic man denouncing the villain being the most
popular. In comedy this is not necessary, but, even there, it should be at
some moment of dramatic significance." To the audience "it is the concentrated summing-up of the whole act."[18] However, the tableau of situation and effect appeared independently of what came to be called the
"tableau curtain," if Puff's evidence can be trusted at all. We know from
the text that Puff has a drop curtain at his disposal as well as the ordinary
closing-in of flats for a change of scene, and we know that he is a master
of "situation," or tableau-marked stage effect. But Puff uses quite another convention for terminal punctuation and managing an exit. After
the English warriors in quintet kneel seriatim and chorus their immortal
pre-Armada prayer in the first scene (making an admirable picture), the
author suggests that the actors go off kneeling—"It would have a good effect . . . and would vary the established mode of springing off with a
glance at the pit." But the tradition-bound actors refuse, and Puff therefore has them repeat the last line standing up "and go off the old way."
Later Tilburina has a similar exit at the very end of a scene. Parting from
Whiskerandos, she goes out "without the parting look," to Puff's intense
annoyance. As corrected, she speaks her exit line "Aye for ever. . . .*Turning
back and exeunt. Scene closes* "—leaving her confidante to get off as best she
can.[19] Puff, especially in the prayer, created excellent tableau situations
before there was a closing tableau convention. As a hack genius, Puff is
both the first to take up the new and the last to lay down the old. His
practice, like Sheridan's, suggests the priority of more general cultural and
stylistic currents over limited material causes and utilitarian inspiration in
the development of a pictorial dramaturgy. That is, the urge to make and

enjoy effective pictures was more important than the availability of a curtain in the creation of a pictorial dramaturgy.

The tableau in drama had a history of its own, separable from the ferment which surrounded its incorporation in the new dramaturgy. There is, for example, a striking instance in Racine's *Athalie* (1691). The climactic revelation of Joas enthroned (followed by an opening of the back of the theater to reveal the interior of the Temple and the Levites in arms) is staged as the disclosure of a sacred picture, a divine vision given material, iconic form by the artist, the inspired human instrument. Joad, High Priest, inspired prophet, and here sacred artist, is the manager of the scene and of the curtain that opens to reveal the glorified boy:

> *Le rideau se tire. On voit Joas sur son trône; sa nourrice est à genoux à sa droite; Azarias, l'épée à la main, est debout à sa gauche; et près de lui Zacharie et Salomith sont à genoux sur les degrés du trône; plusiers lévites l'épée à la main, sont rangés sur les côtés.*[20]

The disclosure has a special function and rationale in this play, whose principle *topos* is pentacostal epiphany. For the audience it is theophanic through its allusion to a familiar genre of sacred picture. Racine, however, goes out of his way to remind us of the immense distance between this sacred child, Joas, and the one Joas foreshadows; and he implies a similar gap between his own new art of the sacred image—still staged, imitated, and built of mortal material—and the sacred reality. The gap is inherent in the deliberate archaism of Racine's resort to a dramatically obsolete iconic mode.

The masque and the *auto* had made large use of the emblematic tableau, as had medieval theater and Renaissance pageantry before them. But there was no continuity and little similarity in iconic method between these theaters and the pictorial theater of the nineteenth century. Intervening uses of the climactic tableau (as in *Athalie*) tend to have a special character function. In England, the most important use of the climactic tableau apart from the masque was in the "discovery" scene of the post-Restoration theaters. As the Elizabethans used it, the discovery took the form of an internal show—the Duchess of Malfi's waxworks, Prospero's Ferdinand and Miranda at chess. The post-Restoration discovery scene was an English compromise between neo-Classical decorum and genuine classical sensationalism in which the scene opens to show as done what could not be shown a-doing, chiefly slaughter and mutilation. Aaron Hill's *Merope* (1749-50) offers an example. After the audience has been treated to a vigorous verbal description of the butchery and its setting, the scene opens to show the bloody result, with *"Eumenes discover'd on the Altar with the Axe of Sacrifice in his Hand. Merope kneeling. Priest. Attendants and Guards."* These form a tableau of the living set among a tableau of the dead.[21] So special a use is unlikely to have entered directly into the creation of the later pictorial dramaturgy, where the tableau is, among other things, typically resolved out of its elements before the spectator's eyes. More pertinent to the development of that dramaturgy, though it too was a form of discovery or initial tableau, was a practice Davenant instituted to take advantage of the front curtain in the new prosceniun theater, a curtain that was drawn once and for all after the prologue and might be used to reveal a striking "scene."[22] In either form, the tableau-discovery had predictive affinities with still another related phenomenon that reached its characteristic peak in the nineteenth century, the so-called *tableau vivant.*

The rise of a new pictorial dramaturgy coincided with the pervasive European fashion of the *tableau vivant.* It was not the product of the *tableau vivant,* however, nor should the latter form of picture-making be confounded with the dramatic tableau of effect and situation. What they have in common bespeaks a common appetite. Both presented a readable, picturesque, frozen arrangement of living figures; but one arrested motion, while the other brought stillness to life.

The *tableau vivant* apparently took hold as a widespread genteel social entertainment on the order of charades after Goethe published *Die Wahlwerwandtschaften* (1809), but it had its predecessors in Lady Hamilton's "attitudes," and the related art of Ida Brun.[23] Earlier still, Baron Grimm, swelling Diderot's *Salon* of 1765 with his own remarks, reported:

> Au reste, j'ai vu quelquefois des sociétés choisies, rassemblées à la campagne, s'amuser pendant les soirées d'automne à un jeu tout-à-fait intéressant et agréable. C'est d'imiter les compositions de tableaux connus avec des figures vivantes. On établit d'abord le fond du tableau par une décoration pareille. Ensuite chacun choisit un rôle parmi les personnages du tableau, et après en avoir pris les habits il cherche à en imiter l'attitude et l'expression. Lorsque toute la scène et tous les acteurs sont arrangés suivant l'ordonnance du peintre, et le lieu convenablement éclairé, on appelle les spectateurs qui disent leur avis sur la manière dont le tableau est exécuté.[24]

The theater is generally quick to notice what society finds altogether interesting and agreeable. Consequently the *tableau vivant* had its own distinct life in the theater, so that, for example, a fascinated David Wilkie could write home from Dresden of the *tableau vivant* as an entr'acte entertainment:

> I have been much interested by an exhibition at one of their little Theatres, of what they call a Tableau. The curtain is drawn up between the acts, the stage darkened, and at the back is a scene resembling a picture frame, in the interior of which most brilliantly lighted from behind, men and women are arranged in

appropriate dresses, to make up the composition of some known picture. One I saw the other night was an interior after D. Teniers. It was the most beautiful reality I ever saw. . . . We were quite delighted with it; but so evanescent is the group, that the curtain drops in twenty seconds, the people being unable to remain for any longer period in one precise position.[25]

Later Wilkie directed the getting up of such "beautiful realities" in Anglo-Roman society and at Hatfield.[26] It is surely relevant that Wilkie is one of what must be a goodly company of painters—J. L. David and Holman Hunt, Tintoretto, Poussin, and El Greco among them—who are reported to have made models of figures and interiors for their paintings, like a miniature waxwork tableau or a stage with a missing fourth wall.

At Hatfield, Wilkie made his own drawings of scenes and characters from Walter Scott's novels for the tableaux.[27] The turn to literary illustration had found countenance in even higher circles. For example, in Berlin, on the occasion of the reception of the Grand Duke (later Czar) Nicholas (1821), the two courts joined to present a pictorial version of Moore's *Lalla Rookh*. "The different scenes and events of the Poem were represented in tableaux vivants and the effect of all was heightened by appropriate and touching music."[28] Public entertainments which were similarly illustrative albums of living pictures drew patrons to theaters in Britain and on the continent for the next fifty years. Mrs. Yates, for example, varied the fare at the Adelphi Theatre (1837) by a program delineating the Passions, each set in its appropriate scene: Despair in the Dungeon; Hope at the Sea Shore; Revenge and Pity—the Sacked and Burning City; Jealousy—the Garden; Melancholy—the Convent Garden; ending with the "Grand Allegorical Groupe. St. Cecilia Surrounded by the Passions."[29] Many of these associations of locale and emotion correspond to subtypes of the narrative paintings that were so characteristic a feature of the annual exhibitions at the Royal Academy during this era. A generation later, hard on the Franco-Prussian War, the Theatre Royal, Dublin, advertised *The Dove and the Olive Branch*, a "Series of Illustrative Tableaux":

First Tableau	Summoned to the War
2d "	Adieu
3d "	Prayer for Peace
4th "	Conscript Farewell
5th "	Another Sortie
6th "	Cared For

—and so on, in an obvious temporal progression, to the fourteenth "Allegorical Tableau" (the title emblem), all with "Appropriate Vocal and Instrumental Accompaniments."[30]

The *tableau vivant* in polite society gave the respectable an opportunity to taste the pleasures of impersonation and display (George Eliot's treatment of Gwendolyn's performance in *Daniel Deronda* catches the feeling admirably). When the subjects, as often happened, were supplied by well-known paintings and sculpture, the *tableau vivant* also afforded the pleasures of "realization." Most commentators exclaim over successful examples in those terms. Such realization, however, was not confined to the independent *tableau vivant*. Realization is in itself an "effect"; and consequently the representation of well-known pictorial images in a *dramatic* context, the union of *tableau vivant* and dramatic tableau of effect and situation, was not at all unusual. Taxonomically rather than historically, the curious phenomenon of the *tableau vivant* mediates between the picture, painted or engraved, and the nineteenth century's pictorial dramaturgy.

Dramaturgy Evolving

The close identification of "effect" and "situation" in Mayhew's treatise of the 1840s lasted a generation. The accumulating influence of writers like Thackeray and changes in audience, production, and the models of current dramatic excellence then helped alter the language of criticism. A distinction between "situation" and "effect" is a basic assumption in the 1870 equivalent to Mayhew's handbook, Percy Fitzgerald's *Principles of Comedy and Dramatic Effect.* For Fitzgerald, "situation" is the proper vehicle for character and its vagaries, and he reproves T. W. Robertson for his neglect of vigorous, comprehensive situation in spinning out his conversations and manipulating his eccentric personages. On the other hand he deplores "a too common vice of the stage—the getting broad, coarse effect, at the expense of the situation."[31] He deplores especially the sensational Boucicaultian melodrama of the day and the literal-minded realism that he feels has in general displaced illusion. "All is material, scenes, construction, furniture, and, above all, the play, and the acting. We go not so much to hear as to look. It is like a giant peep-show, and we pay the showman, and put our eyes to the glass and stare." The fundamental confusion in this spectacular theater "arises from the idea, that the closer reality is imitated, the more nearly *effect* is produced. If actual *reality*—the thing itself—can be introduced, the *acme* is reached."[32] In Fitzgerald's critical language, the terms "effect" and "situation" have diverged. While he has no doubt that "effect"—at its best, an *illusion* of nature—is still an essential requirement of theatrical production (witness his title), he sees "situation" as the primary embodiment of the logic of the play.

The primacy of situation and its identification with an inner logic went hand in hand with the contemporary development of the ideal of the "well-made play." The well-made play was the rationalization of effective situation, situation with its causality made manifest. At its heart was a striking conjunction or a seeming impasse, charged with affect or redolent of paradox, and into that situation the whole play was absorbed as preparation or disengagement. At the fulfilling, necessary moment (the so-called *scène à faire*) a skillfully disassembled picture came together with seeming inevitability, a sublimation of the ethos of the tableau.

When situation ideally had become singular and absorbed the whole of the play and the playwright found himself burdened with, not a providential or even probablistic causality, but a mechanistic one, a new critical shibboleth crossed the channel to England. As previously "effect" had to give place to its servant "situation," so now "situation" gives place to *its* servant, and the essential art of the play is identified as "construction."

The new shibboleth get its due in Frank Archer's handbook of 1892, *How to Write a Good Play*, the successor to Mayhew and Fitzgerald. Archer was an actor and a practical man of the theater, and his treatise is a guide to what he call the theater's "conventionalism." As such it was a target of opportunity for Shaw, a statement of the thesis to which his *Quintessence of Ibsenism* had already offered the antithesis.[33] Citing T. W. Robertson's comedies and James Albery's refinement on them to different purpose from Fitzgerald, Archer writes critically of "sympathetic plays, in which character and dialogue are the sole elements of attraction and that are undoubtedly successful. Their construction is faulty in spite of considerable ingenuity in what are called 'situations.'" Later he describes the "Crummles system, writing up to certain 'situations,' scenes, and 'effects,'" in which "whether it be in connection with a house on fire, a sinking ship, an explosion in a mine, or a race-course, it is the exception, rather than the rule, to find good construction or delicacy and truth in characterization."[34] In Archer's mind, if not his heart, "construction" is the essential contribution of the playwright, and he gives it primacy over "situation" and "effect" which in the raw are associated with defective causality. That "construction" might be no more than the apotheosis of the Crummles system escapes him.

One cannot help but be aware of a severe tension in the theater of the nineteenth century between picture and motion—between the achievement of a static image, halting (and compressing) time so that the full implications of events and relations can be savored, and the achievement of a total dynamism, in which everything moves and works for its own sake, as wonder and "effect." At one extreme is A. W. Schlegel's early comparison of the tragic drama to sculpture, a "free-standing group" (rather than the continuing frieze of epic), brought "all at once" before the eyes. He sees it as separated from natural reality by its placement on a base (the stage) "as on an ideal featureless ground" and as united by one action that combines "motion" and "beauty" (linked to repose), rather as an emblem of action than action itself.[35] At the other extreme is a writer in the *Magazine of Fine Arts* in 1821 who advances an idea of the stage wherein nothing is static, not even the scenery:

> *Theatrical Scenery* has made still more rapid and decided advances towards perfection; but there is yet much left for indus-

try and genius to accomplish. Whenever it can be relieved from the charm which holds it fixed and motionless—like the pantomimic corps, struck by the wand of Harlequin—all that can be desired will be achieved. Let the trees bend gracefully to the kissing breeze,—the animals perambulate the meadows, or browse upon the mountains—and the illusion will be so far complete.[36]

An attempt to reconcile these conflicting aspirations would, and did, produce in the theater something like the serial picture in painting. Given the available models and terminology, any well-intentioned attempt to describe this compromise was liable to involve itself in paradox, conscious or unconscious. For example, the *Times* reviewer of W. B. Bernard's *Robespierre* (1840) declares, "Some admirable tableaux are formed in the course of the drama, which is throughout a moving picture."[37] The reviewer has motion in mind, not affect; and the moving picture, or "picture play," as it was also called, is where hindsight suggests these aspirations are heading. But to put it that way is to do an injustice to prescience and intention. There is more than a little of both, for example, in the formulation of Dion Boucicault, the most cinematic of English melodramatists, when he declares, "The stage is a picture frame, in which is exhibited that kind of panorama where the picture being unrolled is made to move, passing before the spectator with scenic continuity."[38] He invokes an available model; he unwittingly suggests more exotic forms, like the Japanese picture scroll; but it is the moving picture that has taken shape in his imagination. The human habit or compulsion that finds a pattern in dispersed events, which made both Hogarth's series and the drama of effective situation into progresses and serial illustrated fiction published in monthly segments into novels, has its analogue in the perceptual paradox on which the moving picture depends, that turns a succession of briefly arrested images into motion. Nevertheless, the uneasiness we still feel about the achievement of the nineteenth-century theater—despite its great actors, its greatness in scenery and spectacle, its cultural and social importance, and despite Schiller, Büchner, Pushkin, Dumas, Ostrovsky, Ibsen, Verdi, and Wagner—is in its failure to resolve the tension between picture and motion and actualize that resolution in an adequate transforming synthesis. That synthesis had to wait for the organization of the available technical possibilities into a new drama "at once eloquence and a living picture"[39] in the next century.

Notes

1. For the Dissolving Views, which played the theaters in the 1830s before finding a home in the Royal Polytechnic Institution, see W. J. Chadwick, *The Magic Lantern Manual* (London: Warne, [1878]), pp. 61-66, and [Anon.], *The Magic Lantern* (London: Houlston, 1873), pp. 78-92.

2. Mayhew, *Stage Effect* (London, 1840), pp. 44-46. The text of Sheridan's play is an editorial mare's nest; but according to Cecil Price the best evidence ends Charles's line in "wonderful," Sir Peter's in "horrible," and gives Joseph (who has just entered) nothing to say at all. Many early versions supply "damnable," however, in Sir Peter's line; and Mayhew's report of *three* exclamations, using the three terms, probably represents a stage tradition.

3. Mayhew, pp. 50-52.

4. The evidence of the *Othello* promptbooks is also not simple, but the first printed version I have seen to give the *full* cut is H. Garland's edition (ca. 1765). At least two earlier acting versions show partial cuts of the passage, and the full cut becomes standard after 1777. See J. P. Kemble's version of 1804 in *John Philip Kemble Promptbooks*, ed. Charles H. Shattuck, vol. 7 (Charlottesville, Va.: Univ. Press of Virginia, 1974).

5. *The Dramatic Works of Richard Brinsley Sheridan*, ed. Cecil Price (Oxford: Oxford Univ. Press, 1973), 2:544-45.

6. Mayhew, pp. 74-75. Cf. William Archer's later definition, in an essay on Victor Hugo: "Melodrama is illogical and sometimes irrational tragedy. It subordinates character to situation, consistency to impressiveness. It aims at startling, not at convincing, and is little concerned with causes so long as it attains effects." *About the Theatre* (London, 1886), p. 320.

7. *Oeuvres de théâtre de M, Diderot* (Amsterdam, 1772), 1:21. Puff's Lord Burleigh, who comes on the stage to think, is Sheridan's comment on the art of advancing the drama through "dumb show and expressions of face."

8. Diderot, *Théâtre*, 1: 168-70.

9. Ibid., 2:418, 420.

10. See Kirsten Gram Holmström, *Monodrama, Attitudes, Tableaux Vivants, Studies on Some Trends of Theatrical Fashion 1770-1815* (Stockholm: Almqvist & Wiksell, 1967), pp. 24-25, 37, 39. Miss Holmström makes the intriguing suggestion that the pictures in Diderot's " 'peepshow' theatre" were inspired by the art of Samuel Richardson. She also shows Diderot's program to be an extension of transformations in the style of tragedy acting largely inspired by Voltaire and of developments in ballet and its criticism.

11. Holmström, *Monodrama*, pp. 103-4 for Humboldt's letter to Goethe (1799); and William Hazlitt, *Complete Works*, ed. P. P. Howe (London: Dent, 1930-34), 5:184.

12. Henry Irving, *The Art of Acting* (London, 1893), pp. 63-64. My italics. Holmström gives a fuller account of the shift from a rhetorical to "pantomimic and expressive" style, particularly in France, *Monodrama*, pp. 13-39. See also Alan Downer's survey of the evolution of acting styles in England, "Nature to Advantage Dressed: Eighteenth Century Acting." *PMLA* (1943), 58:1002-37, and "Players and Painted Stage: Nineteenth Century Acting," *PMLA* (1946), 61:522-76.

13. Alfred Bunn, *The Stage: Both Before and Behind the Curtain* (London, 1840), 1:224-25.

14. *Athenaeum* (18 June 1853), p. 745. Other reviewers remark on the "ingenious adaptation of those quaint attitudes," notably G. H. Lewes in the *Leader* (18 and 25 June 1853), reprinted in *Dramatic Essays, John Forster, George Henry Lewes*, eds. William Archer and Robert Lowe (London, 1896), p. 25; and the reviewer in the *Illustrated London News* (18 June 1853), 22:493.

15. Percy Fitzgerald, *The World Behind the Scenes* (London, 1881), p. 20. See also Richard Southern, "The Picture Frame Proscenium of 1880," *Theatre Notebook* (1951), 5:59-61. Picture frames behind the curtain were used for "living pictures" earlier in the century. See David Wilkie's report from Dresden, note 25 below and the account of Ducrow's statue-in-a-landscape attitudes in the *Spectator* (18 Sept. 1830), 3:371.

16. *Athenaeum* (30 May 1885), p. 705.

17. C. H. Hazlewood, *Aurora Floyd; or, The Dark Deed in the Woods*, French's Acting Edition, vol. 58, p. 17. The corresponding scene in the novel, an interview between Aurora and James Conyers in the North Lodge (ch. 18), provides no such climatic confrontation or inclusive configuration.

18. "A Dramatist," in *Playwriting: A Handbook for Would-Be Dramatic Authors* (London, 1888), p. 18.

---

19. Sheridan, *Dramatic Works*, 2:528, 535-36.

20. Racine's laconic direction for his part of the scene is *"Le rideau se tire."* The amplification here quoted, from the edition of 1736, assembles elements for the most part explicit in Joad's verbal directions. See *Oeuvres complètes de J. Racine,* ed. Louis Moland (Paris, 1877), 5:244. The frontispiece of the original edition of 1691 combines the two phases of the revelation.

21. Cited in Kalman Burnim's *David Garrick, Director* (Pittsburgh: Univ. of Pittsburgh Press, 1961), pp. 95-96. Burnim quotes a letter showing that the crowd was partly painted, partly personated. The "discovery" and its uses is discussed in Lily B. Campbell's *Scenes and Machines on the English Stage during the Renaissance* (Cambridge: Cambridge Univ. Press, 1923).

22. Emmet L. Avery, A. H. Scouten et al, *The London Stage, 1660-1800;* pt. 1: *1660-1700,* ed. William van Lennep (Carbondale, Ill.: Southern Illinois Univ. Press, 1968), pp. lxxxv-vi. The authors cite Pepys on a production of *Heraclius* in 1663/64: "At the drawing up of the curtaine, there was the finest scene of the Emperor and his people about him, standing in their fixed and different postures in their Roman habits, above all that ever I yet see at any of the theatres."

23. See Holmström for a thorough account of these arts of the concert and salon to about 1815. Richard Altick continues the chronicle, noting theatrical and nontheatrical variants, in *The Shows of London* (Cambridge, Mass.: Belknap Press of Harvard Univ. Press, 1978), ch. 24: "The Waxen and the Fleshly."

24. Diderot, *Salons,* ed. Jean Seznec et Jean Adhémar (Oxford: Clarendon Press, 1960), 2:155.

25. Letter to Thomas Wilkie, 4 July 1826, in Allan Cunningham, *The Life of Sir David Wilkie* (London, 1843), 2:333.

26. Ibid., 2:408, 415; 3:67.

27. Published in *Master Drawings* (Spring 1972), 10, with Francis Russell's "An Album of Tableaux-Vivants Sketches by Wilkie," pp. 35-40. See also my comment in *Master Drawings* (Spring 1973), 11:55-58.

28. *The Letters of Thomas Moore,* ed. Wilfred S. Dowden (Oxford: Oxford Univ. Press, 1964), 2:885-86. Colored engravings of the costumes appeared in an elaborate published account, *Lalla Rûkh. Ein Festspiel mit Gesang und Tanz. Aufgeführt . . . an 27 sten Jannar.*

29. Playbill, Adelphi Theatre, 22 Feb. 1837. British Theatre Museum.

30. *Dublin Evening Mail,* 27 Feb. 1871.

31. Percy Fitzgerald, *Principles of Comedy and Dramatic Effect* (London, 1870), p. 95.

32. Ibid., pp. 15, 28.

33. *Music in London 1890-94* (London: Constable, 1932), 2:90, 93. "The other day an actor published a book of directions for making a good play. His plan was a simple one. Take all the devices which bring down the house in existing plays; make a new one by stringing them all together; and there you are."

34. Frank Archer, *How to Write a Good Play* (London, 1892), pp. 51, 96-97. What follows the latter passage, nevertheless, is a handy catalogue of proven effects and situations.

35. August Wilhelm von Schlegel, *Ueber Dramatische Kunst und Literatur,* Zweyte Ausgabe (Heidelberg, 1817), 1:127-28. Schlegel's lectures were delivered in 1808 and translated into English in 1815. His second lecture, concerned with "Theatrical Effect" *(Wirkung),* according to the rubric, likens the dramatic poet to the orator whose art is to create an audience-involving "rhythmus," which the poet makes visible in the progress of the play. Such a model, oratorical and progressive, belongs to an older conception of the art of the theater seemingly at odds with Schlegel's own analogy from *plastik,* and it informs his disagreement with Diderot. Schlegel's own effort, however, is to reconcile the two models.

36. "Theatrical Costume and Scenery," *Magazine of the Fine Arts* (May 1821), 1:30.

37. *Times,* 6 Oct. 1840, p. 7.

38. Boucicault, "My Pupils," *North American Rev.* (1888), 147:438.

39. Schlegel, as translated by John Black, *A Course of Lectures on Dramatic Art and Literature,* 2d ed. (London, 1840), p. 38.

The Yiddish Theater in New York: 1900

MEL GORDON

The relationship between the worsening social conditions brought about by the Industrial Revolution and the growing popularity of the stage melodrama in the first half of the nineteenth century is a relatively new concern. To be sure, the new working class's general acceptance of increasingly inhuman working and living circumstances—especially between 1810 and 1840—is well known. Overcrowding, disease, child labor, seventy-five-hour working weeks, cut wages—these are all trademarks of urban life in Western Europe and North America in the 1800s. Yet the resulting cultural shock and social malaise led not only to the disruption of communal ties and familial patterns that we would expect but also to an unending obsession with the melodrama.

Mediating between what working people wanted and what they experienced, the melodrama released a powerful psychic spring in the working-class imagination. Although its efficacy differed in various cultures, the melodrama shared a similar and ironclad format whenever it appeared: the forces of morality would always triumph over those of capital. And in the melodramatic ethos, the struggle of classes would be forever linked with not just property but with sexuality.

Most of our information about performances of melodramas is from the published texts themselves or descriptions of much later middle-class varieties. The few documents we have describing the working-class melodramas, or penny gaffs, are usually illuminating as to the stage and audience behavior and deserve to be looked at more carefully.[1] But if actual scenic documentation of English, French, and German cheap melodramas is scarce, then material on Yiddish melodrama seems relatively abundant.

Begun in the 1870s in Rumania just when the Industrial Revolution started to make itself felt among Eastern Europe's seven million Jews, the Yiddish melodrama reached its apogee around the turn of the century in New York's Lower East Side. Trapped by poverty and language, the Lower East Side became a ghetto to over 300,000 Yiddish-speaking Jews. Working in garment factories, little industry sweatshops, in restaurants and brothels, and peddling on the streets, even the most unhappy Jews accepted the Lower East Side as their home since returning to their countries of origin was unthinkable. While the majority of the Jews came from small villages where the synagogue held cultural sway, once in the Lower East Side, the Yiddish theater suddenly became their object of extreme—almost religious—devotion.

Presenting real-life detail within a fantasy structure, the Yiddish melodrama began to dominate the subconscious life of the Lower East Side. Writing in 1901, Hutchins Hapgood reported that "Many a poor Jew, man or girl, who makes no more than $10 a week in the sweatshop, will spend $5 of it on the theatre."[2] For a great many Jews, the viewing of the Yiddish theater, almost entirely devoted to melodramas then, became as important as the eating of bread. Both the intelligentsia and mass audiences spoke of theater constantly. Even the editor-in-chief of the most influential Yiddish newspaper, the *Daily Forward*, doubled as a play reviewer.

Ted Thomas, the son of two well-known Yiddish actors, described this early melodramatic period on the stage, "The Yiddish theatre made the Left Bank of Paris look like a convent. There was every form of degeneration you can imagine: murder, suicide, drugs, sex deviations of all kinds. These were the emergent Jews, after years of living a Torah-cloistered existence, suddenly free—and drunk with it."[3]

But if the melodrama was the single most popular genre on the Yiddish stage, historians, scholars, and translators at the time and after have downplayed its social and artistic merits. Calling it *shund* (esthetic trash) or "onion plays," because of its ability to draw tears, nearly all of the Lower East Side's intellectuals and leading performers fought a life-and-death struggle against the cheap, "three-hankie" melodrama. By 1925, the literary, "thought-minded" performance won out, but at a terrible cost—the lose of the average Yiddish theatergoer.

Varieties of Yiddish Melodrama

Essentially, the Yiddish melodrama, like its English, French, and German counterparts, fell into one of several distinct varieties. The earliest kind—the historical spectacle, a mix of local color, adventure, threatened innocence, sacrifice, tangled sexuality, and tragedy—was also the most lavish in terms of costuming, stage effects, music, and language. Typically set in ancient Palestine or at the courts of Renaissance princes, the historical melodrama pitted the Jewish protagonist, usually a well-known figure, and his lover against a superior Gentile force. Much of the performance's pathos and irony was dependent on the spectator's historical foreknowledge of disaster. For instance, in Avrom Goldfadn's successful melodrama, *Bar Kokhba; or, The Last Days of Jerusalem*, written in 1883, the tragic hero, Bar Kokhba, battling the Romans, makes a prayer, "O, Lord of my fathers, we pray that you do not help our enemy. As for ourselves, we need no help!" Knowing the catastrophe that will follow, the normally noisy audience members cluck their tongues, sigh an "oy," or whisper to no one in particular, "Ah, this will end badly!"

After 1900, domestic subjects were the focus of most Yiddish melodrama. The very short runs for most domestic plays necessitated a rather extensive repertoire. Several dozen of those early texts were not written at all, but, according to the terminology of the time, "baked." A "baked" or constructed drama was formed by the alteration of scenes from other—usually obscure classical—plays, only slightly amended in plot and characterization. In other words, a baker-playwright would outline his story on paper: (1) A henpecked husband and wife arrive in the big city for the first time [funny scene]; (2) a young woman shows her retarded son the grave of his grandfather in a potter's field [pathetic scene]; and so forth. Then the playwright would search through volumes of world literature, in order to find vaguely appropriate scenes and dialogue. So, frequently a Yiddish audience would hear an illiterate shoemaker, who in the first act sounded like a poor Hauptmann character, suddenly lament like a worried Macbeth in the second, and finally commiserate in the words of Ivan Karamazov in the last.

Often the domestic melodramatic characters started off in Russia and by the second or third act found themselves in America. As in the English penny gaffs, the protagonists regularly went through the process of being orphaned, abandoned, humiliated, beaten, raped, cheated, and impoverished. Joseph Lateiner's *The Jewish Heart* (1908) contains many typical elements of this variety.[4] A Jewish art student in Rumania, Yankev, discovers that his archenemy, the anti-Semitic Viktor, is his half-brother. By the end of act one, Yankev realizes that his long-lost mother ran away after his birth, married a Rumanian aristocrat, and bore him a child, Viktor. The play ends with Yankev murdering Viktor to save his "Christian" mother, who later takes the blame for the killing. In the very last scene, Yankev marries a Jewish girl before emigrating to America, as his mother, watching and in chains, dies of heart-rending joy. Just as the curtain falls, Yankev breaks into a song about mother-love, about the Jewish mother.

Most of these melodramas were fueled by standard character types with identifiable accessories and muscial themes: the student (with his ubiquitous open book and skullcap), the marriage broker (and umbrella), the synagogue sexton (and snuffbox), the landlord, the righteous Gentile, the wife-beating Christian count, the political radical, the idiot child, the self-depreciating proletarian father, and of course the Jewish mother. In the last act of each play, at least one protagonist had what was called "the tablecloth speech"—an emotionally charged outburst that summarized or changed every aspect of the plot.

A third kind of melodrama dramatized recent news stories from the Yiddish and English-language press. The most sensational of these portrayed trials of innocent Jews accused of ritual murders in Russia, Hungary, and the American South. Others documented natural and manmade disasters such as the Johnstown flood and World War I battles. Interestingly, many of the *Zaytstucke* (time plays) from the non-Yiddish newspapers revolved around the mispractices of Christian doctors.

Another form of Yiddish melodrama consciously took classical and foreign-language plays and fitted them into nineteenth-century Jewish settings. The *Yiddish Medea*, the *Jewish King Lear*, and *The Rabbinical Student (Hamlet)* were the best known of this variety. In these versions, ancient Greek and Elizabethan characters once again appear as Yiddish theater stereotypes: Hamlet as the young scholar, Claudius as a lecherous and wealthy rabbi, the ghost of Hamlet's father as a vengeful dybbuk, Ophelia as the deranged Esther, and so on. Even Boris Tomashefsky's *Uncle Tom's Cabin*, "Where One Persecuted Race Portrays the Hardships of Another," substituted a red-bloused Cossack for Simon Legree. Curiously, if the mix of Jewish elements in the world repertoire seems comical today, many typical spectators at the turn of the century were not even aware that Shakespeare was a seventeenth-century English writer.

The Yiddish Audience/Actor Relation

The single most unusual feature of the Yiddish melodrama did not involve the plays themselves as much as the audience/actor relationships. Jewish spectators were obsessed with not only the personalities but also the working styles of the actors. As distinct from Irish and Italian theatergoers of the same social status in New York, the Jewish spectators applied strict critical yardsticks for both comic and melodramatic acting. More than any other aspect of the Yiddish theater, this deeply impressed the non-Jewish writer Hapgood:

> The spectators laugh at the exact reproduction by the actor of a tattered type which they know well. A scene of perfect sordid-

ness will arouse the sympathetic laughter or tears of the people.
"It is so natural," they say to one another, "so true." The word
"natural" indeed is the favorite term of praise in the Ghetto.
What hits home to them, to their sense of humor or of sad fact,
is sure to move, altho sometimes in a manner surprising to a visi-
tor. To what seems to him very sordid and sad they will frequently respond with laughter.[5]

Hapgood further explained how even plays with bizarre plot developments, unvarying characters, twisted dialogue, and shoddy properties and
costuming still remained effective:

> The Yiddish players, even the poorer among them, act with re-
> markable sincerity. Entirely lacking in self-consciousness, they
> attain almost from the outset to a direct and forcible expressive-
> ness. They, like the audience, rejoice in what they deem truth.[6]

As the taste for more literary melodramas grew, many of the Yiddish
performers found themselves more and more dependent on the prompter—oddly enough, usually a musician. This created a new kind of acting
style on the Second Avenue stage. Whenever a performer needed a forgotten line, he crossed in front of the prompter in studiously measured
strides, polishing his glasses or playing with a coin or looking out into the
distance as if he were lost in thought. After being fed the remaining dialogue, the actor returned to his place. All of which caused the audience to
remark to one another, "What an actor! He thinks!" or "Such a deep
play!" Sarah Adler called this puffing technique "pecking corn."

The most celebrated feature of the Yiddish theater concerned the
audience's fanatical involvement with the performances and the actors.
Spectators frequently interrupted the plays to comment on the acting or
to warn the protagonists of the coming deluge. Nahma Sandrow even records an instance: after Jacob Adler as the Yiddish King Lear is refused
soup by his ungrateful daughter, a spectator stepped into the aisle, shouting, "Leave those rotten children of yours and come home with me. My
wife is a good cook, she'll fit you up."[7] And since the majority of spectators were familiar with the real-life melodramas of the performers, whenever a similar situation occurred on the stage, audiences exploded in applause and psychological analysis.

The stars of the Yiddish theater usually had large and sometimes vio-
lence-prone fan clubs, or *patriotn*. Members of *patriotn* followed their
idols everywhere, occasionally even taking their names or acting as their
house servants. Rival fan clubs brawled and often ridiculed the performances of their idol's challengers, shouting during the play or carrying signs
in front of the theater. On some occasions, this escalated into even more
direct action, as when *patriotn* drugged a horse on which Thomashefsky
was to ride at the play's finale, causing the horse to sicken on stage. Cer-

tainly, the greatest and best documented events in the Lower East Side before 1920 were the gigantic processional funerals of the Yiddish actors. Even the sweatshop operators understood that these were holidays of epic proportions.

While few historians have attempted to explain the phenomenal popularity of Yiddish melodrama and its performers between 1900 and 1925 and its subsequent decline, except in purely linguistic terms, one explanation may have to do with the lack of Jewish leadership and the ghetto's general political impotence. Until the power of trade unionism was firmly established in New York and elsewhere, until working and living conditions allowed for more intellectual and "esthetic" activity, the Jewish masses sought solutions on the "natural," but melodramatic, stage.

Notes

1. See *Theatre Quarterly*, October-December 1971.
2. Hutchins Hapgood, *The Spirit of the Ghetto* (Reprint ed., New York: Schocken Books, 1966), p. 118.
3. Jerome Lawrence, *Actor: The Life and Times of Paul Muni* (New York: Putnam, 1974), p. 40.
4. Partly translated in Nahma Sandrow's *Vagabond Stars* (New York: Harper & Row, 1977), pp. 116–21.
5. Hapgood, p. 138.
6. Ibid., p. 137
7. Sandrow, p. 102.

Like all contemporary writers on Yiddish Theater, I am indebted to Wolf Younin for original materials.

Melodrama in the
Soviet Theater 1917-1928:
An Annotated Chronology

DANIEL GEROULD & JULIA PRZYBOŚ

In 1929 the Central Committee for the Control of the Repertory in the
USSR published *The Repertory Index: A List of Works Permitted and
Forbidden for Performance on the Stage.* Included in the 122-page index
are some 4,000 plays—new works, translations, adaptations of classics,
both published and unpublished—each assigned a grade, showing fitness
for performance, and categorized as to genre. Compared to the Soviet
classifications, Polonius's distinctions among "pastoral-comical, historical-
pastoral, tragical-historical, tragical-historical-pastoral" are rudimentary.
The *Repertory Index* contains nearly a hundred genres, subgenres, and
mixed genres, including such Soviet specialties as agit-étude, hygienic-agit,
agit-grotesque, atheistic-satire, agit-trial, Red-Army-performance-piece,
cinema-poster, and living newspaper.

Although the venerable genre melodrama constitutes no more than
three or four percent of the total number of plays listed, the importance
of this type of drama in the early Soviet theater far surpasses its statistical
frequency. In fact, the idea of melodrama became a major rallying point
in the impassioned struggle to find the correct path for a revolutionary
new dramaturgy.

But first a word about why the Bolsheviks, immediately after gaining power and during a period of civil war, starvation, and epidemic, were so obsessed with matters of dramatic genre. The new Soviet authorities and cultural leaders were unanimous in their view that of all the arts the theater was the chief form of education for the masses and of propaganda in support of the revolution. Theatermania soon swept the country. In addition to all the previously established theaters, which continued to function after October 1917, there quickly sprang up—with official sanction and encouragement—thousands of new stages and groups throughout the USSR, in army units, workers' clubs, young communist leagues, recreation centers, cultural circles, and private homes.

Although theater flourished on a scale unparalleled in world history, there was a crisis with respect to repertory. The Soviet authorities had to decide how to foster the creation of a new body of revolutionary works suited to a communist society with its vast and unsophisticated audiences. And the wide variety of theatrical contexts—amateur, professional, military, rural, anticlerical, sanitary—demanded differing kinds of plays geared to specific pedagogic goals. Hence, the interest in genre on the part of the Soviet leadership was a practical question of allocating the right play to the right audience.

The shortage of revolutionary works for the stage was acute. The old bourgeois repertory of well-made plays, bourgeois problem dramas, light comedies, and decadent works by the ever-popular and virulently anti-Soviet Leonid Nikolaevich Andreyev continued to be played in the major theaters after 1917, just as it had been before the revolution, quite simply because there was nothing to replace it. The fundamental problem for the ruling cultural commissars was one of selecting the best genre for the new Soviet theater and then of finding ways to assure its growth.

Inspired by Romain Rolland's *Le Théâtre du peuple* (1903, first Russian edition 1908), which extols melodrama as the popular theater of the future, Anatoli Lunacharsky and Maxim Gorky—two of the most influential voices for the revolution—engaged in a prolonged campaign to promote romantic and heroic melodrama as the desirable route for Soviet drama to follow. The ideas of Lunacharsky and Gorky actually antedated the revolution and were shared by members of the democratic Russian intelligentsia, who also considered the theater to be an effective tool of education and regarded melodrama as an entertaining means for promoting progressive ideas, such as the rights of illegitimate children.

The classic nineteenth-century French melodramas by Dumas père, Hugo, Dennery, and Decourcelle had been played widely throughout prerevolutionary Russia, after 1900 appearing primarily in the repertory of the provincial theaters, especially at Christmastime and holidays. Now in the early Soviet period, these plays were revived, often in modern adaptations, for the new urban audiences of revolutionary Moscow and Leningrad. In order to make these old melodramas fully contemporary, their innate theatrical dynamism was frequently accelerated through the use of the mechanistic techniques and frantic tempos of American silent movies, then immensely popular in the Soviet Union. By the mid-1920s there were several dozen movie theaters in Moscow, many of which had names such as Tivoli, Riviera, Union, and Fantomas. Thus the Soviet search for a valid form of revolutionary melodrama was nurtured on nineteenth-century French boulevard hits and contemporary Hollywood films. And it reflected a general preference for primitivism in the arts.

The most talented Soviet directors and designers of the 1920s (Eisenstein, Foregger, Meyerhold, Tairov, Stanislavsky, Akimov) all were interested in the theatrical values of melodrama and tried once or more to realize on stage the scenic possibilities inherent in the genre. Never was there such heated discussion about the nature of melodrama, so much analysis of its structure, so many serious debates about how it should be staged and acted, as during the Soviet 1920s.

The experiment ultimately failed. No new melodramas of any lasting artistic merit were created. (During this period Soviet playwriting achieved its only genuine successes with the satirical comedies of Mayakovsky, Erdman, Bulgakov, and Olyesha.) Nor did a valid new style of melodramatic acting emerge. After 1928, when the previous plurality of approaches to theater started to be ruled out in favor of the monolith of socialist realism (officially proclaimed at the First Soviet Writers' Conference in 1934), melodrama as a possible genre of Soviet drama was quickly wiped off the slate. The flamboyant theatricality of melodrama and its total subservience to the interests of the stage—rather than to those of the state—made the genre suspect to the party ideologues who were in control of the Soviet theater by 1930. The bourgeois Western origins of melodrama and its ties to American film, as well as its sheer exuberance and entertaining qualities, rendered the genre incompatible with the colorless, boring dogmas of socialist realism.

The vogue for melodrama and the great period of Soviet theater coincided. The old genre was temporarily rehabilitated and played a significant role in one of the most exciting theatrical experiments of the twentieth century. What remains of the Soviet melodrama craze is the record of a number of unusual productions, plus many probing assessments of the genre by leading practitioners and theoreticians. The following annotated chronology documents this history and offers an occasion to see what the best creative and critical minds in the Soviet Union had to say about melodrama.

1917–1918

Moscow. Charles Dickens's *The Cricket on the Hearth,* adapted and directed by Boris Shushkevich, plays at the First Studio of the Moscow Art Theater. First created in 1914, with Leopold Sulerzhitsky as commentator, Mikhail Chekhov as Caleb Plummer, and Evgenii Vakhtangov as

Tackleton, *The Cricket on the Hearth* remains one of Stanislavsky's most popluar productions throughout the 1920s and is shown on tour throughout the USSR as well as in many countries of Europe. Indignant at Dickens's middle-class sentimentality, Lenin walks out in disgust during a performance on October 29, 1922, and never attends the theater again.

1919

Petrograd. During the civil war the city is encircled by White armies and for months undergoes a state of total siege. The inhabitants are reduced to eating horses and burning their books and furniture to keep warm; many starve to death or freeze.

January. Commissar of Education Anatoli Lunacharsky publishes the influential article, "What Kind of Melodrama Do We Need?"

> Instead of turning up their noses and averting their gaze, serious-minded people should ask themselves what it actually is that draws the crowd to such shows [movies, music hall, and melodrama] and they should conduct an experiment along these lines, and after having eliminated the intolerable crudity from all these forms of art "for the people," they should try to retain what has nothing in common with crudeness, but which may offend so-called refined taste. Then they will tell me that these qualities in film and melodrama are a fine, gripping subject; next richness of action; character traits defined with colossal relief; clarity and sharp expressiveness of all the situations and the capacity to call forth undivided and total emotional reactions of compassion and indignation; action connected to simple and clear ideological positions.
>
> Melodrama simply as theater is superior to other dramatic genres. It is superior to realistic drama because it is free of laborious and quasi-photographic portrayal of everyday life and of probing into psychological minutiae, which quite simply is not suited to the stage and invariably requires a more or less pronounced transition from a theater of the masses to an intimate theater, and this in and of itself marks the decline of the theater. It is superior to symbolic drama because the latter plays with the reader and sets him riddles. It is superior to so-called tragedy because tragedy—unless it is melodrama—is marked by conspicuous bombast and a purely literary poetic quality, pursues the goal of being noble and impressive, sticks to the heights aspired to by the esthetic avant-garde and therefore quite frequently sins by being bookish.
>
> The playwright who dares undertake melodrama, in our view the sole possible form of tragedy for the new age, should

clearly take sides for and against. For the melodramatist, the world should be polarized. At least while he writes, he should cast off all skepticism and all doubt. On stage there should be no place for doubts.[1]

February. A melodrama contest to encourage young playwrights to create new works in the genre is sponsored by the Petrograd Theater Section of the Commissariat of Education, headed by Lunacharsky. Maxim Gorky is the secretary of the jury, which includes, besides Lunacharsky, the great operatic bass Feodor Chaliapin. The announcement of the contest, written by Gorky and appearing in a number of periodicals, contains the following recommendations:

> Since melodrama is based on psychological primitivism and on simplification of the feelings and the interrelationships of the characters, it is advisable that the authors stress clearly and explicitly their sympathies and antipathies towards the protagonists and antagonists; it is also advisable that they include in the text fine song, rhymed couplets, duets, etc.[2]

The results of the contest are disappointing; of the forty-one plays submitted, only one warrants even a second prize (7,000 rubles). Gorky continues his efforts to promote heroic and romantic melodrama as the genre befitting the spirit of the times and best suited to the creation of a new revolutionary culture, declaring that:

> From the stage words must be spoken about courage, selflessness, about love for one's fellow man and respect for him, about the feeling of friendship, about man as a citizen, but the drama of man as a philistine, about man as a passive spectator of the tragedy of life—this drama should die out.[3]

March. The symbolist poet and playwright Alexander Blok, in charge of the repertory at the Bolshoi Dramatic Theater (formed in 1918 by Gorky, Lunacharsky, and Blok to present "Heroic Theater for Heroic People"), explains in a speech to the actors why an old French melodrama is included in the plans for the season:

> Having done Shakespeare, Schiller, and Hugo, we now wish to finish the season with *melodrama* which grew out of romantic drama. In choosing one of the classic melodramas [Dennery and Lemoine's *La Grâce de Dieu,* not in fact produced], we are planning to organize a kind of theatrical festivity; we need no film studios here for that purpose, although in recent times that is where melodramas have been staged; what is required is a lavish production, authentic old music, unusual ease of movement

from tears to laughter—all those things so becoming to the theater.[4]

Moscow. *October.* The Vol'nyi (Free) Theater is founded by the director Boris Nevolin to further the revival of melodrama. The first season includes four nineteenth-century Italian and French melodramas, all of which had been widely performed in prerevolutionary Russia. Luigi Camoletti's *Suor Teresa* (1848, originally starring Adelaide Ristori)—called *Behind the Cloister Wall* in the Russian version—is the story of an abandoned wife forced to join a religious order. In the convent where she is the abbess, the bereaved mother is reunited to her lost daughter, whose freedom and happiness in marriage she then is able to assure. Doomed to eternal separation from her child, Sister Teresa dies of grief but not before her identity is disclosed to her daughter in a tearful farewell. Paolo Giacometti's anticlerical and humanitarian *La morte civile* (1861)—presented as *The Criminal's Family* in an 1870 translation by Alexander Ostrovsky—argues for divorce and prison reform and attacks the bigotry of the church. The hero, Corrado, a convict serving a life sentence for murder, must commit suicide in order to free the wife and child he loves. Dennery and Lemoine's *La Grâce de Dieu, ou la Nouvelle Fanchon* (1841, Théâtre de la Gaieté)—retitled *A Mother's Blessing, or Poverty and Honor* in an 1842 adaptation by the great social poet Nikolai Nekrasov—is a drama with songs about an illiterate peasant girl who flees her native Savoy mountains because of extreme poverty and sexual harassment by a nobleman only to face still greater threats to her virtue in Paris. Saved by her devotion to her mother and the grace of God, the heroine marries a marquis. Dennery and Cormon's famous *Les Deux orphelines* (1874, la Porte-Saint-Martin) as directed by David Gutman is highly successful with the public, but not with the critics who find it too sentimental and artificial to realize Lunacharsky and Gorky's program for a return to heroic and romantic melodrama. Pointing out the shortcomings of the Vol'nyi Theater, the director, dramaturge, and theater historian Pavel Markov writes of the need to discover new ways of acting and staging melodrama:

> The revival of melodrama, which the Vol'nyi Theater has proclaimed as its artistic goal, is warranted by the very nature of this genre of dramatic composition: melodrama is one of the most theatrical forms of scenic art, being a curious amalgam of drama, dance, and music and therefore offering fruitful possibilities, when it is presented on stage, of combining all those scenic techniques primarily associated with the "left-wing" trend, whose development we have witnessed during the past decade. Thus the return to melodrama, actualized at the present time, appears to be both practically and theoretically a natural outgrowth.
> The principles of structure in melodrama—sharp contrasts, rising action along a path of steady growth and maximal ten-

sion, suddenness as the mode of dramatic creation, and, finally, the presence in each act of one or more striking moments, intended to excite in the extreme the emotions of the spectator—all these elements divide melodrama into a series of rhythmically differentiated parts. And therefore it is possible that the search for new forms to realize melodrama on the stage should take the position of affirming rhythm as the basis of melodramatic action.

On the other hand, melodrama by dint of its powers of emphasis—the characters' grief is infinite, their joy is boundless, their passions are fiery and unrestrained, virtue and vice take on the most highly colored markings—admits application of the grotesque and of the unification of sharply contrasting elements in a convincing and scenically expressive design.

The possible ways of approaching melodrama are varied and numerous: they are united by one general principle—renewal of the forms of melodramatic action by means of the revelation of the distinct elements of theatricality that are richly stored within it, and the creation—by means of their synthesis (as it seems to me, in the rhythm)—of a truly unified production.

Only one thing is not possible—application to melodrama of hackneyed ways of acting and staging, fundamentally different from the theater of vividness and strength which is the theater of melodrama. Hackneyed psychologizing is inherently alien to melodrama, which in its very basis is devoid of the elements of psychological naturalism—melodrama is entirely subservient to the interests of the stage. That is why melodrama has had its greatest success in Russia in the provinces, where its proponents were our provincial tragedians: the Poltavtsevs, the Miloslavskiis, the Rybakovs—actors of exaggerated passions, broad gestures, and brightly colored speech. The forms of their stage action are foreign to us at the present time, and there are not any actors who can equal them in elemental talent.[5]

1919-1920

Petrograd. At the Alexandrinsky Theater there are revivals of Edouard Brisbarre and Eugène Nus' *Les Pauvres de Paris* (1856, Ambigu; in Dionysius Boucicault's English adaptation known as either *The Streets of London*, or *The Poor of New York*, depending on the place of production) and Edward Sheldon's *Romance* (New York, 1913).

1920-1921

Petrograd. Sergei Radlov, an organizer of mass spectacles and director formerly at Meyerhold's Studio (subsequently famous for his *King Lear* in Yiddish with Solomon Mikhoels at the Moscow State Jewish Theater in 1935), opens his Theater of Popular Comedy where, during its two years of existence, he creates more than a dozen circus comedies and *commedia* scenarios based on detective stories, penny dreadfuls, and adventure films. Radlov's aim is to return to popular folk traditions and revive marketplace theater in modern guise by utilizing the techniques of urban eccentricism (circus terminology for novelty numbers exploiting the ludicrous, illogical, and surprising), whose fast tempos, tricks, and special effects are "the product of Anglo-American genius." Working without fixed texts, Radlov develops performance pieces in conjunction with his actors during rehearsals. His melodramas, *The Adopted Child* and *Love and Gold*, are based on motion pictures and on motifs taken from the popular French novelist Pierre Decourcelle (1856-1926), author of the celebrated late nineteenth-century melodrama, *Les Deux Gosses* (1896, Ambigu-Comique, running for a record-breaking 758 performances), which was immensely successful in Russia before 1917 and was in fact playing in both Petrograd and Moscow at the time of the October Revolution, as well as of *Les Mystères de Saint-Petersbourg* (1904, Alhambra, Brussels, written in collaboration with Stanislas Rzewuski). In *Love and Gold*, Radlov uses cinematographic techniques of rapid cutting to move about the streets of Paris and to penetrate into its sewers and underworld haunts swarming with apaches and police agents.

1922

Moscow. The Romanesque Theater is founded by Valerii Bebutov, a director who had worked with Meyerhold on his productions of Verhaeren's *Les Aubes* and Mayakovsky's *Mystery-Bouffe*. Inspired by Lunacharsky's theories, the Romanesque Theater is dedicated to the production of romantic melodramas. During its one season of existence, the company presents *The Tour de Nesle* and *The Count of Monte Cristo* by Dumas père. Discussing the Romanesque Theater in an article entitled "The Right Path," Lunacharsky, who claims to have attended almost all the rehearsals of *The Tour de Nesle*, writes:

> The fact is that for almost twenty years now, both verbally and in my writing, I have stressed the great significance of the melodrama and romantic drama of France in the 1830s, '40s, and '50s as the basis and starting point for the creation of a genuinely popular theater.
> A theater of strong effects, contrasts, broad poses, sono-

rous words; intense beauty and caricatural deformity, a theater relying at one extreme on titanic emotions, and at the other, on reckless buffoonery, is the only basis for a truly popular theater and, what is more, the highest form of theater as such.

That is why we must learn from those who so brilliantly began this work, from those who created, in the true sense of the word, in actual practice the very laws of holding an audience's attention and of keeping the spectators enthralled.

I say that in the field of the theater we must go back to Dumas père, and in the field of the novel back to Sue.[6]

In the autumn of 1922 Nikolai Foregger, an experimental director and choreographer, together with the young Sergei Eisenstein and Sergei Yutkevich (designer, director, and later filmmaker), establish a small theater, Mastfor (Foregger's Studio), which presents highly stylized productions combining dance, song, acrobatics, music hall, circus, clowning, and modern *commedia* masks. One of the first productions is Eugène Grangé and Lambert-Thiboust's *La Voleuse d'enfants* (Ambigu-Comique, 1865), the story of Sarah Waters, a child thief, who unwittingly sells her own illegitimate daughter Jeanne to a masked nobleman, Lord Trevellian, whose child has just died. Arrested and deported for her crimes, Sarah returns to London fifteen years later and spends the rest of the play seeking to find and reclaim Jeanne, who has been brought up as Lady Helen Trevellian. Foregger stages the play at a frantic tempo, as though it were a silent film, using spotlights in front of which rapidly rotating discs create the impression of a movie projector's flashing light. According to Yutkevich:

Eisenstein created costumes that did not belong to any precise period, but that sought to reveal the basic traits of the characters: the black silhouette of the villain, recalling the contours of figures by Daumier (who, by the way, was Eisenstein's favorite graphic artist), the brightly colored horsewoman with scarf and top hat for "the virtuous heroine" [Jeanne as the nobleman's supposed daughter], the picturesque rags of "the thief," etc. . . .[7]

1923

Moscow. *October. The Festival of Blood*—an adaptation by the playwright S. I. Prokofiev of Ethel Lilian Voynich's novel *The Gadfly*— is presented at the Mossoveta Theater as a melodrama in six acts and a prologue, bearing the epigraph, "Religion is the Opium of the People." A former governess and music teacher married to a Polish revolutionary, the Anglo-Irish Voynich (b. 1864 in Cork, d. 1960 in New York) knew Engels and Plekhanov and lived in Russia from 1887 to 1889. Written in 1897, *The Gadfly* is a romantic radical novel about revolutionaries in Italy during the 1830s and '40s. Arthur, the gadfly hero, who rebels against the combined power of church and state, dies a martyr to the cause of freedom, defying to his last breath his archenemy, Cardinal Montanelli, who is also his father. Enormously popular in Russia both before and after the revolution and selling many millions of copies, *The Gadfly* was banned from the stage by czarist censorship prior to 1917 (in England, it was dramatized by Bernard Shaw as *The Gadfly, or, The Son of the Cardinal,* to protect Voynich's copyright and presented at Victoria Hall, Bayswater, in March, 1889). The Soviet *Festival of Blood* brings the class struggle up to date in agit style. *The Gadfly* appears throughout the USSR in dozens of other versions, operatic as well as dramatic.

October. Alexander Faiko's *Lake Lyul,* a modern "urbanistic" melodrama using cinematographic techniques and the accelerated tempo of big city life, is presented by Meyerhold at the Theater of the Revolution. Set on an island in the West or the Far East, where different races meet and technological civilization holds sway, *Lake Lyul* (the code name of a revolutionary conspiracy) is the first of a number of Soviet "island" plays with foreign settings used to expose the hypocrisy of the glamorous bourgeois world. In a luxury hotel (with functioning elevators and flashing advertisements), elegant villa, and fancy department store called the Excelsior, intrigues are hatched by business tycoons and political operators in frock coats and top hats, with an avaricious glint in their eyes. The charming and innocent variety show entertainer Georgette Bien-Aimée dances and sings (in Russian, French, and German) her way through the cold, rapacious world of decadent capitalism, which is menaced by social upheaval. When the adventurer-hero Anton Prim betrays the cause and his fellow revolutionaries, he is shot and killed by Maisy, the hotel chambermaid. In *Izvestia* the Central Repertory Committee attacks *Lake Lyul* for its "schematism, abstract-stylized portrayal of revolutionary activity, and anarcho-foxtrot ideology." Although Faiko fears that the production will be stopped, the controversy contributes to the play's success; it is presented by many theaters throughout the Soviet Union and continues in the repertory of the Theater of the Revolution through the 1927-28 season. *Lyul* cigarettes are manufactured and sold. The Central Repertory Committee only requires that certain revisions, cuts, and additions be made in the text. The supplementary material about the workers' movement is supplied by the head of the Central Repertory Committee himself; the playwright simply is asked to edit the changed version. Of the play's reception, Faiko writes:

> On stage an out-and-out melodrama was being played, with incidents of arson, police raids, bankruptcies, treason, and murder, and in the audience there reigned an animated, festive mood, characterized by willing belief and enthusiastic participation.[8]

Commenting on the season, Paval Markov describes the new masks of melodrama:

> The theater has followed not the drama, but the adventure novel and the movies. What was stereotyped in literature and film became still more stereotyped in the theater. Urbanism was perceived as popular Americanism—Americanism of the exterior, not of the essence. Everywhere there could be heard the foxtrot and the sound of automobile horns; movements were sharply focused and vivid. Before the eyes of the spectators there passed a procession of energetic individuals in motoring caps and knitted scarfs, with pipes clenched between their teeth, unusually sinister or—on the contrary—exaggeratedly comic multimillionaires, beautiful adventuresses, etc. These new theatrical masks were added to the available supply of previously developed masks of the contemporary world: the drunken priest, the profligate landowner, the honest worker, and the noble-minded peasant girl.[9]

1924

Petrograd. *January.* In an article entitled "Melodrama or Tragedy?" the critic, playwright, director, and Greek scholar-translator of Aeschylus and Aristophanes, Adrian Piotrovsky, asks whether melodrama, rather than tragedy, can deal with the recent experiences of revolution, social upheaval, and civil war.

> What is melodrama? The most important example of this dramatic genre and the latest in time was the system of bourgeois drama at the beginning of the last century. In it the triumphant bourgeoisie asserted itself vis-à-vis the aristocracy. The criminal marquis and the virtuous steward—here is the basic antithesis of melodrama. And this antithesis still lives out its days here and there in the outlying theaters. And, of course, it is convenient to replace that antithesis with a new one, to put a multimillionaire in the role of the marquis and a socialist in the place of the steward. But we should keep in mind that this is the least of the reforms facing the revolutionary theater.
>
> Melodrama is the child of transitional epochs. Chance and relative morality, these are its driving forces.
>
> Melodrama by its very nature is individualistic. There is no fatality.
>
> Short-sighted optimism, easily attained self-satisfaction—these are the psychological roots of the contemporary propaganda offered by melodrama.[10]

Moscow. *February.* Sergei Eisenstein directs Sergei Tretyakov's *Gas Masks* for the Proletkult at the Moscow gas works near the Kursk railway station on the outskirts of the city. The play concerns a bourgeois factory manager who out of negligence and greed fails to provide safety equipment. When a major gas leak occurs, the workers must attempt to control it without wearing gas masks; they succeed in their dangerous mission, but in the process the manager's heroic son is killed. With the audience seated on the floor of the plant, the melodrama is played among the machines and equipment, which in the course of the action become crucial elements in the story. The setting of the play and the performance area are the same.

1924–1925

Moscow. *December.* Victor Hugo's *Marion de Lorme*, called a melodrama in four acts, as translated by I. A. Rossov, with changes in the text by the poet and director Pavel Antokol'sky, is presented at the Vakhtangov Theater, where it plays through 1929.

1925

Moscow. *January.* In a speech to his company about Faiko's work, Meyerhold discusses melodrama as a form of total spectacle:

> A reconsideration of the basic laws of dramatic art is being undertaken in our theaters, and the trend toward melodrama, which has appeared in recent times, has much to justify it. We take up melodrama, not as Vadim Shershenevich [translator of Dumas père and Sardou and author of *The Lady with the Black Glove*, given at the Workshop of the Experimental Heroic Theater in 1922] has done or anyone else who trots out on stage the mechanical devices of melodrama because melodrama has always been successful—we do it not for that reason, but because mankind itself demands from the theater that all its elements, to which humanity has been accustomed since ancient times, be operative in the theater. In the theater there always had to be musical accompaniment and dance.[11]

The Mystery of Kenilworth Castle, a melodrama adapted by E. E. Matern from Victor Hugo's play *Amy Robsart* (1822), is presented at the Studio of the Malyi Theater.

December. Harriet Beecher Stowe's *Uncle Tom's Cabin*, adapted by the playwright Alexander Brushtein and the director Boris Zon as a melodrama for children, is staged at the Studio of the Malyi Theater; it is also

---

presented in Leningrad at the Theater for Young Spectators in 1927. Stage versions of *Uncle Tom's Cabin* had been popular in prerevolutionary Russia and continue to play in provincial theaters in the USSR well into the 1950s.

Leningrad. *March. Gavroche: The Story of a Single Barricade*—Alexander Brushtein's dramatization of episodes from Hugo's *Les Misérables*—is presented at the Theater for Young Spectators.

October. Citizen Darnay, an adaptation of parts of Dickens's *A Tale of Two Cities* by the actor, director, and playwright Leonid Makaryev, is staged at the Theater for Young Spectators.

1926

Moscow. *March.* Victor Hugo's *Notre Dame de Paris*, adapted by Nikolai Krashennikov as a melodrama in four acts, is presented at the Malyi Theater, where it continues in the repertory through 1929, despite complaints that too much Hugo is being shown and that the pseudomelodramatic style of staging his works is unsatisfactory.

October. At the Kamerny Theater Andrei Globa's *Rosita*, starring Alice Koonen, is directed by Alexander Tairov, with songs on national Spanish motifs by Nikolai Medtner. Globa's play is based on Ernst Lubitsch's first Hollywood film, *Rosita* (1923, originally to be called *The Singer of Seville)*, in which Mary Pickford plays a street singer in nineteenth-century Spain who becomes involved in court intrigues as the result of a satirical song lampooning the king. The film itself is an adaptation by Lubitsch's scenario writer Hans Kräly of a famous nineteenth-century melodrama, *Don César de Bazen*, by Dennery and Dumanoir (1844, Porte-Saint-Martin, with Frédéric Lemaître), extremely popular in prerevolutionary Russia. In the French original, the singer is named Maritana, the action takes place in the Renaissance during the reign of Charles II, and the swashbuckling hero is taken from Hugo's *Ruy Blas*. A second American film version of the same play, called *The Spanish Dancer*, with Pola Negri, Adolphe Menjou, and Wallace Beery, also appeared in 1923. Inspired by these Hollywood melodramas and their movie stars, Globa (one of the most talented and original playwrights of the Soviet period) gives the colorful drama a modern setting and a political theme. The Soviet Rosita is an anarchist who climbs on top of barrels in poor quarters and sings songs that not only tug at the heartstrings, but also offer the people hope and challenge them to struggle against oppression. During carnival time, the king falls in love with Rosita, sets the police to pursue her, and has her abducted. In Spain a single step can lead from laughter to murder, from a carnival joke to full-scale rebellion. Tairov conceives the production as prototypical melodrama mixing love songs and comic episodes with tragedy and revolutionary passion. In an address to his company, Tairov declares:

Melodrama is in origin and in essence a revolutionary type of drama. Its fundamental laws are mockery and abuse of evil, philistinism, and meanness of spirit, and affirmation of justice and truth. In Globa's play we are shown the contemporary Spain of Alphonse XIII, about whom Blasco-Ibáñez wrote his famous pamphlet. Spain provides splendid material for melodrama. We are emphasizing those aspects of the play appropriate to the type of melodrama performed in the public marketplace. This requires its own special techniques. The development of the action must be swift, and the rhythm precise. The performance must be fiery and thrilling.[12]

Leningrad. *December.* Boris Romashov's *The End of Krivorylsk*, directed by Nikolai Petrov with sets by Nikolai Akimov, is presented at the Leningrad Academic Theater. Called a satirical melodrama, Romashov's play is about the transformation of a small provincial town whose ludicrous czarist past is eradicated as new revolutionary values are implanted; the town is renamed Leninski. As the result of the play's success, a vogue for satirical melodramas is started.

1927

Moscow. *October.* *The Sisters Gerard* is presented on the Small Stage of the Moscow *Art Theater.* Written by Vladimir Mass and directed by Nikolai Gorchakov, with Pavel Markov as literary manager, this historical melodrama is based both on Dennery and Cormon's *Les Deux orphelines* and D. W. Griffith's film version, *Orphans of the Storm* (1921, with Lillian and Dorothy Gish, first shown in the USSR in 1925), set at the time of the French Revolution, in Griffith's words, as anti-Bolshevik propaganda to show the dangers of mob rule and Robespierre's rabble-rousing demagoguery—a reflection of the recent "red-scare" hysteria in America. Restructured as prorevolution, *The Sisters Gerard* is still officially criticized as an obsolete specimen of bourgeois culture no longer of any interest to Soviet theatergoers and an inappropriate choice for a theater famous for its realistic traditions of acting. In his remarks to the actors, Stanislavsky discusses the theatrical values of the genre and the proper techniques of melodramatic acting:

> In melodrama dramatic scenes are invariably interspersed with comic ones; otherwise it would be impossible to watch. The overcoming of difficulties and misfortunes by the melodramatic hero inevitably imparts to the genre a romantic coloration.
>
> In melodrama the actor must absolutely believe in everything that takes place. No matter what the author has devised, the actor must assume that it has all actually happened. Then and only then will the audience believe all of it. But if the actor winks at the audience throughout the performance to indicate

that he is doing all of it simply because he is playing in a melodrama today, but will be appearing in a real drama tomorrow, then the spectators will be bored.

In melodrama we are very often supposed to laugh at the villain.

A second-rate actor cannot play melodrama. In melodrama the actor must give a great deal of himself; a second-rate actor, without a vivid personality, has nothing to add to his role.

That is why the birth of a melodrama has always depended on the participation of outstanding actors and has always occurred with elaborate settings.

It is of fundamental importance for the actor in melodrama to be able to execute in an interesting fashion all the physical actions indicated by the author.

When a melodrama is to be performed, there can be no coldness or apathy in the theater. On the night of the performance everything must be extraordinary and unexpected. Thus the spectator becomes electrified in advance and a few sparks are then enough for everything to flare up so that creativity and inspiration start to take place on stage—this is yet another way for the actor to acquire a sound creative method. Melodrama does not tolerate any conventionality.

Watching a melodrama, the audience should assume that everything shown in the play has inevitably happened in *real life*, and not on the stage. And that is why theatrical conventionality is the antithesis of melodrama.

Melodrama has always arisen when audiences were filled to the brim with lofty and noble feelings and needed ways to express them and find an outlet for their emotions. And that is why your play should be a great success. Now, after the revolution, many beautiful sentiments have been aroused in our audiences, and the public wants to see exactly the same fine and noble things and just such strong emotions coming from the stage.[13]

1928

Moscow. *February.* Alexander Faiko's *The Man with the Briefcase*, directed by Alexander Dikii with sets by Nikolai Akimov, is presented at the Theater of the Revolution. This mystery adventure melodrama traces the rise and fall of Professor Dmitrii Granatov, a cynical opportunist and ruthless individualist, who hypocritically mouths Bolshevik sentiments and attempts to manipulate the new regime for his own selfish purposes. After committing a number of crimes, Granatov is finally unmasked and driven to suicide. The first Soviet play to deal with an intellectual as an enemy of the people plotting underhandedly against the Revolution, *The Man with the Briefcase* is praised for raising an important issue but severely criticized for its manner of doing so. In the view of the critics, the outer form of exciting but unreal adventures does not suit the material and results in oversimplification, improbability, and lack of motivation. Faiko's attempt to present a serious picture of contemporary life in such an amusing and sensational form leads to the triumph of entertainment over realism. The old nineteenth-century form of melodrama is no longer regarded as suitable for dealing with the complex problems of Soviet reality; it is impossible to put contemporary life and its social conflicts into the crude and factitious mold of traditional bourgeois genres. The critic and theorist Boris Alpers expresses the now widespread feeling that melodrama is an obsolete form that cannot be adapted to revolutionary ideology:

> On stage a French melodrama of the adventure type was being played according to all the established laws of the genre. The hero of the play was endowed with all the attributes of the traditional theatrical villain, committing crimes exactly as the hero of Pixérécourt's melodramas commits them. The social and psychological fabric of the portrayal was hidden under a web of entertaining stage situations taken from the arsenal of classic melodrama and developing not by virtue of the concrete conditions of life today but by virtue of the stage logic inherent in this genre.
>
> A biting political theme from our own days was forced into the framework of an adventure drama of a past century, which in its time had been firmly based on concrete social reality and shaped by it.
>
> The events shown in *The Man with the Briefcase* for that reason belonged to a significant degree to a fictional stage world, theatrically entertaining and striking but which had lost touch with everyday reality.
>
> The Theater of the Revolution caught precisely this aspect of Faiko's play by creating in a series of episodes a stylized quasi-fantastic set, which still more markedly pushed the action of the drama into the plane of theatrical make-believe.
>
> The heroes of Faiko's melodramas, adventurers and villains, followers of extreme individualism, for all their negative qualities appear on stage invested with a romantic halo. They are placed in a beautiful tragic pose.[14]

Despite the savage attacks by the critics, *The Man with the Briefcase* was a great popular success, remained in the repertory for many years, and played in a large number of theaters throughout the USSR. But the vogue

A. T. Anders as Jacques and M. A. Titova as Marianne in Vladimir Mass's version of *The Two Orphans* called *The Sisters Gerard* at the small stage of the Moscow Art Theater in 1927. *Courtesy Alma H. Law Collection*

for melodrama came to an end as the result of this production and the official responses that it elicited.

Notes

1. A. V. Lunacharsky, *Sobraniye sochinenii* (Moscow: Khudozhestvennaya Literatura, 1964), 2:213-215.
2. Reprinted in "Dramaturgicheskie Konkursy," ed. N. S. Plyatskovskaya, in *Russkii Sovetskii Teatr 1917-1921: Dokumenty i Materialy*, ed. A. Z. Yufit (Leningrad: Iskusstvo, 1968), p. 359.
3. *Arkhiv A. M. Gor'kogo* (Moscow: Goslitizdat, 1951), 3:220-22.
4. Quoted in S. Mokul'skii, "V bor'be za Klassiky," *Bol'shoi Dramaticheskii Teatr* (Leningrad: Bol'shoi Dramaticheskii Teatr, 1935), pp. 49-50.
5. P. A. Markov, *O teatre* (Moscow: Iskusstvo, 1976), 3:7-8.
6. Lunacharsky, *Sobraniye sochinenii*, 3:112-14.
7. Sergei Yutkevich, *Kontrapunkt rezhissera* (Moscow: Iskusstvo, 1960), pp. 233-34.
8. Aleksei Faiko, *Teatr* (Moscow: Iskusstvo, 1971), p. 516.
9. Markov, *O teatre*, 3:176.
10. Adrian Piotrovskii, *Teatr, kino, zhizn'* (Leningrad: Iskusstvo, 1969), pp. 64-65.
11. V. E. Meyerhold, *Stat'i, Pis'ma, Rechi, Besedy* (Moscow: Iskusstvo, 1968), 2:76.
12. Quoted in Alisa Koonen, *Stranitsy zhizni* (Moscow: Iskusstvo, 1975), p. 309.
13. Quoted in N. Gorchakov, *Rezhisserskie uroki K. S. Stanislavskogo* (Moscow: Iskusstvo, 1950, pp. 296-314.
14. B. Alpers, *Teatral'nye ocherki* (Moscow: Iskusstvo, 1977), 2:208, 230.

The Two Orphans
in Revolutionary Disguise

ALMA H. LAW

In 1926, Konstantin Stanislavsky invited Nikolai Gorchakov and Pavel
Markov to try their hand at directing a production with the Moscow Art
Theater's young performers. The play the two young directors finally
selected for staging (with Stanislavsky's blessing) was *Les Deux Orphelines*
by Adolphe Dennery and Eugène Cormon. Written in 1874, this very
popular nineteenth-century melodrama tells of the vicissitudes that befall
Henriette and her blind sister, Louise, on their arrival in Paris where they
have come to live with their uncle Martin. Martin, who has been drugged
by the police detective, Picard, fails to meet them, and the two girls become separated when Henriette is abducted. Henriette is taken to the Marquis de Presles's chateau where she is presented to the assembled guests as
his latest find. When Henriette begs to be taken back to the square where
her sister is waiting, she is rescued by the Chevalier de Vaudrey who set-
tles her in a room in Paris and promises to help her find Louise.

Meanwhile, Louise has been snatched by La Frochard who forces the
girl to go out begging with her crippled son, Pierre. Pierre soon falls in
love with Louise only to be thrust aside by his brother, Jacques, who

decides to take Henriette for himself. Events reach a climax when de Vaudrey's mother, Countess de Linières, visits Henriette and discovers that Louise is the daughter she had abandoned as a baby. At that moment Louise passes by in the street singing. Henriette recognizes her voice and rushes to find her. However, she is stopped at the door by a policeman who, by order of the Count de Linières, takes her to prison.

In prison, Henriette meets Jacques's mistress, Marianne, who gives the girl La Frochard's address and helps her to escape. Henriette rushes to La Frochard's and demands the release of her sister. A fight ensues between Jacques and Pierre over Louise. At that moment de Vaudrey arrives, followed by Picard who arrests Jacques and his mother. Next to arrive are the Count and Countess de Linières along with a doctor. The melodrama ends happily with Louise learning that the Countess is her mother, de Vaudrey proposing to Henriette, and the doctor promising to restore Louise's eyesight.

Well aware that the Moscow Art Theater would invite certain attack for staging something so seemingly frivolous, the directors commissioned a librettist and writer of comic parodies, Vladimir Mass, to do a new, more "socially significant" version of the melodrama. Inspired by *Orphans of the Storm*, D. W. Griffith's 1921 epic film adaptation of Dennery's melodrama, Mass moved the play's action from Louis XV's reign to 1789, the eve of the French Revolution. In this way, Mass was able to transform the melodrama, now titled *The Sisters Gerard*, into a rather politically loaded picture of conflict between self-satisfied aristocratic "haves," and starving, discontented "have-nots," for which the audience could easily find parallels in its own recent history. Typical of the revolutionary color Mass injected into the melodrama were the crowd scenes he added, such as the one with which the play opens, depicting a hungry and very angry crowd milling about in front of an empty bakery demanding bread (this appears in Griffith as well).

Mass also completely reworked the final act of the play to give it more tragic overtones, by having Henriette fatally stab Jacques in order to prevent him from killing his brother. The play concludes with a courtroom scene in which a people's court is trying Henriette for murder. Alas, the only person who can save her is Pierre and he has disappeared. At the final moment, however, when all seems lost, Marianne rescues Pierre from the cellar where La Frochard had locked him and brings him to the courtroom. Pierre just barely manages to testify to Henriette's innocence before he collapses to the courtroom floor and dies. As a hero of the Revolution, he is solemnly covered with the tricolor. The play closes with a speech by the chairman of the people's court which rather hopefully suggests that in troubled times "the people's court must be governed not only by facts, but also must look at what is hidden behind the flood of events. . . ."

By far the most interesting change Mass made in the Dennery melodrama was to transform the gathering of aristocrats (act 1, scene 2) from a rather stuffy affair to a full-blown orgy (also in Griffith), which in the production culminated with little blackamoors carrying in a huge tray laden with fruits that were then removed to reveal the half-nude body of the drugged Henriette. Not only did this orgy satisfy Stanislavsky's love for staging complicated scenes with large numbers of actors—and he, himself, actively took part in creating and rehearsing the orgy—but it also provided just the kind of spectacle that audiences in the still austere world of Moscow loved to see.

Actually, to call this an orgy is something of an exaggeration. "What is an orgy?" Stanislavsky asked at one rehearsal. "It is the scandalous behavior of a group of morally corrupt people, a series of disgusting actions almost always carried out under the influence of narcotics."[1] As Stanislavsky well knew, however, it would be impossible to present such behavior directly on the stage of the Moscow Art Theater. The solution to this problem was to suggest much but to reveal very little. In other words, to tease the spectators and let their imaginations fill in the rest.

The setting for the orgy is a room in the Marquis de Presle's house, lighted by candelabra with special shades that allowed the room to be plunged quickly into darkness. Here and there screens are strategically placed to half-conceal little niches. At both sides are doors leading to inside rooms and at the back is a series of curtains which separate the room from the hall where the orgy is taking place. The effect is that there are a great many people in the house but that most of them are in the main hall behind the curtain and in the niches hidden from the spectators.

As the orgy opens, couples enter and run past. Voices, shouts, and noises are heard from the hall. Little blackamoors appear carrying drinks and bowls of fruit. Music is heard playing continuously.

Scene 1

Two MARQUISES *and a* GIRL *come out from behind the curtain and sit in one of the niches on the stage.*
FIRST MARQUIS. The fluidity and grace of your movements when you dance allow one to suppose that in situations accompanying love you favor the fortunate one with inexplicable joys.
SECOND MARQUIS. You have no rivals in the art of dancing. What, then, can one expect from you in the art of love?!
GIRL. My grandmother taught me. Her suitor was Louis the Beloved himself.
[A little BLACKAMOOR *serves them wine. The first* MARQUIS *moves the screen so that all three are hidden from view.]*

Scene 2

In another niche several claps of the hand are heard and

the BLACKAMOOR *hurries there. He opens the screen behind which are sitting* ROGER, *a* MIDDLE-AGED ARISTOCRAT, *a* GIRL, *and two other men. The little* BLACKAMOOR *receives an order and runs off leaving the niche open.*

MIDDLE-AGED ARISTOCRAT *(holding the* GIRL *on his knees, and unnoticed by her, undoing the back of her bodice. He speaks grandiloquently).* Yes, gentlemen. I am definitely sorry that the Prince of Orleans is not among us. He would have the proof that all his talk about the Parisian riff-raff on the verge of rebelling, about the hunger, and about the growing dissensions among us are all the fruits of his imagination, frightened by events in America. Dissension among us. Where is it? I see a friendly and gay society! Hunger? I see bowls full of ripe fruit!

ROGER. But the mob . . .

MIDDLE-AGED ARISTOCRAT. Oh, the mob! The mob will always remain the mob. We have mercenaries ready to take care of it!

ROGER. You are forgetting about Palais-Royal. I don't want to be a prophet, but the people's anger is growing day by day. The people's thinking is taking the form of firm decisions. It is already finding leaders. Centier and Legendre are not of the mob. Neither mercenaries nor the Bastille will save us when they decide to act instead of talking!

MIDDLE-AGED ARISTOCRAT. Ha-ha!! Legendre! Invite Mr. Legendre here and he'll forget about his demagogy in an instant!

GIRL *(noticing that the* MIDDLE-AGED ARISTOCRAT *has undone her dress).* Oh, Count, what are you doing? You are merciless! I have nothing else on! *(She runs off.)*

MIDDLE-AGED ARISTOCRAT *(running after her).* Stop, stop! Where are you going? *(He runs after the* GIRL. *The entire group follows after him.)*

ROGER. Leave her alone. *(He exits to the opposite side, behind a curtain.)*

Scene 3

An OLD GENTLEMAN *coming out of the door at the left meets the* MARQUIS DE PRESLES *who has come out from behind the curtain. They exchange bows.*

DE PRESLES. Where are you coming from, Count? Why are you so late?

OLD GENTLEMAN. I've just come from Versailles. You can't imagine how distasteful it was for me, who favors the fine old traditions of the court, to be present at his majesty's party!

DE PRESLES. What upset you so?

OLD GENTLEMAN. There's not the least trace left of the former refinement of address, the former elegance of manner, the former etiquette, and the former courtliness. During the minuet, the ladies almost touch their partners with their breasts.

DE PRESLES. Impossible! *(He moves away.)*

Scene 4

The first GIRL *runs out from behind the screen with a penetrating squeal. The two* MARQUISES *from scene one play with her, teasing her in every possible way.*

GIRL *(fighting them off).* Marquis, that exceeds all limits. You're tormenting me. Aren't you ashamed to torture me like that?

FIRST MARQUIS *(to the other).* More boldly, Marquis, more boldly to the attack!

GIRL. Oh, it hurts! I'll be left with bruises and I won't be able to wear this dress any more. Do you think I wouldn't dare pay you in kind? *(She begins to defend herself forcefully.)*

FIRST MARQUIS. Oh, you bitch! How dare you scratch when we play with you. We paid you and have the right to do anything we want.

GIRL. Don't tear my dress. You won't buy me a new one, will you! I can live only a day on what you paid me.

DE PRESLES *(again coming out from behind the curtain).* Enough, gentlemen! Why are you making such a noise, Jeanne? Do you want me to forbid you to come to this house? house?

[The GIRL *and the* MARQUISES *are about to answer him when their attention is caught by an extravagantly dressed* LADY *who is riding on the back of the* OLD GENTLEMAN *from scene three. The* OLD GENTLEMAN *is bridled with ribbons like a horse. A* YOUNG ARISTOCRAT *is driving him with a little whip. A part of the gathering runs out from behind the curtain and follows after them. General laughter.]*

Scene 5

LADY. Well, carry me, count. Show that you're still good for something.

[The YOUNG ARISTOCRAT *whips the* OLD GENTLEMAN *more strongly.]*

OLD GENTLEMAN. Viscount, your whip makes itself felt more than is necessary. It's no longer play. I won't be able to carry our charming kitten.

DE PRESLES. My old friend, allow me to help you.

OLD GENTLEMAN. Thank you, my dear Marquis, thank you!

[COUNT DE LINIÈRES *appears in the doorway. The men lower the* LADY *to the floor. All greet the Count.*]

Scene 6

DE PRESLES. Greetings to you, dear chairman.

[COUNT DE LINIÈRES *exchanges bows with those present.*]

DE LINIÈRES *(taking the* MARQUIS *aside).* Did you manage the abduction, Marquis?

DE PRESLES. I still don't know. I'm expecting Picard any moment now.

DE LINIÈRES. That girl from the provinces made an impression on me. I should like to know how much she would cost me?

DE PRESLES. Dear Count, for you . . . Oh, we'll come to terms.

DE LINIÈRES. But still?

DE PRESLES. My brother, Viscount Blizet, is anxious to get the position of tax collector in the department of the Seine.

DE LINIÈRES. And he isn't afraid the mob will tear him to pieces? The people are in a very militant mood. I warn you, we can't give him any protection. Every soldier of ours is accounted for.

DE PRESLES. He'll hire people with his own money.

DE LINIÈRES. Excellent! Let him submit an application and I'll sign it.

DE PRESLES. And I'll be happy to give over my find to you this very day.

DE LINIÈRES. What, she'll be here?

DE PRESLES. I hope so.

[DE LINIÈRES *exits into the hall. Noise and greetings are heard behind the curtain.*]

Scene 7

[FLORETTE *appears in the door at the left.*]

DE PRESLES *(turning and seeing her).* Ah, Florette Bergère! *(All applaud her.)*

GUESTS. Another new dress!
        Bravo, Florette, charming!

FLORETTE. Gentlemen, gentlemen! A revolution! There's been a revolution!

GUESTS. What?!!
        What are you saying?

FLORETTE. Yes. A revolution. A revolution in hairdos. We are returning to curls. *(She turns and shows her curls.)*

GUESTS. Bravo, bravo, Florette!
    Enchanting!
    What an invention!
    Such taste!
[All pass with FLORETTE *into the hall.]*

Scene 8

[A VISCOUNT *appears with a* YOUNG GIRL *on the forestage.]*
VISCOUNT. I beg you. Your answer?
YOUNG GIRL. I love you!
VISCOUNT. Could I dream of such bliss! I believe in the sincerity of your avowal. But I'm poor, I have nothing.
YOUNG GIRL. I despise gold. Real love is unselfish.

Scene 9

An outburst of shouts from the hall. At that moment gold coins fly through the air from behind the curtain. From various sides women greedily rush to catch them and fight for them. The YOUNG GIRL *runs to join the crowd of women. Some of the guests, including* ROGER *and* DE PRESLES, *come out from behind the curtain.*
ROGER. What happened?
DE PRESLES. Count de Linières's favorite amusement. He is still sufficiently wealthy to allow himself this entertainment.
*[*COUNT DE LINIÈRES *comes out and again throws some money. A new outburst of shouts. The women again fight to catch the coins.]*
ROGER. Father, stop. That is unworthy of you.
DE LINIÈRES. Roger, learn not to poke your nose where it's not wanted.
ROGER. The money you are throwing away belongs to the family and not to you.
DE LINIÈRES. I'm not asking your advice. I have the right to do as I wish with my means.
ROGER. My duty is to restore your self-restraint which evidently has left you.
DE LINIÈRES. You blathering pup! Who gave you the right to talk to me like that?

Scene 10

The GUESTS *gather on stage.* MARQUIS DE PRESLES, *sensing an imminent quarrel between* DE LINIÈRES *and* ROGER, *tries to detract attention. He turns to the guests.*
DE PRESLES. Gentlemen, a moment of attention! There is an

outsider among us.

GUESTS. Who? Who?

DE PRESLES. Viscount Roger, the son of our chairman, Count de Linières. He is at our feast of the "Awakened Fawns" for the first time tonight.

GUESTS. Ritual! Ritual!
Wake the new fawn!
Perform the rite of initiation!

ROGER. Stop, gentlemen, this is ridiculous! Everything going on here is extremely unpleasant to me, and I'll retire with pleasure if you'll allow me.

GUESTS. Not for anything!
Don't let him go, don't let him go!

[The ritual begins.]

(Song of the Fawns)

Oh, Pan, great god of the beasts
And honored among people,
Quickly accept the uninitiated
Into your family.

He knows everything and loves life,
Who is initiated into the fawns,
Who knows the rite of love,
Who remembers your law.

Let lips cling to lips,
Love is always right,
Our own we must take,
And not give a care!

Life is short,
After it, nothing,
Sadness be silent,
Passion flare up.

Everything forgotten,
Let's soar to the heights,
All those who live,
Twirl in dance!

Clear is the road to joy
Whose spirit is drunk with love.
Be with us again!
Wake up from sleep!
Awaken, great Pan!

Teach us, oh goat-legged one
Appear here before us.

Let springs of seething love,
Well up in each heart.

Like night, all in the future is dark,
So catch, then, the hour of happiness,
Let the wine foam noisily,
And the passionate dance go on.

> Burn, heart
> In this is your paradise.
> Passion,
> Overflow.

Everything forgotten,
Let's soar to the heights,
All those who live,
Twirl in dance!

[The MARQUIS DE PRESLES *gives a signal and during the first stanza, the little* BLACKAMOORS *distribute to the guests the grotesque masks of the fawns.* ROGER *is led to the music into the hall to the statue of Pan for initiation. Behind the curtain, figures flash in a wild dance. Suddenly everything is plunged into darkness. Shouts. Another moment and* ROGER *runs out on the fore-stage shouting in revulsion, "How disgusting! I'm not going to do that!" The* GUESTS *and* DE PRESLES *follow after him!]*

ROGER. Turn up the lights. Stop this disgrace!

DE PRESLES. What's the matter with you, Roger?

GUESTS. What happened to him?
      What frightened him so?

ROGER. How can you fail to understand that this is repulsive, that it's boring! I can't bear it!

GUESTS. You gave your son too refined an education. He lost his taste for jest!

DE LINIÈRES. I've always regretted that we put his teacher, Doctor Gilbert, in the Bastille so late.

ROGER. Again, you insult him by mentioning his name here. Yes, I owe everything to him, and not to you. He taught me to see what you don't see. He was the first to open my eyes to the life of our society and to the future of France . . .

GUESTS. Viscount, have pity on us. We want to have fun! . . .
      We're not at all interested in knowing what your
            teacher taught you! . . .
      Let's go on with the game! . . .

ROGER. Enough! I don't want to take part in such madness. Aren't you afraid to wallow here in this mindless vice, this disgusting licentiousness, when an abyss is opening up under us, when perhaps tomorrow the mob will burst into your houses and cut off your heads?

[General laughter]

DE LINIÈRES. You are tiresome, you pup. This is not your Palais-Royal.

ROGER. I know, father, that in the dirtiest hovel, in the meanest quarter, it is cleaner than here!

DE LINIÈRES. You're crazy, I'm ashamed for you. You don't understand what you are saying.

GUESTS. He thinks he's a street orator!
  Danton's laurels don't give him peace. He wants to exceed him in demagogy!
  How ridiculous! The son of the minister of justice!

ROGER. Shame, father! You are marring the honor of the French nobility.

DE LINIÈRES. You, least of all, have the right to speak about the honor of the French nobility. The son of the minister of justice and a frequenter of Palais-Royal, ready like a dog to lick the hands of hungry fanatics!

ROGER. The minister of justice in the role of chairman of the League of Fawns, ready to be at the head of any disgrace by this den of iniquity!

DE LINIÈRES. Miserable misfit!

ROGER. Minister of debauchery!

DE LINIÈRES. Roger!

DE PRESLES. Count! Viscount! Calm down! Why get excited! Our code doesn't allow political arguments. Long live France. We all love her equally. Hail to the King! Hail to the Queen!

[A servant whispers something in the Marquis's ear.]

DE PRESLES. Furthermore, our program is not yet over. I prepared a surprise for you whose success I can vouch for. *(to the servant)* Have her brought in! Attention, gentlemen!

Scene 11

Music. Four little blackamoors, with PICARD *at the head, carry in* HENRIETTA. HENRIETTA *is in a faint. All, except* ROGER, *approach her with curiosity.*

GUESTS. How lovely!
  Where did you find her?
  She's nothing special!
  There's no end to your ideas, Marquis! You are full of surprises!
  She's sweet!
  I don't understand who could like such skinny ones!
  I don't like her!
  Nor I!
  Nor I!
  Nor I!

DE LINIÈRES. Well, if our ladies dislike her so much, then she is indeed perfection.

DE PRESLES. She is innocence itself, Count.

ROGER. A new actress in a new comedy!

DE PRESLES. Viscount, you're a skeptic! I swear there's no trickery here.

GUESTS. She's asleep!
She's in a faint!

ROGER. She's simply pretending in order to play her role better.

DE PRESLES. Picard, I convey to you the gratitude of our entire lodge. You carried out my commission so cleverly. There, gentlemen, I recommend him to all who want to freshen their table with new dishes.

PICARD. Allow me to disturb the sleep of our country Venus?

ALL. Please, please!

MIDDLE-AGED ARISTOCRAT. Let's put on the masks!

DE PRESLES. A brilliant idea! I can imagine her astonishment when she awakens.

[The guests put on the masks. PICARD gives HENRIETTA a vial with some kind of liquid to sniff. HENRIETTA opens her eyes. Those present silently observe her awakening. HENRIETTA looks around. She is frightened. She doesn't understand where she is. Then she sits up.]

HENRIETTA. Heavens! I've gone out of my mind!

[One of those present approaches her imitating the bleating of a goat. All laugh.]

HENRIETTA *(frightened).* Oh, what is this? *(She cries, then her eyes rest on PICARD.)* Are you Uncle Martin? . . . *(All laugh.)* You . . . You ordered me seized . . . You separated me from my sister! . . . Where is she?

MIDDLE-AGED ARISTOCRAT. You have a sister! Ha-ha-ha! She has a sister! And what, is she as pretty as you?

HENRIETTA. What do you want from me? Why did you bring me here? Let me go! She's alone! She's on the square! Near the river! Let me go, let me go!!! I must go back immediately!

ROGER. How vile! To squander your talent playing such a vulgar farce!

HENRIETTA *(to PICARD).* Take me back to my sister! If you have even a drop of pity, take me back. . . . How long have I slept? She's waiting for me! She's calling me! I implore you, order that man to take me back.

DE PRESLES. Dear child, you have no reason to blame him. We all wanted to see you in our circle. He only carried out my orders.

HENRIETTA. Oh, I recognize you! You are the same lord who helped me alight when our stage coach broke down . . . yesterday . . . there, in the forest, and it blocked your way . . .

DE PRESLES. I am exceedingly flattered that you remembered me so well!

HENRIETTA. Then help me now. Let me leave!

DE PRESLES. Part with you? Not for anything! You are an honored guest here. Everything you see, including us, belongs to you. You are the queen of our feast by right of youth and beauty.

HENRIETTA. But I'm no queen. What do you want me for? Why are you keeping me here?

DE PRESLES. How can you ask that? You don't know your own worth! Your youth and beauty are an inexhaustible source of pleasure for each of us. But you'll see that we know how to show our gratitude.

HENRIETTA. Oh! I think I understand what kind of people you are! You kidnapped me. You want to make me your toy and to pay me for that . . . But I don't want to. I don't need to. I don't need anything from you . . . Let me go!

DE PRESLES. Oh, that's not so terrible and it's easily forgotten!

HENRIETTA. Take me back! Heavens, you don't understand that what you've done is doubly cruel! My sister! What she is feeling at this moment! I'm her only support, you see. She has been left alone! Without my help she can't take a single step! What will happen with her. She's blind, you see!

ALL. Blind!!!

HENRIETTA. Yes, blind, blind! Alone in Paris! We just arrived here . . . She doesn't know anyone, absolutely no one! And now she is wandering around the city without money, without help . . . She may be run over by a carriage . . . She could fall, or drown . . . Do you hear? Oh, have pity on us!

GUESTS. Poor girl!
　　　This is indeed terrible!

ROGER. A clever plot for a comedy, and a lot of ingenuity. Is it possible she's not acting? No, could it be real?!

DE PRESLES. Calm down. We'll send people. I'll give an order, they'll find this girl and bring her to you. And meanwhile, forget your unhappiness. Don't let's sink into a gloomy mood. There are so many brilliant gentlemen here. Any one you honor with your choice will be happy to spend several cheerful hours with you.

GUESTS. Who do you like here best of all?
　　　Which one of us do you choose?

[DE LINIÈRES gives a sign. The men form a circle.]

ALL. Red lips, blue eyes,
      Why is it you tarry?
      Choose. You'll not find a route
      Closer to happiness.
      Choose, then quickly,
      Which one you like the best!

[All dance around HENRIETTA.]

HENRIETTA. Don't you dare touch me . . . I don't want to!
Isn't there anyone among you who will take pity on me?

ROGER. This is terrible, if she should be telling the truth.

HENRIETTA. Won't anyone defend me? What did I do to
you? I have no father, no mother, won't you have pity on
me? Can it be possible you have neither shame nor pity?
Save me, someone! You don't understand my despair!
Don't you hear my sister's cries? Haven't you even a shred of
honor . . . in order to defend a poor girl? Isn't there anyone . . .

ROGER. You are mistaken, young lady. Give me your hand. I
believe you. Let's get out here.

HENRIETTA. Oh, thank you. Let's go, let's go quickly!

DE PRESLES. Wait, I'm the master here. I won't allow you to
take her away!

ROGER. Please make way.

DE PRESLES. No. No one has ever left my house at this hour!

ROGER. Fine. Then we'll be the first. Let me go, Marquis. I
order you!

DE LINIÈRES. Roger, leave this girl immediately! She's not
yours. If you don't like it here, you can get out alone.

ROGER. I am leaving only with her.

DE LINIÈRES. You are mistaken. We won't let her go!

[ROGER tries to pass. The COUNT DE LINIÈRES blocks
his way. ROGER draws his sword.]

DE LINIÈRES. What! You want to fight with your father because of this country girl?

ROGER. I'll fight with every scoundrel who prevents me from
carrying out my duty.

[THE COUNT draws his sword. DE PRESLES and several
GUESTS throw themselves between them.]

DE PRESLES. Count, you haven't the right to risk your
life . . . To fight with your son! The king would never forgive you if something happened to you at such a difficult moment for France. As master of the house I am more insulted
than you. You must cede to me the right to fight this defender of oppressed innocence.

[DE LINIÈRES hands the sword to DE PRESLES.]

DE PRESLES (standing opposite ROGER with drawn sword).
Try to pass!

ROGER. As you wish.
[They cross swords.]
GUESTS. Gentlemen, stop!
No, he needs a lesson!
What a blow. He'll kill him!
Look, look!
HENRIETTA. Heavens, have pity on us!
[The MARQUIS DE PRESLES *falls. All rush to support him.]*
ROGER *(drawing* HENRIETTA *away).* Let's go quickly!

Curtain

The Sisters Gerard proved to be a particularly difficult production for the Moscow Art Theater. As a result, the theater spent three times longer on it than Stanislavsky had expected. After a year of preparation and several postponements, *The Sisters Gerard* had its premiere on the Art Theater's "little stage" (the former Second Studio) on October 29, 1927. The production was almost universally panned by the critics, who in addition to raising the question of "Who needs this melodrama?" also criticized the directors for their failure to capture the romantic pathos this genre demands. "All the intonations were right out of Chekhov and Ostrovsky," the critic O. Litovsky observed, adding that "these intonations, their 'naturalness' in places where the text is especially naive, sounded almost like a parody."[2] Nevertheless, according to Vladimir Mass, *The Sisters Gerard* was extremely popular with audiences.[3] They were all too happy to overlook its shortcomings and to simply enjoy the many twists and turns of this melodrama in revolutionary disguise. The production remained for a number of years in the Moscow Art Theater's repertoire.[4]

Notes

1. Vladimir Mass, *The Sisters Gerard* (Sestry Zherar) Moscow: Izdatelstvo MODPIK, 1927.
2. Uriel, "The Sisters Gerard" (Sestry Zherar), *Sovremennyi teatr* (1927), 11:166.
3. In conversation, February 3, 1978.
4. Further discussion of the Moscow Art Theater's staging of this production can be found in Nikolai M. Gorchakov, *Stanislavsky Directs* (New York: Minerva Press, 1968), pp. 277–349, and in David Magarshack, *Stanislavsky on the Art of the Stage* (New York: Hill & Wang, 1961), pp. 297–304.

Old Forms Enter the New American Theater: Shepard, Foreman, Kirby, and Ludlam

JAMES LEVERETT

Sam Shepard

In 1968 *Melodrama Play* became the fifth work by Sam Shepard to win an Obie award within four years.[1]   The young author, then only twenty-five, was well on his way to being recognized as the most gifted and original among a whole chorus of innovative, iconoclastic voices rocking the American theater at that time. Our mainstream tradition—dominated for a generation by Inge, Miller, and Williams—had been judged by the newcomers and found wanting. Mere realism could not contain the vast, tumultuous, often terrifying currents that they felt moving all around them. So, in order to revitalize an art and move it forward, the young artists, consciously or not, looked backward, as is often the case during a cultural revolution. Shunning the immediate past of neat dramas in box sets, they reached beyond to older traditions of more exuberant theatricality.

When he called his creation a "melodrama" play, Shepard was evoking a genre that had fallen into great disfavor. The name still summons up rather simpleminded apparitions in which mustache-twirling villains menace lily-pure damsels who are rescued in the nick of time by heroes whose single attribute is their sterling behavior. This fantasy of utter vice and perfect virtue is served up in an overblown style: cataclysmic disasters, outlandish coincidences, hairbreadth escapes, all drawn with huge gestures and climactic tableaux delineating unmistakably the conflict between good and evil. The picture, as lurid and silly as it might be, still strikes within us an immediate, deep chord of recognition and undeniably begs our emotional participation.

Shepard is conscious of the contradictory responses that his title might elicit. He says in the introduction to the play: "A production . . . should not be aimed toward making it strictly satirical but more toward discovering how it changes from the mechanism of melodrama to something more sincere."[2] Melodrama in his eyes is thus something to be "played" with and not accepted as truthful. The author even puns on the title, going back, whether he knows it or not, to the early nineteenth-century origin of the word—a dramatic piece with music. *Melodrama Play* calls for a rock-and-roll band ("suspended from the ceiling in a cage over the audience's head" is Shepard's suggestion[3]), which backs up the actors' songs and performs some solos of its own. What is more, the play is a drama *about* music. One could call it "The Perils of Duke Durgens, Rock Star."

Duke has one hit record to his name: "Prisoners, Get Up Out of Your Homemade Beds." He claims that this song combines the social message of a Bob Dylan with the poetic appeal of a Robert Goulet (both of whose poster-sized photographs, mysteriously eyeless, dominate the rudimentary set). With the help of his girlfriend, the loyal but dense Dana, Duke is unsuccessfully trying to turn out another blockbuster for his coming concert in Phoenix. Floyd, his manager, appears to give his client some gentle persuasion in the form of pressure at the back of the neck. Two guitarists are on the way, he says, to help out with the creativity. At their rental rates, there had better be results. After Floyd leaves, Duke tells Dana to get some scissors and trim his mane of rock-idol hair. She must also buy him a black suit and tie and a white shirt. He is going to change his image. Before she can follow directions, however, the musicians arrive: Drake (Duke's brother) and his sidekick, Cisco. Drake obliges his brother with a haircut and lets it slip that he really wrote Duke's hit. Floyd returns, finds nothing accomplished, and brings in Peter, a security guard, to see that nobody leaves until some new material is written. When Floyd discovers that Duke has lost his hair, evidently the star's only identifying mark, he decides that Drake must fill in for him in Phoenix. (But inexplicably Drake has introduced himself as Cisco and vice versa.) In the confusion and protest that follow, Peter, the guard, obediently knocks Duke out with a billy club and blows Dana's brains out. The latter bit of mayhem even upsets Floyd who will have to dispose of the body. He leaves, ordering Peter to allow no one in or out until his return. They should all get back to writing songs. Abruptly Peter lines up everyone and forbids them to move until they tell him what they think of him. Both Duke and Cisco get bludgeoned as they try to get past this new incomprehensible threat. In an effort to make some kind of personal contact with Drake, Peter tells him of a chilling dream: He is walking down a street at night when he notices an eyeless man crawling in the gutter beside him. On the man's request, Peter directs him toward Arizona. The man disappears into the distance. A policeman accosts Peter, evidently because he has had something to do with the blind man. He is dragged into a building and told to take off his pants. The dream is interrupted by Floyd trying to enter. Peter will not unlock the door. Drake, petrified with terror, cannot respond to Peter's repeated requests that he should say what he thinks of him. The play ends with Drake cowering under Peter's raised club.

At their best, plot summaries are not easy to follow, but this one is particularly difficult because of the exchanges of identities, arbitrary and elliptic action, and sudden shifts of focus. The play seems more like a vivid, inscrutable hallucination than like any usual notion of melodrama—" . . . the most conventional, schematic and artificial genre imaginable" as Arnold Hauser describes it.[4] But, examined more closely, there are certainly melodramatic elements at work here, even if they do not add up to a traditional formula. There are clear pairings of adversaries: brother against brother, star against manager, and finally the guard against everyone else. A heroine, with a good heart if not particularly unstained honor, is imperiled. There are also moments of inflated gesture and extreme language (which shall be discussed later in more detail) and the obvious climactic tableau of Peter threatening Drake. What is missing is a plainly structured system of good versus evil. All of the characters are caught in a struggle to maintain power and position regardless of what is required to do so. Even Duke, the figure who seems to start as the hero, has robbed his only successful song from his brother. The aggression and frustration, barely held in check by the rest, explode through the character of Peter, more obviously dangerous only because he is more overtly violent and psychotically unpredictable. Everyone battles to control circumstances but, instead, is controlled by the battle. Contrary to what we have come to anticipate in melodrama, the hero gets clobbered, the heroine murdered, and we are left with a scene of irrational, unresolved fury.

However, without the moral parameters of melodrama and with only a few external characteristics of the genre—and those arranged in a way more confusing than confirming to our expectations—other, deeper elements of the form become more distinct. The characters' driven natures coincide with a basic point made by Clayton Hamilton writing in the early part of this century—that melodramas are serious plays in which the incidents determine and control the characters. In the violently manipulative world of Shepard's play, the hero is even interchangeable. Duke is replaced by Drake who introduces himself as Cisco.

As customary distinctions like hero and villain blur, and with them a clear moral framework, the ingredients of aggression and anxiety—the ground bass of all melodrama—assert themselves to the point of distorting all else. In such an ominous atmosphere, Peter's dream of the blind man does not seem at all out of place. It is really a thematic distillation of the whole play from the eyeless posters on the wall to the journey to Arizona where Duke's concert is to take place. One turns inevitably to Eric Bentley's classic pronouncement: "... *melodrama is the Naturalism of dream life.*" Delving still further into Bentley's pioneer analysis of melodrama, one finds adjectives like "childish," "neurotic," "primitive," "narcissistic," and "paranoid" applied to the genre—descriptions hardly inappropriate to this play, indeed to the whole extravagant world of popular entertainment from which it is derived.[5]

Before we go into the implications of the play's subject, let us go back to examine some specific ways in which Shepard experiments with the conventions of melodrama in his *Melodrama Play*. In the introduction already cited, the playwright states that within the play the "mechanism of melodrama" changes "to something more sincere." Furthermore, "This change does not just occur slowly from one thing into the other in the course of the play but rapidly as well as very frequently, especially in the case of Dana (the girlfriend). There are no stage directions indicating when these changes should take place because some of them appear obvious to me and many of them do not."[6] One of the rapid, frequent shifts might be seen in the counterplay between Dana's excessive posturing and Duke's terse replies in this excerpt:

> DANA. But Duke . . . *(there is a loud knock at the door)* Who
>   is it? *(Another knock)*
> DUKE. Go see. (DANA *crosses to the door.*)
> DANA. Who is it, please? *(A voice comes from the other side.)*
> DRAKE'S VOICE. It's Drake, baby. Open up.
> DANA. Duke, it's your brother. What shall I do? Oh what
>   shall I do, Duke? Oh what can I do?
> DUKE. Let him in.[7]

The effect is one of comic deflation of melodramatic overstatement. So is the following:

> FLOYD. Dukie! Oh Dukie baby, they've killed your girl.
>   They've killed your sweet little girl by just plain old not co-
>   operating. Look what they've done to Dana, Dukie. Just
>   look at that . Isn't that a shame?
> DUKE. She's dead. Oh my God.
> FLOYD. Yes, Duke, I'm afraid so.
> DUKE. Did she get my suit?[8]

However, the basic thrust of the play is toward anything but a parody of melodramatic hyperbole. As Shepard states, the shift, both in the short byplays and in the action as a whole, is away from satire and toward something deeper. I take that to mean away from the histrionics of the rock-and-roll world and toward a pervasive, frightening vision of existence. The transition is from melodrama as a set of extravagant conventions which can be easily recognized by the audience and played with for sheer enjoyment to melodrama as an expression of a violent, vivid, portentious reality which operates more like a dream.

This kind of thematic modulation can be found in many of Shepard's plays: An artist or other creative person has come to an inspiration impasse—a crisis that not only expresses something about the processes of human invention but also has broader existential implications. *Melodrama Play* begins with a popular idol with feet of clay, at the mercy of forces quite antithetical to the poetry and social relevance to which he purports to aspire. The play ends with a general nightmare of paranoia and witless brutality in the dress of law and order. On one level, the work is a parable of arrested creativity, especially in a modern pressurized world. On another, it is an apt theatrical metaphor for a culture in political, social, and spiritual collapse (particularly appropriate in 1968 when the play was first produced).

In *Mad Dog Blues* (1971), another rock star is involved in a wild hunt for gold with figures from American myth—Mae West, Jesse James, Paul Bunyan, and Captain Kidd. The play is a quirky takeoff on John Huston's classic American film melodrama, *The Treasure of the Sierra Madre.* Two charismatic figures—Hoss, an old (1950s vintage) rock-and-roll rebel in black leather, and Crow, more in the newer glitter-rock vein with earrings and velvet—battle it out for American mythic supremacy in *Tooth of Crime* (1972). Their struggle is a fantasia on the theme of two underworld figures duelling over territory. *Angel City* (1976) is a disaster play about making a disaster movie. It ends as a green ooze seeps from an Indian medicine man's bundle to envelop Los Angeles and with it the movie industry, America's myth-making apparatus. *Suicide in B^b* (1976) uses the melodramatic conventions of a detective story to explore the annihilation of a famous jazz musician's identity. This piece contains an unusually direct statement of how Shepard links the chaos and dissolution of the creative individual with a broader social and philosophical reality. While reading the following selection, however, do not confuse the reactionary raving of this character, one of the detectives in the story, with the author's own point of view. Shepard is depicting a profound, paralyzing fear and loss of direction which he senses has pervaded all of reality. This is only one of its voices:

> PABLO. How does it relate to breaking with tradition! To
> breaking off with the past! To throwing the diligent efforts
> of our fore-fathers and their fore-fathers before them to the

winds! To turning the classics to garbage before our very eyes! To distorting the very foundations of our cherished values! *(Piano breaks in with loud atonal chords at random intervals.)* To making mince-meat out of brilliance! To rubbing up against the very grain of sanity and driving us all to complete and utter destruction! To changing the shape of American morality! That's where it's at! That's where it's at isn't it![9]

Note the explosive language and the music that goes with it. The movement beneath this hyperbolic speech is still to "something more sincere"—a deeply disturbing sense of confusion and terror.

None of these plays, nor any of the many others in Shepard's oeuvre which uses similar material, is conventional melodrama.[10] But they all use melodramatic forms, particularly those with strong claims on the American imagination—the mystery thriller, science fiction, the western. Shepard uses the familiarity and direct appeal of these popular genres to attract his audience and involve its responses. However, he fragments the structure of these genres, removes from them their traditionally clear social and moral frames, and in the process releases from them their primal theatrical energy: Aggression, paranoia, infantilism, narcissism are all parts of their melodramatic souls. They are also the very aspects of our society which Shepard repeatedly explores.

Other contemporary artists also use these energies but in strikingly different ways. However, the approaches are often surprisingly parallel: to break up melodrama into its components and use these elements analytically rather than synthetically—in other words, not to write melodramas but to explore some aspect of the melodramatic in our existence. The next section concerns a playwright whose idea of theater could not be further from Shepard's but who has also found a place for melodrama.

Richard Foreman

In his provocative essay on the "Aesthetic of Revolution,"[11] Wylie Sypher criticizes nineteenth-century Marxism as untenable within an authentic twentieth-century world view precisely because it is melodramatic: "Hero Labor" struggles with "Villain Captial" and the climax is Revolution. Sypher suggests that the dramatic dualism which gives structure to this philosophy is characteristic of the most vital thought and art of Marx's time. The clearly drawn moral polarity is an informing principle for Dickens, the Brontës, Carlyle, Nietzsche, Kierkegaard, and Dostoevski, to name only a few. The present century, on the other hand, sees events as arranged densely in a "continuum" of experience and too complexly interrelated to admit the extremes of melodrama. Whatever one might think of Sypher's political evaluation of Marxism, the application of his thought to art is quite rewarding. Cubism, his ideal example of a modern esthetic, is abstract and analytical in its approach. It destroys the object in order "to reduce it to a study of intimate and manifold relationships, a fragmentation within a continuum of forms until the definition of the 'subject' remains equivocal."[12]

This Cubistic process could be extended to include Shepard's fragmentation of melodramatic forms. However, the concept of a continuum is more easily applicable to Richard Foreman's work in his Ontological-Hysteric Theatre.[13] Theoretically, Foreman's art would seem to exclude melodrama completely, because it claims to eliminate conflict of any kind and certainly that conflict between hero and villain. Still, his idiosyncratic dramatic productions are loaded with melodramatic elements and do, in fact, depend on conflict but in a way redefined much in accord with Sypher's idea of a continuum. The following is a typical—and fundamental—excerpt from Foreman's "Ontological-Hysteric Manifesto I" (April 1972):

> Conflict at root of drama. OK. It's all so simple, really. Now— art can't be based in conflict. Old art aroused, empathized with that, made our inner nature vibrate to that in such a way that it was "profound." The grounds of conflict are now seen as . . . not between entities, but within the single unitary occasion which could exist—could not exist. That oscillation replacing "conflict."[14]

This "single unitary occasion"—or continuum, for I think that we may substitute Sypher's term—is the heart of Foreman's theater and is as difficult to describe as it is full of wit and resonance. Foreman, the playwright, generates a text by choosing segments from a continual log which he maintains of the content and processes of his consciousness. This way of writing uses character and action as we usually think of them only in the most fragmented manner. It is, as it were, doodling—a stream of consciousness set down as nearly as possible without the active intervention of the writer in the manner of rewriting or polishing. The material thus generated only begins to assume a theatrical shape when Foreman, the director and designer, starts to edit it, assign sections to actors, and subject it to a great range of staging devices which have become the hallmarks of his theater. His aim—inspired by the work of Gertrude Stein, Bertolt Brecht, Minimal Art, and contemporary experimental film—is to bring the stuff of personal consciousness into the theater in such a way as to make the spectators aware of their own mental processes.[15]

"Do you think you are really not interested in murders?" is a line assigned to an actor in *Book of Splendors: Part II (Book of Levers) Action at a Distance* (1977).[16] Simply by reading it in the text, one would not find out that, in Foreman's production, it is a signal for everyone on stage to menace one another with rubber knives, for hands holding daggers to appear from the wings, and for threatening looks to be cast in all directions. This sequence has no apparent context; it refers to nothing before itself nor will it become a coherent part of a subsequent plot narrative. Yet the act of multiple intimidations, isolated and blatantly artificial (both the knives and the attitudes are obvious fakes), sets off a chain of associations which the spectator experiences from any number of different angles. A dynamic is established among many categories of experience: reality and artifice, reality and parody, unity and diversity, and the abstract and the concrete are but a few. The process of fragmentation and analysis of perception is identical both to the one that Sypher ascribes to Cubism and to Foreman's own theory of "oscillation" within a "single unitary occasion."

The motor that runs the cognitive interplay outlined above is fueled by the sheer theatrical vitality of melodramatic image—even images isolated from normal contexts of meaning. Foreman depends on the expectations that raised knives and threatening looks arouse in order to distance and dissect these very responses—and to point out how we succumb to any response automatically and without reflection. Both he and Shepard, though in very different ways, are using the raw aggression underlying all melodrama as a critical tool, sometimes even to examine itself.

In his theoretical writings, Foreman's words for this aggressive force are "ordeal" and "rigor." He is referring to the ordeal of the spectators and the rigor which they must exercise in order to watch the plays properly—that is, in order to maintain a special awareness of private cognitive processes at work in the watching. There is, then, a definite conflict in Foreman's work with a specific moral content: The struggle is between the spectator and the play; good is alertness; evil is slipping back into automatic response. This is a didactic theater of consciousness; the plays are epistemological *Lehrstücke*. A scene from *Vertical Mobility (Sophia= Wisdom) Part 4* (1972) illustrates this audience challenge clearly: During a "tennis game" sequence, harsh white lights are aimed into the auditorium. The performers wear dark glasses and raise their rackets in menacing gestures at their opponents, the spectators. Foreman would have his actors seem to ask the audience, "What are you doing about this piece of art you are watching?"[17]

The large arsenal of staging devices which Foreman has developed are essential to keeping the audience off balance in the midst of its own perceptual processes. Bright lights, loud noises, surprising visual and auditory effects—all can be traced to a creative reading of Brecht's theories of estrangement without implying they are directly copied from Brechtian theater practice. However, the visual inspiration for a large number of these devices comes from nineteenth-century melodrama. Let us start with the shape of the Ontological-Hysteric Theatre itself: very conventional in its audience-stage relationship with the spectators sequestered on risers in front of a clearly delineated playing area. Within the large frame of the stage, other incidental framing devices are moved on and off in order to set off particular elements and underscore the audience's distance from them. One of the most common and effective of these contrivances is that perennial of melodramatic staging, the tableau. The knife sequence described above is a good instance—a striking picture framed by its own rigidity. Not only is the conventional structure of the tableau used, but its melodramatic sense of menace and anxiety is preserved.

The general performance style of these productions is, in fact, permeated by a sense of anxious rigidity, though in other ways it appears unmelodramatic because of its coolness, impersonality, and abstractness. Rhoda, the heroine of most of Foreman's plays, has been played since 1972 by the inimitable Kate Manheim. Without doubt, she has been most successful at inhabiting Foreman's theatrical world and making it part of her own personal statement. The "Rhoda-look" which she has perfected radiates a highly concentrated energy which often translates itself into tension and apprehension—a peculiar mixture of curiosity and solicitude.[18]

True to the Foreman esthetic, however, Rhoda cannot be spoken of as a coherent character in the usual sense—it would be difficult to identify her according to clearly motivated needs and feelings that result in unified action. Still, the force of Manheim's presence causes a conjunction of thoughts or themes which coalesce around the role. To place her in the mainstream of Western thought, Rhoda may at particular moments call to mind the eternal feminine, the temptress Eve, sensuality (not intellect), and intuition (not reason). Interpreted in this way, we can see another kind of conflict taking shape—the classic one between the masculine and feminine. Indeed, as Manheim's part in making this theater has grown more autonomous and assertive, this sexual conflict has tended to eclipse the one between play and audience. As a result of the increased importance of this more traditional dramatic conflict, and the fact that the spectator has been taken off the spot in a way, Foreman's later plays have become somewhat less rigorous to watch and therefore more accessible and attractive.

However, Foreman has hardly begun to write conventional battles of the sexes. Sexual conflict in his theater, along with the audience's ordeal, are ancillary to the dramatization of consciousness. Conflict itself, like all other elements, is but a part of the complex oscillation within the continuum of experience. Moreover, it is fragmented in the Cubistic process described earlier: Insofar as the play is a projection of Richard Foreman's consciousness, the figure of Rhoda is an occasionally contentious feminine constituent in that masculine consciousness. Insofar as the play is a paradigm or, perhaps, allegory of all human consciousness, Rhoda represents what we think of as the feminine pole of cognition—intuitive, sensual, synthetic. Insofar as Rhoda is a distinct character, she is a consciousness in which feminine and masculine elements interact. All of these possibilities exist more or less simultaneously but never as more than momentarily colliding aspects of an ongoing experience: Foreman dramatizes the multiplexity of consciousness by eroticizing it. And the introduction of sexual conflict, no matter how sundered and abstracted, automatically opens the door to melodrama.

We have traced the aggression that pulsates through these plays to an energy released by a kind of fission of melodramatic structures. The eroticism comes from the same source; in fact, it often appears to be at one with the aggression. Ontological-Hysteric plays are filled with (usually female) nudity, often presented with a nineteenth-century racy postcard sensibility—part seduction, part ravishment.[19] Various poses suggest character types from conventional melodrama: the vamp (the temptress who is the female counterpart of the villain) and the innocent heroine whose virtue is in jeopardy. Provocative images of the seductress flicker through Foreman's works, but it is the latter, the embattled female, who really claims attention.

Rhoda has grown into that heroine and Manheim's portrayal of her—anxiously open to experience but also defenseless before it—is particularly resonant. She has always been the object of an aggressive, even obsessive desire in the Ontological-Hysteric plays. But as such, she seems to participate in a special knowledge, to be sought after but never wholly within grasp, and somewhat awe inspiring. In Foreman's earlier plays, Sophia is a principal role that also evokes this elusive wisdom. Here is a sequence from *(Sophia = Wisdom) Part 3: The Cliffs* (1971): Sophia pulls Rhoda, who is wearing only a blanket, to a post and places her hands through two loops hanging from it. While Rhoda is helplessly fastened with her blanket slipping off, Ben (a character who often seems to stand in for Foreman himself) approaches her slowly and, without quite touching her, runs his hand along her legs.[20] The scene is pure melodrama just as it is pure erotic fantasy.

However, there are hints in this sequence that Rhoda, as the object of this domination, is also the subject of some strange ordeal with allegorical overtones—perhaps a rite of passage. Sophia, for the moment at least, is the mistress of ceremonies. The sense that Foreman's plays are allegorical—albeit disjointedly so, with no clear relationship to a hierarchy of ideas—becomes more pronounced in the later works. *Pandering to the Masses: A Misrepresentation* (1974) contains this passage:

> VOICE. . . . In this play for instance, you will see that the naked Sophia and the naked Eleanor are in possession of a certain kind of knowledge to which Rhoda, not yet certain that she needs or desires it, will be soon, painfully, initiated.[21]

The title of another play, *Rhoda in Potatoland (Her Fall Starts)* (1974) is reminiscent enough of *Alice in Wonderland* to prepare us for a funny, humiliating, excruciating, inscrutable adventure of some kind—perhaps a journey of initiation. If neither Alice nor Rhoda conforms to our usual idea of melodramatic heroines, they still undergo some distinctly melodramatic ordeals. However, whereas Alice ends up safely at home, Rhoda never reaches a destination but keeps moving along an ambiguous, densely populated continuum of experience, a road where we may rejoin her from play to play.

We are taken along with Rhoda on a trip toward awareness, but the didactic goal is the trip itself. The engine that propels us is energized by the sheer theatrical power of melodrama. However, this is melodrama in a modern vein, stripped of its clearly delineated superstructure where good vies with evil and pervaded by the relativism of twentieth-century thought and art. The result of this breaking up of forms is almost axiomatic: When the moral shell is fragmented and removed, an aggressive, erotic, even fetishistic force is released—an energy that we could well call the soul of melodrama.

What one experiences in a Shepard play is poles away from what one encounters with the Ontological-Hysteric Theatre of Richard Foreman. Both artists were chosen for this analysis because they differ so radically in their intents and results, yet their attraction to melodramatic material is evident and their ways of using it have important similarities. Other artists working within the various areas of American experimental theater can also be cited for the same reasons.

Michael Kirby

Michael Kirby has created a series of mystery plays for his Structural-ist Theater. These pieces have nothing to do with medieval religious drama. Instead, they are derived from popular genres of melodrama—the spy thriller, political intrigue, mystery, and horror tale.[22]

In *Double Gothic* Kirby crosscuts two Gothic horror tales not only to reveal something about the typical components of that melodramatic genre but (as did Foreman) to involve the audience actively in a high degree of cognitive and perceptual play.[23] The ingenious feature of this presentation is the way in which architecture is used to construct formal relationships between the two stories—relationships that take precedence over the actual content of the narratives.

The performance space is a large black box divided longitudinally by eight corridors of dark scrim. The audience sits on two opposite sides of the box and one section cannot see the other. The corridors are lit from above so that a scene taking place near one side of the audience can be seen clearly by that side, but one performed in a more distant corridor seems to float in shadow and obscurity. The Gothic mood is enforced not only by the murky setting but also by ominous organ tones and occasional lightning flashes.

The two tales are told in discrete scenes alternating with one another, one beginning in a corridor on one side of the box, the other in the opposite. Thus, depending on the side where a spectator is sitting, one story begins clearly and recedes into obscurity as it progresses from corridor to corridor; the other moves forward and becomes more clear.

The narratives themselves are simple but mysterious and drenched with anxiety. They parallel each other closely both in content and the sequence in which they are played: (1) A woman's car breaks down on a lonely road; another woman, a deaf-mute, appears to lead her to a mansion where a sinister older woman waits in a wheelchair. (2) A young woman is met at a train station by a blind woman and taken to a hospital where she meets a mysterious woman doctor. The stories echo each other in many subtle ways: The mute can really talk, the blind woman can see; one young woman has hurt her foot, the other has a sore eye; one is forbidden to go downstairs, the other to venture outside.

The scenes correspond with each other in a way that takes the spectators' attention away from the emotional involvement demanded by the conventional Gothic tale and focuses it on the themes and variations as they unfold themselves: One woman undresses and studies a portrait, the other looks into a mirror; if the bed is on the left side in a corridor near one audience section, it is on the right side in the corresponding scene in the more distant corridor.

The play does not end with the resolution of plot—it ends when the spatial and temporal scheme has completed itself—in other words, when the scenes have progressed through all of the corridors. (The women, warned of impending danger, flee into the night, one carrying a flashlight, the other a lantern.) Kirby even gives his work an overture and a coda which are more musical than dramatic. It opens with a statement of tersely fragmented themes from the two narratives and ends with a similar device. Two Gothic mysteries are intimated but not solved. Whatever feeling of completion and closure that the audience experiences is arrived at formally, not emotionally. What does remain of traditional emotional response to the Gothic tale is an undefined implication of danger to the two innocent young women. The nearest we can come to pinpointing this is an intuition that they are somehow targets of Lesbian rape. After our discussion of Foreman, the situation is familiar: Aggression and eroticism seep through the interstices of the fractured structure of conventional melodrama.

Photoanalysis is not only a good example of Kirby's elegant, provocative theater, it is a further demonstration of the experimental use of melodrama.[24] In it, as in *Double Gothic*, two story lines move toward one another: (1) Carl has supposedly drowned, but his wife discovers signs of his (or someone's) continued existence in her large, white frame house located somewhere in the eastern United States (a ghost melodrama?). (2) Carlos is perhaps a foreign agent or political terrorist. A young woman becomes unwittingly involved with him and others in a large, white frame house in San Francisco (a political melodrama?). The two women (each played by three actresses) recount their stories in fragments. Behind them flash slides that seem to relate to the narratives but are never referred to by the women. The two plots appear to touch at one point when the California girl makes a mysterious trip east. (Are Carl and Carlos the same person?) But they recede from one another again, leaving only a sugges-ion of espionage and conspiracy which even its agents understand only in part.

The slides are expounded upon by a central figure (also played alter-nately by three performers) who lectures the audience on the "new sci-ence" of photoanalysis. From the pictures the speaker purports to derive objective data through the explication of details, light, angles, and so on. It is pointed out that structure exists in every photo, no matter how acci-dental its origin. Furthermore, the image within the frame alludes to a continuing reality beyond itself and can suggest things like color, sound, motion, and emotion although such factors are objectively absent from the photo itself. Of course, each point of analysis immediately extends to the elliptical narratives whose splintered paths we are also following: To explain the slides is to explain the stories and vice versa.

The irony is that the thing being demonstrated is really the insistence of the consciousness of each audience member to give sequential structure and logical causality to the stream of details which confronts him or her. The objective facts that the lecturer claims to discover from each photo are only random points around which the viewer builds a system of possi-ble relationships based on far deeper, subjective cognitive structures. The surface of constantly shifting associations is the only thing that the "sci-ence" of photoanalysis can reveal. It is the parody of a structure beneath which far more profound ones exist.

If *Photoanalysis* is a witty analysis of the processes of consciousness, it also contains implicit social commentary: The data that it offers us comes from a world of violence and intrigue deliberately shown to stretch from coast to coast, and by extension across all existence. Our response to what happens in the play is essentially paranoid even though there are almost no substantial facts to back up what we feel. The story that we provide to explain what we see is inevitably conditioned by a daily diet of television, film, and headlines. This is how we have come to *know* real-ity . . . melodramatically.

The artistic kinship between Kirby and Foreman is readily evident. The subject of their work is human consciousness. The conventions of melodrama, used in a fragmented manner and estranged from any clear moral context, provide both subject matter and a charged theatrical atmo-sphere in which to dramatize it. The plays of both artists are suffused with not only feelings of anxiety, aggression, and eroticism—the roots of melodrama—but also fundamental energies in all human reaction and per-ception. These artists stand at once in the midst of these elemental forces of consciousness and back far enough to examine them.

Shepard also uses similar methods of fragmentation but for the pur-pose of criticizing cultural and political realities rather than that of episte-mological and ontological exploration. However, by charging their work with an extreme sense of paranoia, both he and Kirby reflect something profoundly problematic—they raise questions not only about how modern man perceives the world but, specifically, about what has happened to the American vision of it.

Charles Ludlam

Finally, an antic epilogue. As I hope is evident from the examples in this essay, a great deal about the work of these artists is witty and deftly comic. We have seen elements of parody and satire in Shepard's outrageous rock-and-rollers, in the extravagant tableaux of Foreman, and in Kirby's witty exposé of "scientific" attitudes. The presence of this satiric element is understandable in plays that depend so much on distancing, irony, and an analytical stance.[25] There is also a historical rationale for this—parodies of melodrama go back to the mid-nineteenth century and a love of the genre seems to go along with an affectionate desire to send it up.

Of all the experimental theater artists, Charles Ludlam is the one who sets out most directly to write melodrama—and to write parody. Undoubtedly his classic is *Bluebeard*, created for his Ridiculous Theatrical Company.[26] This parody of a melodrama steals unabashedly from H. G. Wells's novel *The Island of Dr. Moreau*, the legend of Bluebeard's castle, *The Bride of Frankenstein*, with generous helpings from other works of high and low art. His *Stage Blood*[27] follows the so-called Ridiculous esthetic (which has been called a theatrical manifestation of Pop Art), by making *Hamlet* a murder mystery played out in a ramshackle Shakespearean touring company. The play, extravagantly performed by Ludlam's company, manages to send up not only Shakespeare but also method acting and, in a brilliant bit of in-jokery, even Richard Foreman.

Structurally, both *Bluebeard* and *Stage Blood* follow rather conventional melodramatic lines, but they make fun of themselves in doing so. As with the other artists discussed here, it is the great theatricality of melodrama that attracts Ludlam, and its very exuberance plays right into his hands. For him and the others, this most basic kind of theater provides an endless supply of conventions, an unparalleled repertoire of stock responses, which speak to all of us so directly because they are so much a part our own imaginations—of our dreams, as Eric Bentley cannily opined. Melodrama is a form that endures no matter how much it is stretched out of shape, forced from its traditional moorings, broken up and spread over new theatrical territories—endures to entertain and to enliven.

Notes

1. In 1968, *Melodrama Play* shared the Obie with the Theatre Genesis production of *Forensic and the Navigators*. For the chronological information about Shepard in this essay, I must thank George Ferencz and his coworkers who prepared a compre-

hensive checklist of performances for their "Shep in Rep" series at The Center for Theatre Studies, Columbia University (August 1979). The dates in parentheses after the play titles indicate the time of the first performances.

2. Sam Shepard, *Melodrama Play*, in *Five Plays by Sam Shepard* (New York: Bobbs-Merrill, 1967), p. 126. The introduction was written for the anthologized version of the play before its premiere by the La Mama Repertory under the direction of Tom O'Horgan.

3. Ibid.

4. Arnold Hauser, *The Social History of Art*, vol. 3, *Rococo, Classicism, Romanticism*, Vintage Books (New York: Random House, n. d.), p. 203.

5. Eric Bentley, *The Life of the Drama* (New York: Atheneum, 1970), pp. 205, 216.

6. Shepard, *Melodrama Play*, p. 126.

7. Ibid., p. 138.

8. Ibid., p. 148.

9. Sam Shepard, *Suicide in B^b*, in *Buried Child & Seduced & Suicide in B^b* (New York: Urizen Books, 1979), pp. 130-31.

10. I have left certain more recent plays such as *Curse of the Starving Class* and *Buried Child* out of my discussion. These works use melodrama in a more conventional way in that they stand clearly in the tradition of the generation-conflict drama. Melodrama in the plays discussed in this article is more a consciously theatricalist element.

11. Wylie Sypher, "Aesthetic of Revolution: The Marxist Melodrama," *Kenyon Review* (1948), 10:431-44.

12. Ibid., p. 435.

13. The Ontological Hysteric Theatre was founded in 1968 by Richard Foreman. I distinguish its rigorously experimental work from Foreman's more commercially aimed efforts. Of the latter, *Hotel for Criminals*, with music by Stanley Silverman and based on the French silent film serial *Fantomas*, is definitely a melodrama—a quirky, idiosyncratic one, yes, but firmly and consistently enough ensconced in the genre so as not to be problematic. (The 1972 original of this work was revised as *American Imagination*. It appears in *Performing Arts Journal* (1979), 4[1&2]:177-99.)

14. Richard Foreman, *Plays and Manifestos*, edited by Kate Davy, *The Drama Review Series* (New York: New York University Press, 1976), p. 70. This collection also contains an excellent introductory essay by Ms. Davy. I am indebted to her chronology (pp. 227-29) for the completion and production dates of the various plays mentioned in this essay.

15. Kate Davy, "Foreman's 'Vertical Mobility' and 'PAIN(T)'," *The Drama Review* (June 1974), 18(2):26.

16. Richard Foreman, *Book of Splendors: Part II (Book of Levers) Action at a Distance*, in *Theater* (1978), 9(2):79. This issue also contains my article touching on the subject of melodramatic forms in Foreman's work and describing other aspects of his theater: "Richard Foreman and Some Uses of Cinema," pp. 10-14.

17. The description of this sequence can be found in Florence Falk's article, "Ontological-Hysteric Theatre: Setting as Consciousness," *Performing Arts Journal* (Spring 1976), 1(1):58. In the question to the audience concerning what it is doing about the art that it is watching, I am paraphrasing a question Foreman actually used in directing this sequence. It is quoted in the Davy article, p. 34, along with a description of a scene in which Foreman instructs his performers to glare at the spectators like "large hostile birds."

18. Kate Davy, "Kate Manheim as Foreman's Rhoda," *The Drama Review* (September 1976), 20(3):37-50.

19. If Richard Foreman utilizes the energy of the melodramatic without actually writing melodramas, he also harnesses the force of pornography without being prurient. He disrupts our responses to nudity in the same way that he distances us from the expectations called forth by melodramatic conventions.

20. Michael Kirby, "Richard Foreman's Ontological-Hysteric Theatre," *The Drama Review* (June 1973), 17(2):23. This is the first thorough account of Foreman's theater and remains the most complete description of its means.

21. Richard Foreman, *Pandering to the Masses: A Misrepresentation*, p. 21 in *The Theatre of Images*, edited by Bonnie Marranca (New York: Drama Book Specialists,

1977. This collection also contains introductory essays by Ms. Marranca which discuss various aspects of the new theater.

22. A thorough treatment of this series has been done by Noël Carroll, "The Mystery Plays of Michael Kirby," *The Drama Review* (September 1979), 23(3):103-112. The plays discussed are *Identity Control*, which has its roots in the spy thriller, *Revolutionary Dance* and *Photoanalysis*, which cull motifs from the world of political intrigue, and *Double Gothic*, which depends on the conventions of the horror tale.

23. *Double Gothic* was played at the Performing Garage in New York in the winter of 1978-79. I am indebted to Noël Carroll for his excellent description and evaluation of the production, "Twice-Told Tale," *The Soho Weekly News*, January 4, 1979, p. 52.

24. Michael Kirby, *Photoanalysis: A Structuralist Play* (Seoul, South Korea: Duk Moon Publishing Co., 1978). This, unfortunately, is the recondite source for the only published Kirby script. It also contains all of the slides used in the production.

25. It is noteworthy that Northrop Frye, who otherwise gives melodrama short shrift and a bad name (he links it unfavorably to mob psychology), takes the trouble to show the strong relationship between melodrama and ironic comedy. *Anatomy of Criticism* (Princeton, N.J.: Princeton Univ. Press, 1957), p. 47.

26. Charles Ludlam, *Bluebeard*, in *More Plays from Off-Off Broadway*, edited by Michael Smith (New York: Bobbs-Merrill, 1972), pp. 359-409.

27. Charles Ludlam, *Stage Blood*, in *Theatre of the Ridiculous*, edited by Gautam Das Gupta and Bonnie Marranca (New York: Performing Arts Journal Publications, 1979), pp. 51-105.

PART 3

THE MYSTERIES OF LONDON AND PARIS AND *THE SECRET AGENT*

10

The Mark of the Beast:
Prostitution, Melodrama,
and Narrative

PETER BROOKS

Descent into the Parisian Depths

Monsieur Rodolphe—otherwise Son Altesse le Grand-Duc Rodolphe de Gerolstein—is on one of his errands of general and incognito mercy in the social depths of Paris at the outset of Eugène Sue's *Les Mystères de Paris* when he meets Fleur-de-Marie, the prostitute known to her low-life companions as "La Goualeuse" (slang for "La Chanteuse") from her irrepressible love of song, and hears her story in a typically sordid *tapis-franc*, or cabaret, of the Ile de la Cité, in the company of assorted housebreakers, murderers, pimps, stool pigeons, and other unspecified gallows birds. The destiny of Fleur-de-Marie, prostitute with a heart of gold, virginal flower anomalously growing in the urban slime, is one of the principal guiding lines through the labyrinth of multiple plots and realms that constitute *Les Mystères de Paris.* When she declares herself an orphan of unknown parentage, and when we learn that Rodolphe takes a special interest in her because she is just the age that his daughter would have been had she lived, instead of dying as an infant in mysterious circumstances, we can already, if we are attuned to the necessities of melodrama, divine the higher pathos of this confrontation which, all unbeknownst to its actors, is of father and daughter.

While this information will be explicitly furnished to the reader after a few hundred pages, it will take Rodolphe over 3,000 pages to bring it to light, through a series of peripeties, dramatic ironies, coups-de-théâtre, and startling coincidences, motivating the convergence of nearly the whole cast of characters and all the lines of plot on the loss and recovery of this unfortunate creature who, after a battered and starving childhood begging on the sidewalks of Paris and a term in prison, was made drunk with eau-de-vie and sold into prostitution. Rodolphe's discovery is the occasion for a full articulation of the antitheses and oxymorons of Fleur-de-Marie's existence: the hereditary princess destined to a life of beggary and blows; the pure, blond child delivered to the hands of a putrid mob of convicts and degenerates; the imprisoned singing bird; the "angelic and candid" girl of sixteen smeared with all the filth to be found in the underbelly of Paris. In Fleur-de-Marie, all social and moral extremes meet, in a rhetoric of pathos and excruciation.

When all has come to light, Rodolphe undertakes not only to rehabilitate Fleur-de-Marie (a process already well advanced earlier when, before knowing her to be his daughter, he removed her from the Ile de la Cité and placed her in the model farm of Bouqueval, a place of virtue, industry, and simplicity, from which, alas, she is abducted once again by her former associates and tormentors) but also to restore her to her rightful place in his palace in the Duchy of Gerolstein. But the plan cannot succeed: despite the kindnesses which Rodolphe lavishes on her, Fleur-de-Marie remains a victim of past remembrances. When Rodolphe and his new bride, Clémence, explain to her that she is blameless, a victim of social misery, constrained to degradation, she replies: "But, that infamy . . . I experienced it . . . . Nothing can efface those frightful memories."[1] The past persists, ineffaceable; and when Fleur-de-Marie receives an offer of marriage from Prince Henri of Herkaüsen-Oldenzaal, whom she loves, the promise of final happiness only reveals its final impossibility in the ultimate oxymoron of the prostitute-become-mother, making a *mère* of what was once a *fille:* " 'I a mother,' replied Fleur-de-Marie with a desperate bitterness, 'I respected, blessed by an innocent and candid child! I, once the object of everyone's contempt! To have me thus profane the name of mother . . . . Oh! never' " (10:151). The inexorable logic continues with her decision to seek refuge in the convent. Yet even this compromise cannot subsist. She no sooner takes the veil than she succumbs to the secret illness that is sapping her from within and dies.

When she is explaining to Rodolphe and Clémence why she can never marry Prince Henri, Fleur-de-Marie concludes her pathetic confession: "I love Prince Henri too much, I respect him too much, ever to give him a hand that has been touched by the bandits of the Cité" (10:153). The formula recapitulates the antithesis that governs her existence, and suggests the uncrossable bar separating the terms of the antithesis. Using Freud's explanation of the "displacement upwards" that can occur in the symptoms of hysteric neurotics, one can say that "hand" here is a metonymy, a euphemism that displaces the place of uncleanness, of *souillure*.[2] The despoiled can never again be made whole. One can, of course, see in Fleur-de-Marie's refusal to give her soiled body to a legitimate husband, and in her decorous choice of death as the only solution to the oxymorons of her existence, a simple sign of Sue's capitulation to conventional bourgeois morality: there are limits beyond which even such angelic creatures as Fleur-de-Marie cannot be revirginized. Yet something more appears to confront us in the death of Fleur-de-Marie: what we may want to read as a symbolic representation of the impossibility of ever effacing the mark of the Cité, of the lowest of the social depths, once one has descended into them. There is at the end of *Les Mystères de Paris* perhaps at once a dissent from the romantic cliché of the redeemed prostitute, a bad-faith capitulation to bourgeois morality, and a representation of how the novel itself—and its author—have undergone marking by the indelible trace of misery, crime, and the sold body. That these conflicting messages should all be encoded at the end of *Les Mystères de Paris* is, I think, typical of the book as a whole, in its presentation of the Parisian underclass from initial motives that must appear sensationalistic and exploitative but which change considerably as the novel pursues its protracted course of composition and publication in the *Journal des Débats*—in the audacity of Sue's enterprise which one feels to be tempered not so much by caution as by unacknowledged ambivalences and blindness and which must ultimately be judged a curious mixture of the daring and the conventional. We are left saying that if Fleur-de-Marie cannot escape the mark, the indelible trace of the Cité, this may on the one hand be a sop to morality and a sign of loss of novelistic nerve, yet on the other hand it may stand as a sign of a certain realism about the limits of redemption and also perhaps a personal confession that certain *souvenirs* are indeed ineffaceable.

Earlier in the novel, when the society lady Clémence d'Harville is preparing to visit the prostitutes confined in Saint-Lazare prison (it was reserved for female thieves and prostitutes) to work toward the rehabilitation of those whose "degraded souls show the slightest aspiration toward good" (5:99), Sue draws an explicit parallel between the mission of charity ladies and his own. The gesture in both cases is one of *descent*, indeed of condescension, from the heights into the very abysses of society, to bring the lamp of knowledge and reform to the darkest recesses of the social order. A contemporary reviewer caught the movement and meaning of Sue's novel when he wrote: "Up until now, the novel, almost exclusively lordly, had kept proudly to the social summits, without deigning to look down . . . . This is the first time it has stirred up so profoundly the social slime, and that it has descended into these somber abysses where human suffering seems forever cast away from the pity of man and the justice of God."[3] The descent is first of all carried out by Rodolphe himself, who in expiation of a personal sin has undertaken to succor the virtuous poor, by exercising a "police of virtue" which, as the novel goes on, becomes (in the manner of so much else in the novel) a blueprint for a new social organization: a bureau of the police charged with discovering and rewarding unrecognized virtue. The obverse of Rodolphe's vigilantism of virtue is his arrogation to himself of the power to punish those who cause the sufferings of the persecuted virtuous, most notably in the horrendous and immediately famous scene in which he has his private physician blind the archvillain, the Maître d'Ecole. The blinded evildoer will be rendered harmless and will in darkness meditate his sins. As urban Robin Hood, Rodolphe exercises power over the body, and in this case we recognize Freud's equivalence between blinding and castration, since the Maître d'Ecole represents a powerful sexuality as well as a thoroughly perverse criminality. Rodolphe thus redresses the wrong of Fleur-de-Marie's having been subjected to power over the body. The descent, which ever matches criminality with punishment, as it matches the aspiration to virtue with rehabilitation, constantly juxtaposes fear and power.

The original motives of Sue's descent must appear somewhat suspect, possibly less well intentioned than Clémence d'Harville's. Sainte-Beuve saw the situation accurately: "It is doubtful that in beginning his famous work, this man of wit and invention made claim to doing anything other than persisting more than ever in his pessimistic line, and, bringing together all its secrets, to create a spicy and salty novel for the consumption of good society. I imagine that he wished to see, in a kind of wager, just how far, this time, he could lead his pretty women readers from the outset, and if great ladies wouldn't recoil from the *tapis-franc* .... The result of his success has been to make of someone who was an ironical and skeptical aristocratic writer—or aspired to be one—a popular author henceforth enslaved to his public."[4] The comment perceptively suggests Sue's point of departure as the fashionable dandy, read by a bourgeois audience with aspirations to gentility, who sought a *frisson nouveau* in the novelistic exploitation of the social underbelly. Sue at the inception of *Les Mystères* can validly be accused of slumming and with more frivolous intent than his hero Rodolphe. Yet there is good evidence that as he went on, not only did he become the slave of a popular audience that waited eagerly to read—or to hear read—each of the 147 installments of the *Journal des Débats*, but he also developed a new concern with the causes of the social phenomena he was describing and with the fate of the vast body of the underclass. While he began *Les Mystères de Paris* with the vaguest of ideological orientations—and without knowing at all how the novel's plot and meaning would evolve—Sue emerged from it ready to give some consistency to his declaration of allegiance to socialism. He would indeed go on to become a deputy from a working-class district of Paris during the Second Republic and then figure among the banished from Napoleon III's Second Empire. Sue's personal relations with such socialist writers as Félix Pyat were certainly a factor in his "conversion," as were the enthusiastic reviews in the reformist and socialist press that greeted the early installments of the novel, and also Sue's vast fan mail, which, along with letters pleading that the novelist alleviate Fleur-de-Marie's sufferings or that he bring Le Chourineur back from Algeria (Sue submissively complied) or that he dispatch Rodolphe to succor some real-life victim, included urgings from reformers and students of urban misery to persist in the exploration of this new terrain as well as testimonials from the people themselves, recounting anecdotes of their lives.

Sue began to imitate his fictive hero Rodolphe, to put on worker's clothes and to visit garrets and workshops and prisons. He began to inquire into the causes of misery, prostitution, and crime; he discovered the precariousness of the artisan's condition, the lack of social resources for those living on the brink of pauperization, the unequal hand of justice, and the iniquities of the penal system. Sue became more than a simple entrepreneur of the new industrial literature: working within its conditions, he became aware of the general conditions of which it was a part, the world of rapid urbanization, nascent industrialism, and exploitative capitalism.[5] A novel which had begun as a descent into the Parisian underbelly in search of exciting and amusing quarry became as it went along a "popular novel" in terms of its subject, as well as its audience and its mode of production. The sensationally melodramatic led to an inquest into the system responsible for the melodramatic contrasts of urban life. In an increasing number of polemical digressions as the novel advanced, Sue put forth a series of proposals: for model cooperative farms, workingmen's interest-free loan associations, penal reform, and, of course, the police of virtue. The social reformism of the novel is not at odds with its melodrama of tone and presentation; as in the stage melodramas of Félix Pyat and a host of other playwrights, melodrama becomes a chosen vehicle for the attempt to change the world. The results may be consonant with the curious blend of boldness and conventionality, the ambivalence and the blindness, which we found in the death of Fleur-de-Marie, and which can perhaps best be addressed in the question of prostitution as Sue's chosen way into representation of the social inferno.

Deviance and Prostitution: Last Refuge of the Narratable

To begin to elucidate the place of prostitution in *Les Mystères de Paris*—and beyond that, its peculiarly privileged place in the nineteenth-century novel in general—we should say something more about the indelible mark that prostitution confers on Fleur-de-Marie. Karl Marx, in some brilliant and scathing pages of *Die Heilige Familie* (1845), demonstrates how Rodolphe "saves" Fleur-de-Marie by first transforming her from prostitute into repentant sinner, then from repentant sinner into nun, then from nun into corpse. Marx argues that Rodolphe teaches Fleur-de-Marie to internalize her "fault," which in large measure means abstracting her fault. That is, to Fleur-de-Marie prostitution is originally a lived situation, a situation external to her humanity, not an abstraction in terms of which she must condemn herself. Rodolphe—when he begins her rehabilitation at the model farm of Bouqueval—turns Fleur-de-Marie over to the Abbé Laporte, who makes her aware of her condition as one of sin inhabiting within. "In making me understand virtue," Fleur-de-Marie tells him, "you have also made me understand the depths of my past abjection" (3:61). To which the good priest replies: "However generously endowed by the Creator, a nature that has been plunged, if only for a day, into the slime from which we rescued you, keeps from it an ineffaceable stigma." Whereas, comments Marx, Fleur-de-Marie knew herself as human before, she now knows herself as fallen: the filth that previously had only soiled her on the outside now has become her internal essence; God, and then death, are the only answers. Fleur-de-Marie's *sold* body has become the Abbé Laporte's *sinning* body: perhaps because she is Sue's *erotically deviant* body.

Marx's analysis here is characteristically remarkable but perhaps not wholly faithful to Sue's script. Marx makes too much of the Abbé Laporte. Fleur-de-Marie herself assigns the precipitating cause of her feeling of inner *souillure* and unworthiness to her meeting with Clara Dubreuil, an innocent young girl of her own age, and the sense of distance between the two of them: "For the first time, I felt that there are blots that nothing can efface" (3:56). In particular, Fleur-de-Marie describes the horror she feels when Clara recounts the story of her "simple, calm, happy life," and then asks Fleur-de-Marie to narrate her own life. The Abbé Laporte essentially confirms what Fleur-de-Marie has discovered in juxtaposition and contrast to the normal existence of the unsullied girl of her age: that her own life, her own past, is not *narratable*. The story of the mark she bears cannot be told, the past cannot be recuperated in a full, candid narrative of her life. Hence the mark is ineffaceable, the past irremediable.

The apparent paradox here is that the unnarratable life is the very one Sue has chosen to narrate: the novel after all is concerned with Fleur-de-Marie's story, not Clara Dubreuil's. What Sue has chosen to narrate to his audience—what comprises the very definition of the narratable in *Les Mystères de Paris*—is the deviant, the shameful, the criminal, that which most clearly diverges from the "simple, calm, happy life." The situation is by no means confined to this novel; it is at least characteristic of the nineteenth-century novel and perhaps in some degree of all narrative. Narrative in general has precious little use for the simple, calm, and happy, which are essentially unnarratable; and there is a certain novel, of which Sue, along with Balzac, Dickens, Hugo, Wilkie Collins, Dostoevsky, might be considered a most notable practitioner, which in full contrast seeks the narratable in that which deviates most markedly from the normal—in the criminal, the outside-the-law, the unsocialized, and ungoverned. In this context, Sue's descent into the Parisian depths can be read as a foray into that world which remains potentially storied, where there is to be found the greatest fund of the narratable. If we think of traditional storytelling as allied with travel, with the reports of those coming from afar, and with the marvelous, the realm of the folktale and its story of victory over hostile forces, we may conceive that in the banal nineteenth century, where (as Balzac, for instance, frequently complains) everything is becoming standardized and boring, the world of the social depths—of the professionally deviant, so to speak—comes to appear the last place of stories ready to hand, the last refuge of the narratable. Deviance as a question in social pathology offers an opportunity for tracing its arabesque figure as plot.[6] If the wretched of the earth are Sue's subject of predilection, it may be first of all because, for a bourgeois public at least, they are eminently the stuff of story; though—to preserve the full measure of ambiguity in Sue's descent—their stories may lead to a new understanding of the causes of that deviance which is the object of representation.

When one reflects upon the place of prostitution in this context, one begins to perceive its special and exemplary role in the nineteenth-century narratable. As Albert Béguin remarks in *Balzac visionnaire*, where he notes that the percentage of prostitutes in a census of *La Comédie humaine* far exceeds their proportion in the world outside the novel, the prostitute is preeminently someone with a destiny: a special, idiosyncratic form of life.[7] The prostitute's plot is by definition a deviance, and in literary terms she is often seen as herself defining the idiosyncratic trajectory through the world, the plot by which her life achieves a style and meaning not previously defined. Within the limits set by her social role and function, the prostitute is conceived as an essentially theatric being, capable of making mask into meaning. Balzac's prostitutes—occasionally the lowest class of streetwalker which Fleur-de-Marie represents but more often courtesans, expensive kept women, or dancers, *rats d'opéra* and the like—have a special capacity to cross social barriers, to exist in all milieux, to make it to the top but through a kind of demonstration that the top is in essence no different from the bottom.

The prostitute in this view would deserve that sobriquet applied in American gangster lore to the automatic pistol: the old equalizer. Balzac's Fanny Beaupré, Jenny Cadine, Tullia, Florine, Suzanne du Val-Noble, and the touching Esther Gobseck play a compensatory social role which Balzac explicitly, if ironically, compares to socialist ideology in a phrase from *Splendeurs et misères des courtisanes*, where he describes the banker Nucingen's passion for Esther and notes that an honest bourgeois wife cannot understand "how a fortune melts between the hands of these creatures whose social function, in the Fourierist system, is perhaps to make up for the sorrows caused by Avarice and Cupidity."[8] For the prostitute speculates on the *libido universalis*, on the capacity to make everyman succumb to his erotic needs, each according to his means. The journalist Etienne Lousteau describes Esther's magical powers near the start of *Splendeurs et misères:* "At age eighteen, that girl has already known the highest opulence, the lowest misery, men on each social storey. She has a manner of magic wand with which she unleashes the brutal appetites so violently suppressed in men who, while concerning themselves with politics, science, literature, art, still are passionate at heart. There is no woman in Paris who can say as well as she does to the Animal: 'Come out! . . .' And the Animal leaves its cage, and wallows in excess'' (p. 21). The underlying image here is no doubt Circe, turning men into pigs. In her transformational role, in her capacity to provoke metamorphoses, the prostitute is not only herself narratable, she provokes the stuff of story in others.

Prostitution may well be as old as human civilization. Yet as an organized and everyday phenomenon, it would appear to have special affinities with industrial capitalism. Georg Simmel makes the point that prostitution and money are counterparts in terms of the social relations each engenders: "The indifference with which [money] lends itself to any use, the infidelity with which it leaves everyone, its lack of ties to anyone, its complete objectification that excludes any attachment and makes it suitable as a pure means—all this suggests a portentous analogy between it and prostitution."[9] Prostitution in Paris took on new dimensions with the large increase of population in the first half of the nineteenth century and the creation of an impoverished urban proletariat. As Louis Chevalier writes, "Prostitution was a basic phenomenon of urban life, more particularly of working-class life, during the first half of the nineteenth century."[10] It had, in Paris at this time, a discernable geographical organization, considerable diversification of function, and it had become regulated by the police. The extensive and serious study of prostitution published in 1836 by Dr. A.-J.-B. Parent-Duchatelet, *De la Prostitution dans la ville de Paris*, details the different categories of prostitutes, running from the *"fille à carte"* (the common streetwalker obliged to carry her police card) to the *"fille à numéro"* (occupying a brothel) on up to the *"femme galante,"* *"femme à parties,"* *"femme de théâtres."*[11] From Parent-Duchatelet's work emerge the contours of an entire subsociety, a subterranean world with its own social organization, its manners, even its language—its special slang—analyzed and documented with remarkable detail and authority. It is not surprising that the study was of the greatest interest to those novelists fascinated by the social underground—the "subbasement of society," as Balzac sometimes called it—and that such as Balzac, Dumas, and Sue put Parent-Duchatelet's research largely to profit. Having read Parent-Duchatelet, one can easily recognize the frequent moments at which the novelists liberally borrow from him, working from suggestive details on the prostitute's manner of life to the creation of such characters as Esther or Fleur-de-Marie.

Parent-Duchatelet's work is one of the most remarkable of an impressive group of contemporary inquiries into the miseries of the people, and the work of novelists—most fully, no doubt, Sue and Hugo—went very much in the same direction and belonged to the same movement. The great question of the nineteenth century was to be that of social destitution, or as Victor Hugo expressed it in the working title to his great novel, "Les Misères." As translated into the ordinary bourgeois perception of the world, the issue tended to be, as Louis Chevalier has so well demonstrated, most immediately that of criminality: the threat from the dangerous classes. The criminal act and the criminal mind, I have already noted, become major novelistic themes from Balzac to Dostoevsky and beyond. The novel tends to maintain itself between admiration for the maximal, most daring social deviance on the one hand, and the counter discipline of the police on the other: it is no surprise that the detective novel and cops-and-robbers fiction are nineteenth-century inventions. While Sue eventually discovers the powerless, what really interests him more are the discontents of power, those in the depths who use it in reverse, perverse ways. Ultimately, as Fleur-de-Marie's profession and the Maître d'Ecole's symbolic castration together imply, the deviant power of the underworld is in essence sexual. This suggests further motivation for the fact that access to the underworld passes most readily through the Circe's den of prostitution.

Sexuality, Money, and Storytelling

The subject of prostitution is perhaps necessarily and of itself fraught with the ambiguities we noted in Sue's descent into the realms of social misery: does the novelist's interest lie with the sold body or with the deviant body? Social misery, the working class, criminality, approached through their relation to, and manifestation in, prostitution, are gilded by the erotic. The descent of the novel here mimes the traditional descent of bourgeois men who, buying the erotic through money, enter a special world which is at least on the threshold of the nether regions. There is also a parallel imagery of psychological descent into the unavowable erotic, where in darkness and secret the beast is liberated. One can speculate that portrayal of prostitutes allowed nineteenth-century novelists to deal with the dangerous and fearful subject of female sexuality in a manner not possible when portraying women of the upper and middle classes. Balzac is perhaps the most striking case here, in that such sublime and flaming creatures as Ester, Coralie, or the sequestered Paquita Valdès of *La Fille aux yeux d'or* are vehicles for the exploration of intense female sexuality, extending even to its "perverse" forms. But Balzac's treatment of the subject appears daring in good measure because the courtesanesque potential is present even in his well-bred women, who, as Proust noted, tend to behave like *filles* when moved by passion. Sexuality circulates across class lines, the low and the high meet, extremes converge.

In Sue, Fleur-de-Marie, promised to attempted redemption, is preserved from too much personal sexuality (as opposed to the male sexuality she has merely endured) by pairing her with La Louve, the She-Wolf, whose sexuality is explicit, and explicitly violent and bestial, both scary and exciting: "La Louve was a large girl, twenty years old, agile, strapping

in a virile way, and of quite regular features; her rude black hair shone
with reddish tints; the ardor of her blood blotched her complexion; dark
down shadowed her full lips; her chestnut eyebrows, thick and coarse, met
over her large savage eyes; something violent, fierce, bestial, in the expression of the physiognomy of this woman; a kind of habitual mocking grin
which, pulling back her upper lip during her fits of anger, revealed her
widely-spaced white teeth, explained her given name, the She-Wolf"
(5:133). Female sexuality is handled in this passage by its assignment to
animal sexuality: rhetorically, the whole description is constructed to explain and justify the animal nickname, which in turn explains and justifies
the presence of such overt sexuality. La Louve's sexual presence acts as a
"lightning rod" to draw away any undue worry on the reader's part about
Fleur-de-Marie's inner relationship to the sexuality on which her trade is
founded and allows her to speak of the degradation of prostitution uniquely in moral terms. Indeed, Fleur-de-Marie always, with the possible exception of her first scene in the *tapis-franc* of the Ile de la Cité, appears so
sweet, so passive and virginal, that it is hard to credit her identity as prostitute. Yet, of course, it is she who will eventually succumb to the mark of
the beast, die repining for an unrestorable virginity. Whereas La Louve,
rehabilitated through Fleur-de-Marie's good offices, is married off to
Martial who, originally a poacher and prostitute's consort, becomes a
gamekeeper, legitimate husband, and father of a numerous progeny. The
reason La Louve can survive rehabilitation, while Fleur-de-Marie ultimately cannot, must be attributed to social class: a prostitute can be reclaimed
for the proletariat, become an honest working-class wife, but not for the
bourgeoisie. There are limits. La Louve shows Sue's humanitarian liberal-
ism, whereas Fleur-de-Marie suggests its profoundly bourgeois character
and its limitations.

Parent-Duchatelet's *De la prostitution* is itself not exempt from these
contradictions. As a piece of social-scientific research, it is extraordinarily
advanced, consciously rejecting prejudice, received ideas, and hearsay, in
favor of a scrupulous examination of records and statistics. The sections
concerning the physiology and medical histories of prostitutes show a considerable freedom from prejudice and folklore concerning female sexuality, and the discussions of the causes of prostitution insist upon poverty,
illegitimacy, lack of education, destitution, rather than moral turpitude.
And yet, Parent-Duchatelet can turn around and talk about the moral degradation of these shameful creatures who lend themselves to unspeakable
practices and who suffer all consequences as an inevitable result of "a first
lapse from the most important of duties," that is, female chastity. Many
chapters begin or end with sententious moral homilies, and the introduction to the study makes its apologia concerning the matieral to be treated
by comparing this investigation to Parent-Duchatelet's earlier inquiry into
the condition of the Paris sewer system: "Why should I blush to enter this
other kind of cesspool (a cesspool more frightful, I admit, than all the
(others) in the hope of doing some good ... ?" (1:7).[12] Parent-Duchatelet's

report, we realize, itself marks an exercise of power over the lower depths: its scientific and moral discourse of prostitution constitutes a surveillance of the criminal body (to use terms suggested by Michel Foucault's *Surveiller et punir*). It belongs to a larger nineteenth-century project of policing deviance. Sue's discourse is similar, but more subversive in its attraction to the power of sexuality. Sue can, and does, treat prostitution as a socially generated evil, insisting on its near inevitability in sectors of the proletariat where families are piled together in one room, where incest is common, where a girl's only salable commodity is her body, and he issues a diatribe—which immediately became famous among social reformers—against a system which not only creates and accepts prostitution but goes on to regularize and register it through the Bureau des Moeurs. But Sue's reformism does not exhaust his interest in prostitution, which is first and foremost in *Les Mystères de Paris* the means of access to the lower world, the place where the manhole lid lifts up. The bourgeoisie touches the proletariat in a relation of erotic need mediated by money. This is surely a curious and ambivalent way to open up the question of the social depths, but perhaps historically it was necessarily the first way.

The prostitute, then, stands out as the key figure and term of access to that eminently storied subworld we have already mentioned; she exemplifies the modern narratable. One of Balzac's witty courtesans, Suzanne du Val-Noble, exactly makes the point as she shows her guests around her sumptuously furnished apartment: "Voilà les comptes des mille et une nuits," she tells them.[13] The phrase plays on the "*Contes* des Mille et une Nuits"—the Thousand and One Nights, or Arabian Nights—to suggest that accounts in two senses, the narrative and the financial, are interchangeable; that in the life of a prostitute at least, the accounting gives something to recount, money and story flow from the same nights of sexual exchange. The ramifications of Suzanne du Val-Noble's pun are everywhere in *Illusions perdues*, whose very subject, in George Lukàcs' description, is the "capitalization of spirit"—the transformation into commodity of the products of intelligence—and whose intricate plots turn on recountings of accountings, and accountings for recountings.[14] That this aphorism, which might stand as epigraph to the whole of "La Comédie humaine," should be spoken by a prostitute suggests how the narratable of Balzac's world is found in the conjunction of sexuality and monetary circulation. In the nexus of sexuality, money, and storytelling lie the source and subject of Sue's novel as well, and indeed also, its mode of production.

The *Roman-feuilleton* and the Melodramatic Imagination

To complete our comments on prostitution and narrative, we need to say something about the very way in which Sue's novel was published, which presents some version of the accounts of the Arabian Nights, or vice versa. The *roman-feuilleton*—the serial novel running in regular installments in the daily newspaper—was an invention of capitalism which helped to create modern mass-circulation journalism. The process began when Emile de Girardin founded *La Presse* as the first low-cost newspaper in 1836. His idea was to cut the normal subscription price by half (there were no single-issue sales at the time) and at least to double the number of subscribers, which would then permit an increase in the price and amount of advertising, which would thus take the place of subscription income as the basis of newspaper financing. What permitted the speculation—the oil of this revolutionary new machinery—was the daily dose of fiction in the *feuilleton* printed on the "ground floor"—the bottom quarter of the first page—which aimed to bring in a readership that had never before felt the need for a newspaper. The formula launched by *La Presse* was immediately successful: the paper quickly had four times the usual number of subscribers, and other papers hastened to follow suit. Subscription figures began to reach totals unimaginable a decade earlier. A secondary industry sprang into being with the creation of agencies specializing in collecting paid advertisements and feeding them to the newspapers. The financing of newspaper publishing hence became truly capitalistic, the financial and political power of the press increased immensely, and a shift in the balance of political forces was inaugurated as public opinion, as expressed, interpreted, and aroused by the mass-circulation newspapers, became a potent fourth estate.

Hence the creation of modern mass journalism and its power not only permitted the emergence of the *roman-feuilleton* but it quite directly depended on this first truly industrial form of literature. The successful *feuilletonistes* not only learned to live exclusively by the products of their pens, but because they were paid by the line, they learned to shape their plots to the exigencies of serialization. Each installment had to fit the space allotted, of course, and had to move the story forward to a new moment of suspense and expectation so that the terminal tag, *'La Suite à demain,'* could take its full toll on the reader. Moreover, newspaper subscriptions were renewable quarterly, hence it was important that matters be brought to a particularly dire moment of cliffhanging just before the renewal date so that readers would be sure to sign on for more. In its mode of production and publication, in its audience, and then in many of its themes, the serial novel of this period marks the advent of true industrial literature, conceived for a new mass marketplace, tied to the birth of modern journalism and the information revolution so characteristic of modern times.

If one judges the success of the *roman-feuilleton* by numbers of readers per copy, it is clear that *Les Mystères de Paris* marks an all time high: people literally fought over copies of the *Journal des Débats* as they appeared, from June 9, 1842, through October 15, 1843, and Sue's work incidentally saved the rather staid *Débats* from financial crisis. Sue's novel brought a full realization of the fusion of the "popular" in theme, audience, and mode of production, since Sue's social awareness was born of the writing of the novel itself, and that writing was shaped in an unprecedented manner by the interventions of its readers, in a dialogue that made of the work as it went along more and more of a collective enterprise. The most decisive moment of reader-recognition and reader-participation appears to have come with the introduction of the jewel-cutter Morel, the poor and honest artisan who lives and labors in a cold garret with his four children, his invalid wife and her idiot mother, and whose misfortunes and victimization accumulate with relentless progression: one child dead of malnutrition and exposure; his daughter Louise seduced, made pregnant, then accused of infanticide upon her child's death; Morel himself accused of theft, cleared through Rodolphe's intervention, then reduced not only to penury but to madness by Louise's misfortunes, confined among the insane at Bicêtre prison, and his family left in total destitution. Morel's story unfolds with all the excruciating excess of melodrama, but, again, this in no way contradicts the reality that his situation represented for thousands of Sue's readers. The melodrama is supported by reality: in the situation of Morel, Sue touched on a scandal from which there was no escape through moralizing. Morel was the typical honest artisan, victimized by a system that made even hard labor insufficient to assure protection from pauperization and that guaranteed any misfortune would quickly plunge a whole family into the depths of misery. Here were the powerless, more serious stuff for reformers and socialists than the lurid criminal population of the Ile de la Cité. Yet it is the logic of Sue's descent via the prostitute into the social depths that pauperization should be discovered through criminality, the laboring classes by way of the dangerous classes, the sold body from the deviant body.

It may be significant that the publication of *Les Mystères de Paris* in the *Journal des Débats* ended, following Fleur-de-Marie's death at Gerolstein, with an open letter from Sue to the paper's editor-in-chief, drawing the attention of readers to a new periodical, *La Ruche Populaire*, written and produced exclusively by workers and addressed to their interests, which in its first issue takes its epigraph, concerning the idea of the "police of virtue," and indeed its inspiration, from *Les Mystères de Paris*. Sue, that is, closes his *novel* with announcement of a *newspaper* that will continue his work; and he ends his letter to the editor by recapitulating a four-point legislative program aimed toward the relief of social misery. The novel ends, then, by passing on into the world of its readers, becoming part of the movement toward reform and social justice, putting itself at the service of a world discovered by means of the melodramatic fiction.

Sue's socialism was undoubtedly sincere yet much tinged by romantic sentimental colorings and eminently vulnerable to the Marxist demolition in *Die Heilige Familie*. Sue's main sympathy goes to the honest artisan who needs a living wage and a helping hand from the state. He makes occasional reference to the Saint-Simonian notion of the "organisation du travail," but the posture remains essentially one of bourgeois paternalism, as the famous conception of the Police of Virtue—which particularly drew

Marx's ire—clearly implies. Sue's portraits and his ideas are based on humanitarian and fraternal sympathies rather than on analytic study of industrial capitalism as a system. Sue's posture, in fact, never wholly ceases to resemble that of Clémence d'Harville condescending to visit the prostitutes in Saint-Lazare—society lady on errands of succor and mercy among a class of beings who are conceived to be both victims of a system and irremediably morally stigmatized, capable of spiritual redemption but only within the limits traced by the definition of the feminine in each social class, and not to the extent of bourgeois marriage; and who offer the adventurer from the upper world excitement, fear, and the opportunity for pity. Ultimately, prostitution and the prostitute most fully express Sue's enterprise in its rich ambiguity and indeed offer an emblem of what is at stake in much of the most interesting nineteenth-century narrative fiction.

Les Mystères de Paris remains a remarkable descent beneath the "vast smug surface" of society (as Henry James would call it in the preface to The Princess Casamassima). Critics have often attempted to separate a concern with serious "social realism" from the melodramatic fascination with the underworld and its menacing potential of violence, but the distinction may finally be untenable. The melodramatic situation and gesture are the forms through which serious social concerns are opened to consciousness and made available to literature. The melodramatic imagination working on the world encounters the need to open up its underworld. That the point of entry into the nether regions should be found in prostitution has the logic of connection, as perhaps of uncanny metaphor. Here sexuality, money, deviance converge to form a powerful potential for story. "Les comptes des mille et une nuits" offer the greatest source of a contemporary Arabian Nights of Paris in the era of capitalist development. In the case of Fleur-de-Marie, we run the whole gamut of melodramatic possibilities, playing out the lowest depths and the highest summits, toward a sublime redemption which cannot work within the social order and veers into death. Along the way of her tortuous narrative path, Fleur-de-Marie receives the ineffaceable stigmata from which she must eventually die. Sue also may have received the mark of the Cité in that his novel does not end in the spirit in which it began, though it ends in full ambivalence of attitude. We have dwelled enough on these ambivalences and the contradictory attitudes evoked by the mark of the beast. We may close simply by reminding ourselves that the same ambivalences inhabit the use of melodrama as vehicle for discovery and representation of social issues. "Sombre et cruel spectacle!" writes Sue in presenting the tableau of Morel and his family reduced to the final extremities. It is in that insistent invitation to see—both to be spectator at, and to bear witness to—this lurid drama of misery that Sue's melodrama displays its possibilities and its limitations, the ambiguous power of half-understood discoveries.

Morel, his daughter Louise, and Rodolphe from a scene in the first edition of *The Mysteries of Paris* (London: Chapman and Hall, 1845-46).

Notes

1. Eugène Sue, *Les Mystères de Paris*, 10 vols. (Paris: Charles Gosselin, 1843), 10:149. Subsequent references will be to this edition, and will be given in parentheses in the text. Translations from the French are my own.

2. For an example of Freud's analysis of such a displacement, see "Fragment of an Analysis of a Case of Hysteria" ("Dora"), *Standard Edition of the Complete Psychological Works of Sigmund Freud* (London: Hogarth Press, 1953-), 7:30.

3. E. Faure, *"Les Mystères de Paris*, par M. Eugène Sue," book review in *La Revue Indépendante* 8 (1843), reprinted in Helga Grubitzsch, ed., *Materialien zur Kritik des Feuilleton-Romans* (Wiesbaden: Akademische Verlagsgesellschaft Athenaion, 1977), pp. 40–41.

4. C. A. Sainte-Beuve, "M. Eugène Sue," from *Portraits contemporains* (1846), reprinted in Grubitzsch, *Materialien, p. 71.*

5. On these questions and all others concerning Sue's life and career, see the excellent biography by Jean-Louis Bory, *Eugène Sue: Dandy mais socialiste* (Paris: Hachette, 1962). See also Umberto Eco, "Rhetoric and Ideology in Sue's *Les Mystères de Paris,"* *International Social Sciences Journal* (1967), 19:4. For some brief remarks on Sue and the popular novel, see my article, "A Man Named Sue," *New York Times Book Review,* July 30, 1978.

6. For some further thoughts on plot and deviance, see my article "Freud's Masterplot," *Yale French Studies* (1978), 55–56:280–300.

7. See Albert Béguin, *Balzac visionnaire* (Genève: Skira, 1946). pp. 151-79.

8. Honoré de Balzac, *Splendeurs et misères des courtisanes* (Paris: Garnier, 1964), p. 251. The original date of publication of the novel is 1838-47. The first section, originally entitled "La Torpille," was offered to Emile de Girardin for publication in *La Presse,* but Girardin refused to publish the story of a prostitute for fear of scandalizing his subscribers.

9. Georg Simmel, "Prostitution" (from *Philosophie des Geldes*, 1907), in Donald N. Levine, ed., *On Individuality and Social Forms* (Chicago: University of Chicago Press, 1971), p. 122.

10. Louis Chevalier, *Classes laborieuses et classes dangereuses* (1958), trans. as *Labouring Classes and Dangerous Classes* by Frank Jellinek (London: Routledge), p. 276. A recent and excellent study of prostitution in Alain Corbin, *Les Filles de noce* (Paris: Aubier Montaigne, 1978).

11. See A.-J.-B. Parent-Duchatelet, *De la Prostitution dans la ville de Paris*, 2 vols., 2ème éd. (Paris: J.-B. Baillière, 1837). I have also consulted the edition of 1857, "complétée par des documents nouveaux . . . par Adolphe Trébuchet & Poiret-Duval."

12. For an example of Parent-Duchatelet's rhetorical blend of observation and veiling of the evidence, physiology and morality, consider these remarks concerning sodomy: "Ces malheureuses, livrées à la brutalité d'une foule d'hommes blasées sur les jouissances que permet la nature, ne refusent pas toujours ces communications illicites qui, pour avoir lieu entre des individus de sexe différent, n'en sont pas moins révoltantes. . . . Je dois avouer qu'il n'est pas un point de la vie et des habitudes des filles plus obscur que celui-ci; on peut dire, à leur louange, qu'elles sont sur ce sujet d'une réserve complète, qu'elles repoussent avec horreur les questions qu'on leur adresse, et qu'elles affectent une certaine indignation lorsqu'on paraît les soupçonner de s'être prêtées à des communications de cette nature" (1:225-26).

13. Balzac, *Illusions perdues* (Paris: Garnier, 1961), p. 467.

14. See Georg Lukács, *"Illusions perdues,"* in *Studies in European Realism,* trans. Edith Bone (London, 1950). It is worth noting that in part 3 of *Illusions perdues,* Balzac invents an elaborate story simply from the circulation of a *compte de retour,* or unpaid letter of credit: "Calembour à part, jamais les romanciers n'ont inventé de conte plus invraisemblable que celui-là . . . " *(Illusions perdues,* p. 588).

11

A Victorian Gothic:
G. W. M. Reynolds's
Mysteries of London

DANIEL S. BURT

Early in the course of G. W. M. Reynolds's melodramatic serial, *The Mysteries of London*, the narrator comments: "Shakespeare said, 'All the world is a *stage*'; we say, 'All the world is an *omnibus*.'"[1] Despite the pun, Reynolds's conception of the world as an omnibus provides an accurate description of his dramatic method as well as his fictional vehicle, which ran through a change of publisher and title from 1844 to 1855 in weekly penny numbers, monthly sixpenny parts, and a reissue of twelve volumes of approximately four-and-one-half-million words. The world that Reynolds dramatized is one in which, as on an omnibus, "The old and the young- the virtuous and wicked—the rich and the poor, are invariably thrown and mixed together" (1:101). Accordingly, the passengers of *The Mysteries of London* include prostitutes, thieves, murderers, paupers, body snatchers, bankers, members of Parliament, clergymen, and even Victoria and Albert. With a cast ever growing and changing, brought together by the contrivance of an exciting, if improbable, plot, the hair-raising ride of the omnibus is underway, resulting in an omnibus of a different sort: an encyclopedia of Victorian thrills, sensation, and sentiment.

By the 1830s and 1840s, melodrama as adapted by novelists in Gothic romances had changed. The Gothic novel was largely subsumed by other popular literary forms for a new working-class readership who demanded more realistic and recognizable sensation. As Michael Sadleir points out, "The Gothic novel crashed and became the vulgar blood."[2] The popular press was quick to offer a dizzying assault of shocks and thrills in cheap periodicals, penny numbers, and multiple volumes. Tales of horror, crime, and villainy were elaborated and expanded weekly by a large complement of hack writers. Like the Gothic novel or the stage melodrama, the penny bloods rapidly became a formula fiction with stock characters and incidents and with excitement created by the simple dramatic situation of virtue threatened by villainy. Among writers who catered to the Victorian readers' appetites for the sensational and the melodramatic, G. W. M. Reynolds was by far the most popular and the most successful. *The Mysteries of London* sold an estimated 40,000 copies a week, and, when Reynolds died in 1879, *The Bookseller* reported that "Dickens and Thackeray and Lever had their thousands of readers, but Mr. Reynolds's were numbered in the hundreds of thousands, perhaps millions."[3] Reynolds's success stemmed from his mastery of the art of fictional melodrama in concocting rousing stories to horrify, instruct, and morally uplift a massive popular audience.

London's Den of Horrors

Modeled on Eugène Sue's *The Mysteries of Paris*, Reynolds's series of novels, *The Mysteries of London* and its sequel *The Mysteries of the Court of London*, dramatize the secrets and thrills of London high and low life. His scope is panoramic, and his subject is crime and villainy:

> The visitor to the Polytechnic Institution or the Adelaide Gallery has doubtless seen the exhibition of the microscope. A drop of the purest water, magnified by that instrument some thousands of times, appears filled with horrible reptiles and monsters of revolting forms.
> Such is London.
> Fair and attractive as the mighty metropolis may appear to the superior observer, it swarms with disgusting, loathsome, and venomous objects, wearing human shapes.
> Oh! London is a city of strange contrasts! (1:58)

Reynolds's multivolume serial provides such a sensational magnification that the entire urban panorama may be studied to reveal its perfidy and wickedness. The narrative is a series of strange contrasts, and a summary of the plot of *The Mysteries of London* would be exceedingly complicated and beside the point. The interest in Reynolds's serial comes not from the working out of its tangled narrative but from its separate episodes, on a multitude of sensational vignettes and short melodramatic stories. To get a sense of Reynolds's fiction it is better to examine representative scenes and characters to illustrate his fictional method and material.

A prime ingredient in any installment of *The Mysteries of London* is its shock value. Reynolds's work is strongly laced with horror guaranteed to cause a shiver or chill in even the most phlegmatic or hardened reader. For his sensation Reynolds resorted to the relatively new subject of the horrors of the modern city and dramatized what Henry Mayhew in *London Labour and the London Poor* examined with statistics, eyewitness accounts, interviews, and a sociologist's eye. Reynolds, like Mayhew, was concerned with the various strata and social groups in London, but he presented his findings with the eye of a sensationalist, taking his readers first-hand into the city's "Den of Horrors":

> Some of the houses have small back yards, in which the inhabit-
> ants keep pigs. A short time ago, an infant belonging to a poor
> widow, who occupied a back room on the ground-floor of one
> of those hovels, died, and was laid upon the sacking of the bed
> while the mother went to make arrangements for its interment.
> During her absence a pig entered the room from the yard, and
> feasted upon the dead child's face!
> In that densely populated neighbourhood that we are de-
> scribing, hundreds of families each live and sleep in one room.
> When a member of one of these families happens to die, the
> corpse is kept in the close room where the rest still continue to
> live and sleep. Poverty frequently compels the unhappy rela-
> tives to keep the body for days—aye, and weeks. Rapid decom-
> position takes place;—animal life generates quickly; and in four-
> and-twenty hours myriads of loathsome animaculae are seen
> crawling about. The very undertaker's men fall sick at these
> disgusting—these revolting spectacles. (1:43)

The horror of such scenes is drawn out to extract the maximum in shock and macabre thrills. Comparing Reynolds's account of the slum of Saffron Hills and Smithfield with Mayhew's study of similar material, the reader senses not so much Reynolds's exaggeration (nothing in fact is more sensational or horrifying than some of Mayhew's interviews and statistics) but his absolute relish for sensational details such as the child's mutilated face and the close-up view of a corpse's decomposition.[4] Reynolds updated Gothic horror by casting it in modern dress and setting it in scenes of London city life that highlighted its monstrousness. In one particularly graphic passage, the narrator describes the activities of a gravedig-ger that demonstrates Reynolds's unflinching realism and his zest for shock effects:

The man returned to the grave, and was about to resume his labour, when his eyes caught the sight of a black object, almost embedded in the damp clay heaped up by the side. He turned it over with his spade: it was the upper part of the skull, with the long, dark hair of a woman still remaining attached to it. The grave-digger coolly took up the relic by that long hair which perhaps had once been a valued ornament; and, carrying it in this manner into the Bone-House, threw it upon the fire. The hair hissed a moment as it burnt, for it was damp and clogged with clay; then the voracious flames licked up the thin coat of blackened flesh which had still remained on the skull; and lastly devoured the bone itself. (1:314)

The Resurrection Man

Cemeteries are favorite settings, and corpses are favorite characters in Reynolds's fiction. One of the novel's main villains is a resurrection man or body snatcher. Although the profession was in decline after 1829 and the notorious trial of the Scottish resurrection men and murderers Burke and Hare, which resulted in legislation to make cadavers legally available to doctors, Reynolds employs a body snatcher who still plies his grisly trade as an all-purpose bogeyman in the novel. Reynolds includes in his presentation "A Body-Snatcher's Song" that illustrates the horrifying thrills in which the novel delights:

> In the churchyard the body is laid,
> There they inter the beautiful maid:
>   "Earth to earth" is the solemn sound!
> Over the sod where their daughter sleeps,
> The father prays, and the mother weeps:
>   "Ashes to ashes" echoes around!
>
> Come with the axe, and come with the spade;
> Come where the beautiful virgin's laid:
>   Earth from earth must we take back now!
> The sod is damp, and the grave is cold:
> Lay the white corpse on the dark black mould,
>   That the pale moonbeam may kiss its brow!
>
> Throw back the earth, and heap up the clay;
> This cold white corpse we will bear away,
>   Now that the moonlight waxes dim;
> For the student doth his knife prepare
> To hack all over this form so fair,
>   And sever the virgin limb from limb!

A scene showing the Resurrection Man at work in one of Reynolds's favorite settings. Corpses and open graves are prime ingredients in the novel's Gothic chills. The illustration and others that follow, by G. Stiff, appeared in the weekly serial and helped to ensure *The Mysteries of London*'s popular success.

> At morn the mother will come to pray
> Over the grave where her child she lay,
>   And freshest flowers thereon will spread:
> And on that spot will she kneel and weep,
> Nor dream that we have disturbed the sleep
>   Of her who lay in that narrow bed. (1:125)

Like his famous Scottish predecessors, Reynolds's resurrection man frequently does not wait for nature to take its course before procuring a new cadaver. Often as many victims are sent to their graves as he takes out. Reynolds gives a description of the method used in preparing a new corpse for sale, in the words of the resurrection man: by " 'holding him with his head downwards in a tub of water . . . till he was drowned. That way don't tell no tales;—no wound on the skin—no poison in the stomach; and there ain't too much water inside neither, cos the poor devils don't swallow with their heads downwards' " (1:124). In one scene the resurrection man retrieves from a pond the body of a murdered girl to torment his fellow murderer, Lady Adeline Ravensworth:

> Then, holding the light in such a manner that its beams fell upon the floor, and withdrawing his arms from Adeline's waist, he exclaimed in a tone of ferocious triumph, "Behold the remains of the murdered Lydia Hutchinson!"
> Lady Ravensworth threw one horrid glance upon the putrid corpse; and uttering a terrific scream expressive of the most intense agony, she fell upon the floor—her face touching the feet of the dead body.
> Tidkins raised her: but the blood gushed out of her mouth.
> "Perdition! I have gone too far," cried the Resurrection Man. (1:390)

Most readers will no doubt strongly agree.

Scenes of Violence

The horror portrayed by Reynolds at times verges on the sadistic, showing a delight in graphic scenes of violence. The domestic life of Bill Bolter will serve as an example. Bolter is a kind of Bill Sikes as a family man. His two children are almost continuously beaten and brutalized, but the violence done to them is nothing compared to that contemplated by their mother. Planning their children's future, the parents decide that young Henry can go into his father's business and will be "so handy to shove through a window, or to sneak down an area and hide himself all day in a cellar to open the door at night,—or a thousand things." Fanny's vocation, however, remains a problem until her mother suggests blinding her to increase her potential as a beggar. As she remarks, ''There's nothing like a blind child to exact compassion.'' As if this were not enough, Reynolds offers a description how the blinding might be accomplished. Fanny's mother has heard of another woman who covered her child's eyes ''with cockle shells, the eye-lids, recollect, being wide open; and in each shell there was a huge black beetle. A bandage tied tight round the head kept the shells in their place; and the shells kept the eye-lids open. In a few days the eyes got quite blind, and the pupils had a dull white appearance'' (1:45). The horror of such a torture suggested by the child's mother is revolting enough even, one imagines, for the strongest stomachs. Mrs. Bolter's friend could have been Mary Arnold, the Female Monster, celebrated in a popular Victorian street ballad:

> Of all the tales was ever told,
> I now will you impart,
> That cannot fail to terror strike,
> To every human heart.
> The deeds of Mary Arnold,
> Who does in a jail deplore,
> Oh! such a dreadful tale as this,
> Was never told before.

> *Chorus*
> This wretched woman's dreadful deed,
> Does every one affright.
> With black beetles in walnut shells,
> She deprived her child of sight.

> Now think you tender parents,
> What must this monster feel,
> The heart within her breast must ten
> Times harder be than steel.
> The dreadful crime she did commit,
> Does all the world surprise,
> Black beetles placed in walnut shells,
> Bound round her infant's eyes.

> The beetles in a walnut shell,
> This monster she did place,
> This dreadful deed, as you may read,
> All history does disgrace,
> The walnut shell, and beetles,
> With a bandage she bound tight,
> Around her infant's tender eyes,
> To take away its sight.

A lady saw this monster,
In the street when passing by,
And she was struck with terror,
For to hear the infant cry.
The infant's face she swore to see,
Which filled her with surprise,
To see the fatal bandage,
Tied round the infant's eyes.

With speed she called an officer,
Oh! shocking to relate,
Who beheld the deed, and took the wretch,
Before the Magistrate.
Who committed her for trial,
Which did the wretch displease,
And she's now transported ten long years,
Across the briny seas.

Is there another in the world,
Could plan such wicked deed,
No one upon this earth before,
Of such did ever see.
To take away her infant's sight,
'Tis horrible to tell,
Binding black beetles round it's eyes,
Placed in walnut shells.[5]

Reynolds answered the ballad's last stanza with his own female monster.

After Mrs. Bolter contemplates blinding her daughter, Reynolds in characteristic fashion pulls back from the scene to moralize on its hideousness and then arranges a fitting punishment for such an unnatural mother. She is interrupted while beating her children by Bolter who is unexpectedly moved by the children's suffering:

The poor lad screamed piteously: the hand of his mother had fallen with the weight of a sledge hammer upon his naked flesh.

But that ferocious blow was echoed by another, at scarcely a moment's interval. The latter was dealt by the fist of Bill Bolter, and fell upon the back part of the ruthless mother's head with a stunning force.

The woman fell forward, and struck her face violently against the corner of the deal table.

Her left eye came in contact with the angle of the board, and was literally crushed in its socket—an awful retribution upon her who only a few hours before was planning how to plunge

Tidkins, the Resurrection Man, often sends as many victims to their graves as he takes out. Here, Virtue, represented by the helpless female, struggles with Vice in the melodramatic manner.

her innocent and helpless daughter into the eternal night of blindness. (1:51)

Reynolds here demonstrates his chilling orchestration of shocking and sensational scenes with moral commentary, melodramatically staging the punishment for the villainy and violence he has so lavishly depicted.

Victorian Peep Shows

In addition to scenes of horror and violence, a staple in Reynolds's melodramatic fare is a kind of semipornographic and titillating depiction of sex. The unfortunate history of the Reverend Reginald Tracy offers a characteristic example. Tracy is seduced by a temptress, and the stages of his moral decline are described at some length. In one scene, Tracy, revolted by his recent lapse into the arms of his lover (discreetly presented in the text by two lines of asterisks), tries to avoid any further temptation. He is, however, called on parish business to the garret of a sculptor where he sees what he takes to be a statue resembling his lover. The scene recalls the *tableau vivant* popular on the Victorian stage where nudity might be presented if it involved classical subjects. Here the subject is Pygmalion: "It was naked to the middle; the arms were gracefully rounded; and one hand sustained the falling drapery which, being also coloured, produced upon the mind of the beholder the effect of real garments." The statue to Tracy's amazement comes rather markedly to life: "the statue burst from chill marble into warmth and life; it was indeed the beauteous but wily Cecilia—who returned his embrace and hung around his neck;—and the rector was again subdued—again enslaved!" (1:395). Such a theatrical way for Cecilia to reclaim her lover is typical in Reynolds's presentation of sex.

Tracy's fall into lust is further dramatized in a scene that is a kind of Victorian peep show. Tracy is attracted to one of the novel's heroines, Ellen Monroe, and Reynolds allows Tracy and the reader a provocative glimpse of her before bathing with her child:

> When the rector beheld her descend in that bewitching *negligee*, her hair unconfined, and floating at will—her small round, polished ankles glancing between the white drapery and the little slippers—and the child, with merely a thick shawl thrown about it, in her arms . . . without a moment's hesitation he stole softly from the recess where he concealed himself, and approached the door of the bath-room.
>
> His greedy eyes were applied to the key-hole; and his licentious glance plunged into the depths of that sacred privacy. (2:26)

The narrator gives a moral commentary and condemnation of the reverend's actions in no uncertain terms, yet the reader still finds himself with Tracy at the keyhold. Reynolds, therefore, has it both ways—moral correctness and titillation at the same time:

> The fires of gross sensuality raged madly in his breast.
> Ellen's preparations were now completed.
> With her charming white hand she put back her hair from her forehead.
> Then, as she still retained the child on her left arm, with her right hand she loosened the strings which closed her dressing gown round the neck and the band which confined it at the waist.
> While thus occupied, she was partly turned towards the door; and all the treasures of her bosom were revealed to the ardent gaze of the rector.
> His desires were now inflamed to that pitch when they almost became ungovernable. He felt that could he possess that charming creature, he would care not what the result—even though he forced her to compliance with his wishes, and murder and suicide followed,—the murder of her and the suicide of himself!
> He was about to grasp the handle of the door when he remembered that he had heard the key turn in the lock immediately after she had entered the room.
> He gnashed his teeth with rage.
> And now the drapery had fallen from her shoulders, and the whole of her voluptuous form, naked to the waist, was exposed to his view.
> He could have broken down the door, had he not feared to alarm the other inmates of the house.
> He literally trembled under the influence of his fierce desires.
> How he envied—Oh! how he envied the innocent babe which the fond mother pressed to that bosom—swelling, warm, and glowing!
> And now she prepared to step into the bath: but, while he was waiting with fervent avidity for the moment when the whole of the drapery should fall from her form, a step suddenly resounded upon the stairs. (2:26)

Ellen's striptease is stopped at the last possible moment with her modesty barely preserved but not before Reynolds has extracted as many thrills as possible from the scene. The reader should note his stage directions as Tracy gnashes his teeth with rage like a melodramatic stage villain. The image of the mother and child with its sacred, madonnalike associations, perversely made so profane by Tracy's monstrous lust, is a further twist or element to heighten and intensify the scene which grotesquely mixes lewdness and morality. The reader can both sin with Tracy and be saved by adopting the narrator's perspective and tone of righteous indignation at such infamy.

If the history of Reginald Tracy shows the reader the early stages in the making of a voluptuary, the depiction of the final moments of the aged Marquis of Holmesford offers a glimpse of the last stage and in the process shows the reader the private bedchambers and excesses of the wealthy. We learn that the Marquis has established a harem at Holmesford House:

> There was the Scotch charmer, with her brilliant complexion, her auburn hair, and her red cherry lips:—there was the English girl—the pride of Lancashire—with her brown hair, and her robust but exquisitely modelled proportions:—and next to her, on the same ottoman, sate the Irish beauty whose sparkling black eyes denoted all the fervour of sensuality.
>
> On the sofa facing these three women, sate the French wanton, her taper fingers playing with the gold chain which, in the true spirit of coquetry, she had thrown negligently round her neck, and the massive links of which made not the least indentation upon the plump fullness of her bosom. By her side was the Spanish houri, her long black ringlets flowing on the white drapery which set off her transparent olive skin to such exquisite advantage.
>
> This group formed an assemblage of charms which would have raised palpitations and excited mysterious fires in the heart of the most heaven-devoted anchorite that ever vowed a life of virgin-purity. (2:400)

Such excitement has no doubt contributed to the Marquis' failing health, and, although close to death, he seeks the company of his harem for one last time:

> "Consider that I am going on a long journey, my dear girls," he exclaimed, with a smile; "and do not let our party be sorrowful. Kathleen, my sweet one, come nearer: there—place yourself so that I may recline my head on your bosom—and now throw that warm, plump, naked arm over my shoulder. Oh! this is paradise!"
>
> And for a few minutes the hoary voluptuary, whose licentious passions were dominant even in death, closed his eyes and seemed to enjoy with intense gratification all the luxury of his position. (2:402)

Reynolds does not neglect the opportunity to note the scene's strange, not to say grotesque, contrast and its moral lesson:

It was a painful and disgusting sight to behold the shrivelled, haggard, and attenuated countenance of the dying sensualist, pressing upon that full and alabaster globe so warm with health, life, and glowing passions;—painful and disgusting, too, to see that thin, emaciated, and worn-out frame reclining in the arms of a lovely girl in the vigour and strength of youth:—hideous— hideous to view that contiguity of a sapless, withered trunk and a robust and verdant tree! (2:402)

Chastened by the narrator, the Marquis nevertheless continues to enjoy his sensual pleasure (as does the reader), and dies, fulfilling his dream to go "with his head pillowed on the naked—heaving bosom of beauty, and with a glass of sparkling champagne in his hand" (2:403).

Virtue's Reward—Vice's Punishment

After several hundred pages such sensational and shocking scenes start to be repeated with fairly tedious regularity. If there is one scene in a graveyard, one hero who falls to what seems to be certain death, one virgin who *almost* loses her honor, there are several such scenes and situations. Incidents displaying the monstrous underside of city life and the formula of villainy's assault on virtue are played out again and again in newer and stranger episodes as Reynolds tries to find fresher stimulants to shock and thrill his audience. Whatever Reynolds concocted to electrify each installment, the outcome is not long in doubt. His moral is as inescapable as the shocks and the blood. " 'Tis done," the narrator proclaims at the end of the first series of *The Mysteries of London*, "VIRTUE is rewarded—VICE has received its punishment" (2:424). After a litany of sensation, Reynolds ends with a homily: "If, then, the preceding pages be calculated to engender one useful thought—awaken one beneficial statement,—the work is not without its value" (2:424). Like the stage melodrama that is part thrilling adventure and part morality play, Reynolds's fiction is also a kind of all-purpose entertainment: a guided tour through brothels, lady's boudoirs, elegant drawing rooms, and gin shops, in which the reader can get his full penny's worth of practical advice, sentiment, and terror that combines the tabloid and the tract.

Reynolds and Dickens

It may be argued that, in Reynolds's fiction, terror and sentimentality have finally found their proper level among undiscriminating readers, beginning a long underground history in subliterary forms that surface today in detective fiction, thrillers, Victoria Holt and Barbara Cartland romances, soap operas, and comic books. Such fictional entertainment, though immensely popular, is critically ignored, recognized as not the sort of fiction from which great art is made. Yet the gap separating popular and serious literature—highbrow and lowbrow art—was not as wide nor as difficult to bridge in the Victorian period as it is in our own. The audience for the best Victorian fiction overlapped in part with the audience for the worst. Reynolds, for example, began his novel-writing career with an imitation of *The Pickwick Papers*, and Dickens's *Household Words* and *All the Year Round* competed for a portion of the same audience as the more lurid *London Journal* and *Reynolds's Miscellany*. The mode of publication for many of the classic Victorian novels in installments was the same as that for the lowest fictional hack work, and it is hard to imagine that a novelist like Dickens who was so conscious of the tastes of the marketplace was not also aware of his competitors in the popular press and their readers' craving for strong scenes full of suffering and sentiment with as many thrills as laughter and tears. Reynolds's novels and the other penny bloods are important, therefore, in giving the modern reader a clear indication of what a majority of the age demanded in popular entertainment—an audience whose taste the major Victorian novelists had to contend with—to cater to, react against, or modify.

Reynolds's popularity and career curiously parallels Dickens's. Both men were the age's bestsellers, though by most accounts Reynolds's sales far outdistanced those of Dickens. And, although Dickens expressed nothing but contempt for Reynolds's novels, which he called "a national reproach," both writers have certain interesting similarities in their melodramatic methods.[6] Reynolds was a passionate reformer, drawn to the temperance movement and the Chartists, and his moral and political concerns crept into even the most extravagantly sensational of his tales. Reynolds used his sensational and melodramatic stories as a vehicle for a certain degree of propagandizing and social satire, much in the same manner as did Dickens. In *The Mysteries of London*, for example, though the incidents verge on the pornographic and the luridly sensational, Reynolds makes it clear that

> We have a grand moral lesson to work out—a great lesson to teach every class of society; a moral and lesson whose themes are
> Wealth. | Poverty. (1:415-16)

Reynolds's social theme and panorama are not far removed from Dickens's in novels like *Dombey and Son, Bleak House, Little Dorrit,* and *Our Mutual Friend.* Both novelists use the melodramatic and the sensational to dramatize a social message; both attempt to show the connection between the lowest members of society and the highest. Reynolds writes:

Crime is abundant in this city: the lazar-house, the prison, the

Bill Bolter and family. In a scene of elaborate poetic justice, Mrs. Bolter who has suggested blinding her daughter to increase her potential as a beggar is herself blinded and killed by her husband, an unlikely but convenient agent of the novel's moral retribution.

brothel, the dark alley, are rife with all kinds of enormity; in the same way as the palace, the mansion, the club-house, the parliament, and the parsonage, are each and all characterised by their different degrees and shades of vice. . . . Crimes borrow their comparative shades of enormity from the people who perpetrate them: thus it is that the wealthy may commit all social offenses with impunity; while the poor are cast into dungeons and coerced with chains, for only following at a humble distance in the pathway of their lordly precedents. (1:2)

Reynolds's diagnosis of the connection between vice and social class resembles Dickens's analysis of society and particularly of the urban slums in *Dombey and Son:*

Those who study the physical sciences, and bring them to bear upon the health of Man, tell us that if the noxious particles that rise from vitiated air were palpable to the sight, we should see them lowering in a dense cloud above such haunts, and rolling slowly on to corrupt the better portions of a town. But if the moral pestilence that rises with them, and, in the eternal law of outraged Nature, is inseparable from them, could be made discernable too, how terrible the revelation! Then should we see depravity, impiety, drunkenness, theft, murder, and a long train of nameless sins against the natural affections and repulsions of mankind, overhanging the devoted spots, and creeping among the poor.[7]

Like Reynolds's microscope, Dickens uses the instrument of his melodramatic plot to reveal the moral climate of his society: the connection, as in Reynolds's omnibus, of rich and poor, the wicked and the virtuous.

Without asserting that Reynolds's novels provided a direct model for Dickens, it is possible to claim a kindred quality in both novelists, as it is between the penny bloods and the work of the major Victorian novelists. Reynolds opened new territory for the novelist in his scenes of city life and perfected the form for the successful melodramatic serial while also developing ways in which a sensational narrative might be extended to encompass other themes and purposes. If Reynolds largely succumbs to the melodramatic and sensational excesses that Dickens and novelists like Wilkie Collins and Thomas Hardy were often able to transcend and develop in more challenging and interesting ways, Reynolds's fiction remains a useful collection of fictional melodrama: a wild assortment of stories, character types, gruesome details, and sentimentality that were the stock elements on the Victorian stage and in the novel.

The Marquis of Holmesford dies in the arms of a member of his harem. The wealthy, in Reynolds's novel, are characteristically debauched, and the novel allows the reader a close look at aristocratic excesses.

Notes

1. G. W. M. Reynolds, *The Mysteries of London*, 4 vols. (London: Geo. Vickers, 1845-48), 1:102. All further references to this work appear in the text.

2. Michael Sadleir, *Things Past* (London: Constable, 1944), p. 199.

3. Quoted by E. F. Bleiler in his introduction to Reynolds's *Wagner, the Wehr-Wolf* (New York: Dover, 1975), p. xiii. Besides his most perceptive introduction to the novelist and his work, Bleiler also provides a useful bibliography to which I am indebted. See also Donald Kausch's "George W. M. Reynolds: A Bibliography," Transactions of the Bibliographical Society, *The Library* (December 1973), 5th ser., vol. 28, no. 4, pp. 319-326. Other useful studies of Victorian popular literature and Reynolds are Margaret Dalziel's *Popular Fiction 100 Years Ago* (London: Cohen & West, 1957); Louis James's *Fiction for the Working Man 1820-1850* (London: Oxford Univ. Press, 1963); Victor E. Neuburg's *Popular Literature: A History and a Guide* (Harmondsworth: Penguin, 1977); and E. S. Turner's *Boys Will Be Boys* (London: Michael Joseph, 1948, rev. ed. 1975).

4. The use of pigs devouring a child occurs again for its shock effect in French and Spanish avant-garde drama. John A. Henderson in *The First Avant-garde 1887-1897* (London: G. G. Harrap, 1971) describes Auguste Linert's *Conte de Noël* (1890) in which "On Christmas Eve an abandoned farm-girl gives birth to an illegitimate child, which, in despair, she proceeds to murder (off stage). She then returns to announce that the remains have been gobbled up by the farmer's pigs, while the neighbours go off to midnight Mass [p. 84]." In Ramón María del Valle-Inclán's *Divine Words* (1913) a child's face is devoured by hogs on stage. It is interesting to note that these shocking examples of avant-garde theater, the last word in repulsive naturalism, were preceded by the popular fiction of Reynolds in 1844.

5. John Ashton, *Modern Street Ballads* (London: Chatto & Windus, 1888), pp. 374-76. I have been unable to determine whether Mary Arnold was an actual Female Monster or a fiction. In any case, whether Reynolds had an actual criminal in mind or this ballad, the similarity suggests the source material Reynolds certainly used throughout *The Mysteries of London*—tales, real or imagined, of striking and shocking crimes and foul deeds.

6. For an interesting essay on the connection between Reynolds's and Dickens's use of mysteries and secrets see Richard C. Maxwell's "G. M. Reynolds, Dickens, and Mysteries of London." *Nineteenth-Century Fiction* (1977), 32:188-213.

7. Dickens, *Dombey and Son*, ed. Alan Horsman (Oxford: Clarendon, 1974), pp. 619-20.

12

Joseph Conrad's
The Secret Agent or the
Melodrama of Reality

ZDZISŁAW NAJDER

Melodrama may be most generally defined as a sequence of events for which "normality" (or verisimilitude, if it is represented or described) is claimed, but which is too spectacularly dramatic, too extravagant to be taken as "normal" or realistic. It is, of course, a culturally and historically relative concept: what is melodramatic for a reader of *The New Yorker* is not so for a reader of *True Stories;* a novel by Smollett or Balzac is, for us today, inherently more melodramatic than one by Sinclair Lewis or Roger Martin du Gard.

There is the melodrama of events and the melodrama of presentation; the two often overlap, but not necessarily. On the one hand, a straightforward description of the plight of the nineteeth-century immigrants to the United States, of the trenches in Flanders in 1916, or of a contemporary labor camp may strike us as melodramatic by the sheer force of facts related. On the other hand, it is possible to describe hidden psychological developments in a manner which has to be called melodramatic; Henry James would sometimes do that, as has been pointed out by several critics.

In its developed literary and dramatic forms, melodrama rests on the principle of unabashed emotionalism. It strives to call forth unambiguous and strong feelings, plays on polarities of moods, selects plots abounding in emotionally loaded situations, uses starkly contrasted characters and impassioned speech; there is hardly any withholding of anticipated emotional gratification and the denouement is psychologically unequivocal. These "ontological" rules tally with the fundamental axiological principle of melodrama: it operates on black-and-white contrast of moral values, or, to put it more adequately, enacts violent conflicts of moral extremes.[1]

The words *melodrama* and *melodramatic* are often used with reference to the work of Joseph Conrad. Usually this is done in an accusatory manner, pointing at his apparent weakness for popular artistic clichés. Thus it won't be superfluous to point out that melodrama appears in Conrad's work in many functions and guises. We find in his stories both the melodrama of events, as in "Typhoon" and the unfinished *Suspense*, and the melodrama of presentation, as in "The Black Mate" and *The Arrow of Gold*. And, of course, there are novels where melodramatic events are melodramatically described, as in the early *An Outcast of the Islands*, in *The Rescue*, and in the late *Victory* and *The Rover*. It is widely agreed that the appearance of melodramatic conventions mars the structure of these ostensibly realistic novels, and in the case of *Victory*, makes the symbolism of this novel obtrusively evident and garishly simple.

That Conrad was not irresistibly and passively drawn to melodramatic conventions is shown by the example of "Typhoon," where he skillfully deflates the latent emotionalism of the plot by detachment and parries black-and-white simplifications by display of gentle irony. It is only in *The Secret Agent* (1907), however, that Conrad demonstrates his dexterity in employing the techniques of melodrama for very different and by no means simply parodistic ends. *The Secret Agent* is also Conrad's only piece with reference to which he himself used the concept of "melodrama": he wrote to R. B. Cunninghame Graham that the novel was "a sustained effort in ironical treatment of a melodramatic subject."[2]

As esthetic categories, melodrama and irony are polar opposites. While melodrama blows up, irony deflates. But what Conrad does, in fact, is not only to present a melodramatic subject in a nonmelodramatic manner but also to convert certain typical melodramatic conventions to a fresh use. And he does all that, I shall be trying to show, not as an artistic experiment or exercise in skills, but to obtain his unusual esthetic effects and, above all, to convey, in this distinctive fashion, a specific intellectual message. *The Secret Agent* was supposed to be, in Conrad's words in the same letter to Graham, "a new departure in genre," an intentionally meaningful departure.

The events forming the plot of *The Secret Agent* are sensational and gory enough: a double, or rather treble, agent serving the anarchist movement, the Russian embassy in London, and the British police; a scientist producing explosives for terrorist purposes; a half-wit blown to pieces by a bomb; a husband knifed to death by his wife; there is provocation, betrayal, robbery, suicide; among the principal characters are anarchist, policemen, foreign diplomats, a statesman, a devoted mother, a loving sister, and an idiot. The narrative, however, goes against the melodramatic grain of the subject matter. The course of action does not resolve the conflicts but makes them more complex and ambiguous; instead of simple contrasts we are faced with manifold deceptions, misunderstandings and ambiguities. The story does not end with a final triumph of good over evil but on scenes of moral confusion and desolation.

The only pure emotions are those of an idiot—and these are cynically aroused and perversely exploited. (By the way, Stevie does not—*pace* Professor Irving Howe—escape Conrad's irony.[3] And he is a literary cousin not so much of Prince Myshkin [the standard association of critics] but of the Romantic "fools," simpletons, and madmen, who understood the world in the terms of their hearts. Stevie is even, ironically, called an "artist.") And the stronger the emotions of other characters, the more muddle they cause. Thus emotions are not, as in melodrama, the locus of a clear distinction between good and evil but a domain of chaos and hopelessness.

The last conversation of the Verlocs, ended by Winnie stabbing her husband, is, as a subject, pure melodrama—but it is written as an antimelodramatic tour-de-force. The Verlocs express their raw, deepest feelings: fear and hatred, disillusionment, weariness and despair. But there are no effusions, no overstatements; the dialogue is languid and convincingly naturalistic, and the pace of the scene is the slowest in the whole book. And in spite of the mutual frankness of the couple, contrasting with their earlier reticence, and total in that they are now not hiding anything intentionally, the scene is a piling-up of confusions and misconstructions. Winnie Verloc's thought "what were words to her now?" (250)[4] is revealing: contrary to the melodramatic principle of a final disclosure of facts and feelings, what does not meet the eye is deemed important. "What could words do to her for good or evil in the face of her fixed idea?" (250). Winnie does not try to deceive her husband, but there is nothing in her words and behavior that would warn her husband about his impending doom; in Adolf Verloc's perorations there is nothing intended to fool Winnie or to arouse her fury. Thus, what is on both sides intended and perceived as a moment of truth, turns out to be a scene of thickening confusion that leads straight to murder.

While in melodrama the initial mysteries and muddles are finally and triumphantly resolved, in *The Secret Agent* mysteries keep multiplying. The perplexities reach their dramatic peak some fifteen pages from the end in the scene where Comrade Ossipon mistakes the corpse of Verloc for the living man. Unlike this last case, most of these mysteries remain ultimately unresolved—for the characters, that is, not for the readers. Robert D. Spector believes that the whole irony of *The Secret Agent* consists in a gradual exposure of the ignorance the novel's characters display concerning each other's motives, plans, and actions.[5] This, however, is only one of the ways in which Conrad's irony works.

Making dynamic use of a secret is, of course, one of the commonest conventions of melodrama. In *The Secret Agent* this convention is blithely and brilliantly transmogrified. Secrecy is used not to heighten the tension, to play on opposites, or to dramatize the basic good-evil contrast; we do not have characters who are overtly good and secretly evil, or apparently evil and in fact good. The thrills of this thriller do not come from unexpected developments and suspense: most of the plot's events are clearly foreshadowed. Secrecy is used to expose the intricate connections and interplays between *good* and *evil.* More importantly, what is secret in the novel is shown to be soothing and stabilizing; to disclose too much or to investigate too deeply—in other words, to blow the cover of secrecy—is imprudent, disturbing, risky. Winnie Verloc believes, in the often quoted phrase, "that things do not stand much looking into" (177). Her attitude amounts to the tacit acceptance of a web of secrets around her. It also makes her more "secret" than her husband: being incurious, she does not provoke any questions about herself either. When the death of her brother compels Winnie to "look into" things, she flies into a murdering rage.

The stabilizing role of the "uninquiring acceptance of facts" (153) and tolerance of secrets is demonstrated by several other characters: Mr. Vladimir and the Assistant Commissioner, Stevie and Inspector Heat. As long as they do not show too much inquisitiveness, things keep to their steady, inobtrusive (and corrupt) course. The acceptance of secrets also forms a part of the irony in *The Secret Agent.* Secrecy is obviously a degeneration of human intercourse and of communal life in general; if it is shown to be a condition of relative peace, then, by the same token, the existing order of things is shown to be degrading.

The "natural" progress of a sensational plot is from secrets and obscurity to discoveries, revelations, and clarifications. In *The Secret Agent* the course is different: we pass from secrets and simplicity to confusion and ambiguity. And while in melodrama such events as murder, suicide, and treason are understood to *represent* reality, in *The Secret Agent* they are shown to *hide* it: they are just its visible outward manifestations, misleading if taken at their face value. This is why Conrad does not bother to keep us in suspense, does not hesitate to describe the reasons and preparations for a crime, to presage the most dramatic events of the story. Again, what does not strike the eye is most important.

The high-pitched language of melodrama is sometimes used in *The Secret Agent* but ironically to deflate, not to build up the mood. When Conrad says that Mr. Verloc "descended into the abyss of moral reflections" (52), or when a flicker in the eyes of Mrs. Verloc is compared to "a ray of sunshine heralding a tempest of rain" (297), the effects are mock-heroic.

A mock-heroic poem or novel (like *Joseph Andrews),* however, is not a burlesque and requires a standpoint from which the heroic is being mocked. Irony consisting of a determined effort to expose shams, to blow covers, to reveal deceptions, implies an assessing authority that commands these devastating actions. It is sometimes assumed that this authority is in *The Secret Agent* a thoroughly nihilistic one, that it undermines and destroys without any positive reason or value in the background, that Conrad does not evaluate but only derides. Such an interpretation puts Conrad on a level with the bomb-producing Professor, the only "perfect" anarchist of the novel.

Is *The Secret Agent* a nihilistic book, a work in which irony turns its corrosive force upon itself, a novel lacking—to quote Irving Howe—"a moral positive to serve literary ends"? Or, in Professor J. Hillis Miller's words, a novel in which "Conrad's voice and the voice of the darkness most nearly become one."?[6]

There are two characters, one minor and the other fairly central, with whom the reader may easily sympathize or even identify: the old lady patroness of Michaelis and the Assistant Commissioner. Neither of them is immune to ironic treatment; in the case of the old lady it is, however, counterbalanced by a dose of respect, and in the case of the Assistant Commissioner it is reduced to the vestigial level of good-humored jokes about his foreign appearance. From neither of these do we fear any duplicity; in the presence of the latter we feel relaxed and confident: here we have, for a change, somebody who is not morally suspect—and who is clever to boot.

But for the vindication of Conrad's claim that *The Secret Agent* "may even have some moral significance,"[7] the end of the novel is more important. The final paragraphs show two characters: Comrade Ossipon, who twelve days ago took all her money from Winnie Verloc, and the Professor. Considered in the terms of their own designs they ought to feel successful, and the Professor sounds very sure of himself. But are they presented as victors? Ossipon, supposedly "scientific" and "free from the trammels of conventional morality" (297), is brought to his knees by nothing more than remorse for having caused Winnie's suicide. Just when he has achieved what he always wanted—money and with it practically unlimited leisure and access to women—he finds himself incapable of enjoying the fruits of his cunning. He cannot bring himself to face other people and is heading straight for the gutter, his punishment for a betrayal of trust.

The Professor ostensibly fares better. The novel closes on him walking "unsuspected and deadly, like a pest in the street full of men." But the Professor feels compelled to avert his eyes "from the odious multitude of mankind" (311). The multitude impresses this Stirnerian hero with fear because it is "invincible." "The resisting power of numbers, the unattackable stolidity of a great multitude, was the haunting fear of his sinister loneliness" (95). It is only when he is fully swathed in his "astounding ignorance of wordly conditions" that the Professor feels confident. When we see him last, he is going on, grotesquely ill-matched to the immensity of his self-appointed task: "His thoughts caressed the images of ruin and destruction. He walked frail, insignificant, shabby, miserable—and terrible in the simplicity of his idea calling madness and despair to the regeneration of the world" (311). He is dangerous, but freakish.

Thus both these characters are ultimately exposed as humbugs: as men of false consciousness at best, despicable frauds at worst.

It is the historical experience of mankind that has shaped the moral ideas to which the Assistant Commissioner turns when balking at Inspector Heat's double-dealings and exposing Mr. Vladimir's plotting. It is this moral tradition from which the irony of the novel takes its fiber—and on which it bases its appeal.

The essential seriousness of *The Secret Agent*—a novel which is much more than an "entertainment"—is sometimes put in question because of the treatment accorded to anarchists. It is true that anarchists in *The Secret Agent* look primitive and one-dimensional when compared with the central personalities of the novel—the Verlocs, Winnie's mother, Stevie, or for that matter even the Assistant Commissioner. We do not, however, have to see this as an artistic failure; it seems more appropriate to consider this an element in the general design of "ironical treatment of a melodramatic subject." The anarchists in *The Secret Agent* are characters of a melodrama; they are physical images—embodiments—of their ideals. Thus Michaelis' obesity and consequent immobility signify his optimistic determinism; the cadaverous Yundt represents the staple of terrorism; the Professor's meager figure contrasted with the strength of his monomaniacal passion points at the monstrous abnormality of his designs. If they are grotesquely overdrawn, simplified, and maligned, this is because the ideas and sociopolitical attitudes they stand for are also grotesque, crude, and malevolent. Their archenemy, Mr. Vladimir, is treated in much the same way—which should acquit Conrad of the accusation that he was particularly unjust to anarchists. In the case of all these characters, melodrama equals realism, just as for Winnie "the very cry of truth was found in a worn and artificial shape picked up somewhere among the phrases of sham sentiment" (298).

The contemptuous treatment of "revolutionary" anarchists in *The Secret Agent* does not mean that the social injustice and political oppression that give rise to revolutionary movements are dismissed in the novel as nonexistent or unimportnat. On the contrary, causes for social and economic grievances are plainly in evidence. "Bad world for poor people" (171) is here a documented statement, bizarre as the context of this verdict may be. Also demands for civil liberties are quite obviously regarded as well founded. If Conrad ridicules his anarchists, this is not because he considers them rebels without a cause; he only thinks they are either wrong-headed, or impostors, or both. Take Comrade Ossipon, "ex-medical student" (44). This professional educationist and writer of leaflets treats education and knowledge with utter contempt. All he believes in is emotional rabble-rousing. "What the people knows does not matter" (50). The terrorist Karl Yundt would like to harness "the suffering and misery of poverty . . . all the hopeful and noble illusions of righteous anger, pity, and revolt" (48) to his program of "no pity for anything on earth . . . death enlisted for good and all in the service of humanity" (42).

They are outside the mainstream of the conflicts between the rich and the poor, the idle and the exploited, the oppressors and the oppressed. They are the lunatic fringe of these conflicts. But marginal as they may be, they are both symptomatic and dangerous. Symptomatic, because they show that the divisions listed above are not identical with the good-evil demarcations, that evil breeds evil—in the form of "sinister impulses which lurk in the blind envy and exasperated vanity of ignorance" (48). Professional oppositionists are at least as prone to moral degeneration as professional rulers. Dangerous, because it is easier to provoke hatred than compassion, to destroy than to reform, to kill than to cooperate. Today, when one reads the Professor's theorizing: "To break up the superstition and worship of legality should be our aim. Nothing would please me more than to see Inspector Heat and his likes take to shooting us down in broad daylight . . . what's wanted is a clean sweep and a clear start for a new conception of life" (73), one is struck by Conrad's uncanny gift of prophecy.

The anarchists as portrayed in *The Secret Agent* may be atypical as revolutionaries or even as anarchists—although nobody can deny that there were, and are, many like them; they are certainly, as I have said, outside the mainstream of social and political movements; but they *can* influence the course of events. They can influence it not by giving to it a fresh impetus, by subjecting it to some new organizing principle—but by derailing it, by making the existent structures dysfunction or even collapse.

Therefore, these melodramatic heroes are both grotesque, almost absurd—and real, significant, portentous. A lunatic fringe represents here some essential sociopolitical issues. And this very fact, that a melodramatic subject matter and melodramatically construed characters are so uniquely suited to expressing serious truths, forms an inherent artistic reason for Conrad's irony. Look here, he seems to be saying, if this is our situation, if such people, such grotesque people as Mr. Vladimir or Mr. Verloc or the Professor can influence our life or cause our death, if we are defended by such men as Heat and governed by such as Sir Ethelred—then irony is indeed the only attitude worthy of a serious person.

Notes

1. See Peter Brooks, "The Melodramatic Imagination: The Example of Balzac and James," in David Thorbutn and Geoffrey Hartman, eds., *Romanticism: Vistas, Instances, Continuities* (Ithaca, N. Y.: Cornell Univ. Press, 1973), pp. 198-220; Daniel Gerould, "Russian Formalist Theories of Melodrama," *Journal of American Culture* (Spring 1978), 1(1):152-68.

2. C. T. Watts, ed., *Joseph Conrad's Letters to R. B. Cunninghame Graham* (Cambridge: Cambridge Univ. Press, 1969), p. 169.

3. Cf. Irving Howe, *Politics and the Novel* (New York: Horizon Press, 1957), p. 97.

4. The numbers in parentheses refer to pages of *The Secret Agent* in the Doubleday edition (Garden City, N. Y., 1924).

5. Robert D. Spector, "Irony as Theme: Conrad's *The Secret Agent*," *Nineteenth-century Fiction* (1958), 13:69-71.

6. J. Hillis Miller, *Poets of Reality* (New York: Atheneum, 1969), p. 39.

7. G. Jean-Aubry, *Joseph Conrad: Life and Letters* (Heinemann: London, 1927), 2:38.

PART 4

FILM:
MELODRAMA
AND
POPULAR CULTURE

13

Melodrama and Farce: A Note on a Fusion in Film

STANLEY KAUFFMANN

Around 1920 American film comedy began belatedly to face a formal crisis. Early in the preceding decade, other kinds of film had faced the same crisis: the change in length of feature films. From about 1903, when the fiction film began to flourish, until 1911, films were at most two reels long and many of them were one reel. A substantial picture ran twenty minutes. Then came longer films from Italy. In 1913 the Italian *Quo Vadis*, which ran two hours, was an enormous success—at a ticket price of $1.50. Proportionately, this is as if a film today ran twenty hours, charged $40, and was a hit. The American film industry of the day immediately divided into two camps: the larger one changed to longer films, built ornate palaces to house them, and prospered; the smaller one saw no reason to tamper with a profitable system, stuck to short films, and soon went broke. From then on, American films—feature films—were almost never less than one hour long.

There was one exception to this general change: comedy. Not comedy in the high comic or romantic sense but farce, the kind of film most generally associated with the terms "slapstick" or "clown." The reason is plain for the clown's reluctance to change. It's relatively easy for the screenwriter of dramas or romantic comedies to invent further complications, add characters and subplots, increase or postpone climaxes, and thus build a twenty-minute idea into an hour film. It's quite different, and in terms of invention much harder, to move from ten minutes of sustained comic pantomime to a sustained sixty minutes. The duration of one gag is only a matter of seconds—rarely as much as a minute—and the number of good gags that can be worked out of one premise is limited. Twenty minutes is a long time for such a film. An hour is gargantuan.

The clowns resisted, fairly consistently, for most of the decade, but at last commercial requirements had to prevail. Farce made the move to greater length. And some of the clowns always regretted it. In his old age, Stan Laurel said of himself and Oliver Hardy:

> We should have stayed in the short-film category. There is just so much comedy we can do along a certain line and then it gets to be unfunny. . . . You can't take a whole, long series of things we do and stick them all together in eight reels, and expect to get a well-balanced picture out of it. We didn't want to go into feature films in the first place, and even though I've got some favorites among them, I'm sorry we ever did go beyond the two- and three-reelers.[1]

But the point of this brief note of mine is that some of the clowns, including the very best, did not "take a whole, long series of things . . . and stick them all together" as did the endearing Laurel and Hardy. They changed their approach completely. When they moved into longer films, they used melodrama as their armature.

Take Chaplin as example, if a genius of his magnitude can ever serve as an example. Through the decade in question, he had appeared in one six-reel film directed by someone else (that in itself was a rarity), had made one four-reel film, but had otherwise clung to one- and two-reel films, with an occasional three-reeler. He said in his autobiography, "As far back as 1916 I had many ideas for feature pictures,"[2] but he never did anything about them until he discovered Jackie Coogan and got the idea for *The Kid*. Released in 1921, *The Kid* was in six reels and was most certainly not a mere extension of a two-reeler by adding more gags. Chaplin said that, while he was making the picture, he often discussed it with Gouverneur Morris, a successful writer of the day:

> He said: "It won't work. The form must be pure, either slapstick or drama; you cannot mix them, otherwise one element of your story will fail." . . . I argued that form happened after one had created it, that if the artist thought of a world and sincerely believed in it, no matter what the admixture was it would

be convincing. . . . Raw slapstick and sentiment, the premise of *The Kid*, was something of an innovation.[3]

But the word "sentiment" is insufficient. Here are the basic plot ingredients of *The Kid:* a baby born out of wedlock and abandoned by its mother; the finding and adoption of that baby by a tramp; the love, as the baby grows, between child and adoptive father; the struggle of the two, against the law's intrusion, to stay together; the final reunion of the child and his mother, together with the suggestion of romance between the mother and the tramp. Those, of course, are all ingredients or derivatives of nineteenth-century melodrama.

Or take Buster Keaton, the only other screen figure who can (and must) be considered Chaplin's peer. Keaton began his film career three years after Chaplin; it was interrupted by army service in World War I. When Keaton resumed work in 1919, long after noncomic features had taken over the screen, he continued with two-reelers. In 1920 he appeared in a feature directed by someone else, *The Saphead*, which was adapted from a Broadway comedy and is not generally esteemed as first-rank Keaton. In 1923 he founded his own studio and turned to feature films. His first, *The Three Ages*, is, structurally, three short films stitched together. But his second, *Our Hospitality*, which is his first organic feature, is based on melodrama. The root conflict is that of a blood feud between two Southern families, and the first six minutes of the film deal exclusively with killing and a vow of vengeance, set amidst lightning and storm—no slightest trace of comedy. At the end the climax consists of Keaton's hairbreadth rescue of the heroine as she goes over a waterfall. (Could the contemporary audience *not* have been reminded of *Way Down East*, which Griffith had made from one of the best-known melodramas of the day?)

Instances could be greatly multiplied from the works of both these great actor-clowns. But the point is clear: when they had to move into a greater length, they did not merely expand the short form, they sought the support of an older form. I don't maintain that none of the Chaplin or Keaton shorts had had melodramatic elements, which is patently untrue, or that these men were the only ones of their contemporaries to employ melodrama in their features. (Compare almost any Harold Lloyd picture.) I take Chaplin and Keaton as paragons of insight, both of whom knew instinctively that the new length needed not a more complicated series of gags but a nonfunny structure on, and out of, which more gags could grow.

The kinships between melodrama and farce are deep and old. First, in theatrical practice there is a long history of the performance of melodrama being followed by the performance of farce that cartooned melodrama.[4] Second, there is a basic anatomical affinity between melodrama and farce (of which the best slapstick is an externalized exponent.) Both of them, as is well known, are built on fear and the threat of violence. In melodrama, someone we care about must be in hazard, the more physical the better; this is also true of farce. In melodrama, things must come out right for the person we care about, and the happy ending is both a theological affirmation and a social emollient. (The heroine's life is saved in *Way Down East*, and this, plus forgiveness for past sin, is the reward for her disregard of life.) In farce, the happy ending is often the result of physical agility and ingenuity, but it too affirms order in a chaotic world. (Keaton's waterfall rescue in *Our Hospitality* is arithmetically precise amidst the tumult.) In both forms, the emotional results, as well as the dramatic kinesis, are the same. The two furthest ends of the dramatic spectrum, melodrama and farce, fit over one another like transparencies on a drawing board.

To follow that figure, the combined transparencies produced a new form in film, not orthodox melodrama or farce. Before this fusion, the film medium had already empowered farceurs to do things impossible on stage: to shuffle places in a snap, to play with gravity, to juggle time. Having altered stage farce, they now had, by "admixture" (Chaplin's word), to alter the melodrama they were employing. I know of no theater melodrama that calls for the hero to execute exquisite comic pantomime and slapstick. A melodrama might easily have had a poor hero who wanted to earn money to help cure a blind girl, as in *City Lights*, but his efforts would not have led him into a hilarious boxing-ring escapade. Many a stage hero rescued his girl from the clutches of a villain but not, like Keaton in *College*, by pole vaulting in through an upper-story window on a clothesline pole, in a track suit. Chaplin and Keaton were leaders in the devising of a new form.

The progeny of the form have been very numerous. I won't attempt a chronicle or attempt to map the changes as the early film comics were gradually replaced by those who were not alumni of the vaudeville/music-hall/burlesque school (because that school was disappearing). Yet the form persists. One 1979 example is *The In-laws*.

The inception of the form marks a historical moment: it was possible only to comics who had done their training in a particular school and who had simultaneously been immersed in nineteenth-century melodrama. And it has another importance. Other film forms, even the western and space-opera, are amplifications of theater forms. This fused form, though based on theater origins, is the only one that was born of, and unique to, film.

Notes

1. John McCabe, *Mr. Laurel and Mr. Hardy* (Garden City, N. Y.: Doubleday, 1961), p. 182.
2. Charles Chaplin, *My Autobiography* (New York: Simon & Schuster, 1964), p. 210.
3. Ibid., pp. 235-38.
4. For a good discussion of this practice, see David Grimsted's *Melodrama Unveiled* (Chicago: Univ. of Chicago Press, 1968), pp. 234-40.

14

Where Melodrama Meets Farce

ALBERT BERMEL

A turbulent river dashes Buster Keaton over rapids and through white water toward a sheer drop. He is tied to a log. At the edge of the water-fall his log catches on a rock. The impact hurls Buster out beyond the vertical torrent, so that he dangles in space and spray, held up by the rope and the trapped log.

Inspired editing offers us a reverse view of the scene from upriver. As we look down past the waterfall at the misted landscape in the dis-- tance, we get an idea of the height of the drop. Hundreds of feet below lie plains and hills and forests of the Sierras, the might and peacefulness of natural scenery.

Buster snaps into action. He goes hand over hand up the rope, hooks his heels over the log, scrambles on top of it, and tries to unfasten the rope. Water has tightened the knot. It won't give. He wants to cut the rope but has no blade. The log now starts to ease itself away from the rock. Buster glimpses a notch in the cliff—a ledge—at the side of the falls. He swings across to it on the rope, which is still tied to the log. When the log breaks loose it will pull him off the ledge. Before he has time to worry about this prospect, he spots Natalie Talmadge flowing downstream. The current has already swept her to within several yards of the fall. He makes a futile gesture: Get back! Then he dives boldly into empty air at the literal end of his tether. In one pendulumlike motion he scoops her in his arms with perfect synchronization, as she goes over, and brings her back with him to the ledge. Within seconds the log finally comes free. It should drag Buster with it. But while his acrobatics loosened it from its fortuitous mooring, they also scraped the rope back and forth across the rock's abrasive surface until, as the log plunges over, the rope parts, leaving Buster safe but drenched, high but not dry, on the cliff face.

Is this sequence from *Our Hospitality* (1923) farce? Or melodrama? The supporting cast—a log, a rope, a rock, cliff ledge, and a limp heroine—inanimate objects all—plus the river and waterfall, two forces of nature, might persuade us that we are watching a typically depersonalized farce, as do the presence and virtuosity of Keaton, as well as his signal to Natalie to go back (by reversing the current, maybe?). But what we are watching is not so much funny as almost intolerably tense. The laughter may be in our mouths, ready to break free, like the log. But so are our hearts.

The emotional high point of *Uncle Vanya* occurs close to the end of the third act. Vanya, outraged by the behavior of his brother-in-law Serebriakov in planning to sell the family estate to which Vanya and his niece have given their lives, and incensed at himself for having once idolized Serebriakov as both a scholar and a man, goes into another room for a revolver. Offstage he fires it once, accidentally, then returns agitated, fighting off his sister-in-law. While the rest of the family panics, he aims at Serebriakov and fires again. As he pulls the trigger he shouts, "Bang!" He evidently wants to make sure that the bullet will be lethal. But it misses. The failed shot sums up Vanya's life. He throws down the pistol in disgust with himself, and the curtain rings down on a scene of confused bathos. It had risen to a feverish, melodramatic pitch, but the melodrama was compromised by Vanya's futility, not only his faulty marksmanship but also his over-anxiety as he cries, "Bang!" The melodramatic pathos has dissolved into farce—but not altogether, for we have been made privy to the depths of Vanya's feelings and cannot quite laugh at him.

Farce or melodrama can infuse a tragedy or comedy (the famous "knocking at the gate" in *Macbeth*; the scene in the portrait gallery in *The School for Scandal*), and they can equally intrude on one another. We are not dealing here with diluting or tainting, only with adding. A moment of farce need not weaken a tragedy. An "impure" tragedy by Shakespeare need not take second place to a "pure" one by Sophocles. It may be superior in some respects. It is certainly different. If I may argue by analogy, melodrama or farce is not like salt, which adds its peculiarity, saltiness, to a mixture while losing its appearance and character as an independent substance. It is more like the lima beans or corn kernels in succotash, which remain what they are.

As a matter of observation, it is hard to find many plays or films that belong wholly to one of the four main formal genres. Tragedy, comedy, melodrama, and farce incessantly tangle with one another, thanks to the unruliness of authors. Numerous works that are not farces or melodramas, such as the two parts of *Henry IV*, incorporate segments and characterizations that are unmistakably farcical and melodramatic. Besides, no farce or melodrama—and *Our Hospitality* and *Uncle Vanya* are illustrations—stays farcical or melodramatic throughout. The zaniest goings-on in a farce require relatively serious preparation during the early scenes if an audience is to follow them; and they require a relatively serious wrapping-up if they are not to strike the audience as being pointless. Even events that are *meant* to seem pointless must somehow make that very point—that they amount to nothing of consequence—or else audiences will go on looking for something of consequence and fail to find it and be disappointed, if not estranged, by the wasted effort.

Thus, when we say that a work is a farce or a melodrama, we have to mean that the farcical or melodramatic effects predominate, not that the work consists of a single genre only. Its most vivid moments, its most forceful impressions, are farcical or melodramatic, and these are substantively what we remember it for. It may well contain moments that belong to other genres, but these moments are secondary.

In that case, where does the realm of one genre end and where do the others begin? In most writings about generic drama there is an unstated assumption: that the genres could be sketched on a two-dimensional map as if they were continents, each with its territorial integrity and with boundaries between them. Farce might be said to exist on the lunatic fringe of comedy and on the ludicrous fringes of tragedy and melodrama. The four continents could then be schematically subdivided into countries (the continent of farce would include such kingdoms, principalities, and provinces as adventure farce, bedroom or boudoir farce, "screwball movies" of the 1930s and 1940s, and farcical fantasies). Between the continents, and even between the countries on this undrawn map would lie borderline areas that are artistic no-man's-land, taking their mixed character, their cultural bastardy, from the territories they adjoin.

The map makes an attractive and graphic picture. But that picture is static, whereas dramatic structure is dynamic. To visualize the *shifting connections* between the four genres we might do better if we imagined them as shapes of more than two dimensions (preferably four), without fixed definition or domain and never at rest, drifting together and apart, colliding and infringing one on the other, combining their individual qualities without surrendering them. If melodrama were blue and farce yellow, a collision that produced a farce with moments of melodrama would be not green but yellow with blue added, and all the more heightened, all the more strikingly yellow, because of the contrasting blue.

Differentiating between generic types can be tricky. It requires that one look closely at characterization and not merely at that ineffable thing we call mood. A tragedy, for example, presupposes a protagonist who consciously or unconsciously wills his or her own downfall, and then, because of certain temperamental deficiences (the "tragic flaw") brings that downfall to pass. If a protagonist brings about the downfall of somebody else, such as an antagonist, or if it's the antagonist who brings about the protagonist's downfall, then the work is not a tragedy but a melodrama. And not inferior for that reason. Certainly not what critics often choose to label it: a "failed tragedy." The element of will or intention is at the heart of this distinction.

These preceding remarks are open to several kinds of question. What about a work that has more than one protagonist? Is Iago as important a character as Othello is, that is a protagonist? If so, his fate is tragic: he is responsible for it, willfully so. Does he cause Othello's downfall or does Desdemona?—in either case, if Othello is the protagonist the play is a melodrama. It is a tragedy only if we interpret Othello as being responsible for his own downfall. Does Hamlet cause his own downfall or is it brought about by the combined efforts of Claudius, Gertrude, Ophelia, Polonius, Laertes, Rosencrantz and Guildenstern, and the ghost of Hamlet's father? In the latter case, *The Tragedy of Hamlet* would be classifiable as a melodrama, even though it's still the same play. Who causes Willy Loman's downfall and death? He himself (tragedy) or society at large (melodrama) or his wife and sons (melodrama again)? It will be noticed that if I seem to be divesting tragedy of its corona of approval and insisting that it is a *type* of play, a genre, and not an automatic name for a finer play, I am also expanding the compass of melodrama so that it takes in not only horror plays and guignol at one extreme but also "high drama," the *drame sérieux*.

Characterization also comes into account when one differentiates a melodrama from a farce. There is always a disparity between the character and his surroundings. In farce, that disparity is laughable: Harold Lloyd, part way up the side of a tall department store in *Safety Last*, hears the crowd below applauding, and lets go with one hand to raise his hat and acknowledge its appreciation—but what is he doing with his hat on up there, anyway? In melodrama the disparity is distressing because it means that the protagonist is in danger. We can't laugh at him; he lacks the protective shell of his farcical counterpart, the indestructibility. We are continually looking ahead fearfully on his behalf, and our fears color our responses. But if the melodramatic actor proves defective, if he loses one jot of the terrific concentration and conviction that melodrama demands, he may slide into ridicule. And then the laughs will come: not the friendly laughter of relief, but the hostile laughter of scorn for poor craftsmanship. The melodramatic actor, like the tragedian, performs on the slippery edge of a pit and its name is farce. The melodramatist works nearer than the tragedian to the edge, if that is possible. For him the pit yawns wider and more inviting. Ah, temptation!

Frédérick Lemaître tells an anecdote about how, instead of avoiding the pit, he plunged recklessly into it. Some authors had brought him a script called *The Inn of the Adrets*. Reading through this "gloomy melodrama," he could not think of a way to induce the public to accept its "mysterious and melancholy plot"; nor could he believe in the character he was to portray, "a highway assassin, frightful as the ogre of any fairy tale, and carrying his impudence to the extent of curling his whiskers with a dagger, while eating a bit of Gruyère cheese!" Then the idea occurred to him of treating the work as a farce, without substantially altering its dialogue. The transformation would depend on the acting. To make a long transformation short, the play turned out to be so successful as a farce that it gave rise to a sequel featuring the same leading character, written by Lemaître in collaboration with two of the three original authors, and entitled *Robert Macaire*, which became one of the smash hits—if not the biggest—in the French theater of the nineteenth century.[1]

How did the actor get this result? Did he go into mugging and hamming? Unlikely. The audience would have resented this and let him know it; besides, Lemaître was an uncommonly intelligent artist who respected his public's discernment. He saw that, because drama depends on enactment, categorizing any play depends on the attitudes of the creator of the dominant role or roles. The term *creator* here is shorthand for a collaboration between the author, director, and actor, or for the reader who is staging the play for himself on an imaginary platform behind his brow. If the creator has sympathy for the character, the play will come out melodramatic; if he has amused contempt, or affectionate contempt, for the character, the play will come out farcical. In melodrama the character is treated as if he were a real human being, and the same is true for tragedy, give or take an infixion of tragic madness. But in older farce the character is treated as a defective human being, the not-so-distant relative of inert objects and machines. In other words, a farce can consist of essentially the same action as a melodrama can. Only the attitudes of the audience will differ as they follow the lead of the creator. If that lead turns out to be a weak one, the audience may convert a farce into a melodrama by declining to laugh, or turn a melodrama into a farce by laughing in the teeth of the creator's intentions. While Buster Keaton does his stunts over the waterfall, and we chuckle, we realize that our palms are sweating as freely as if we were watching a melodrama by Hitchcock—Cary Grant being chased by a plane in *North by Northwest* or the innocent boy in *Sabotage* boarding a bus with a package that has a time bomb in it.

Hitchcock is the heavy influence in contemporary melodrama on films founded on spy stories and chases, not only in his techniques— choices of shooting angle, lighting, and editing—but even more in the blank characters, particularly the women, and in the creator's attitudes toward the material. (The influence is sometimes acknowledged in the form of visual quotations from the master—which also crop up obtrusively in Mel Brooks's farces.) The melting of melodrama into farce practiced by Hitchcock is taken further in James Bond films, which run sedulously along Hitchcock tracks. In *Moonraker*, for instance, a couple of water chases begin melodramatic and rapidly grow farcical. In the first chase, 007 (Roger Moore) is loafing along the canals of Venice in a gondola when the employees of the archvillain Drax tail him in a fast launch and machinegun him. Bond twiddles with levers that convert the sedate vessel into a high-speed motor boat. Then, as his pursuers gain on him, he comes up with another mechanism that turns the gondola amphibious. Crawling out of the canal, it crosses St. Mark's Square to the consternation of the crooks, the crowds in the square, and a pigeon that wags its head in amazement. In the second chase Bond is racing along the Amazon followed by the man with the iron mouth called Jaws (Richard Kiel) and finds himself hurtling toward a waterfall at about sixty knots. At the last second he ejects himself into the air, attached to a hang-glider, and coasts to a safe landing in the jungle, while his boat and Jaws and *his* boat go over the falls.

Both times, as well as in other parts of the film, the farcical intentions of the creator (screenplay by Christopher Wood; direction by Lewis Gilbert) are made plain by a series of side incidents, names like Drax, and sly quotations from, or references to, other films, among them *Close Encounters of the Third Kind* and *The Rules of the Game.* The pursuit boat in the first scene cuts right through another gondola, the two halves of which drift apart. In one half, two embracing lovers don't notice they're going under. A "corpse" raises the lid of his coffin, mounted amid wreaths on a funeral barge, takes aim at 007, and receives a knife in the chest; the coffin is bumped off the barge by a low bridge and floats away like another boat on the canal. In the second scene Jaws mugs like fury as he realizes he can't avoid the waterfall. Here, we have characterizations that wobble back and forth between the genres.

I imagine that in the future we will see many a melodrama that farcically kids itself and its audience as it reaches for thrills and at the same time muffles their impact with laughter. We have already witnessed what a master like Ionesco can pull off when (in *Jacques, The Chairs,* and *The Lesson)* he allies a terrifying melodramatic ending to a farce and makes us swallow our laughter at a gulp.

Note

1. The two authors were delighted with their play's new personality and with the royalities therefrom. The third author, a Dr. Polyanthe, strenuously objected to Lemaître's interpretation, but then, as the actor writes, "if he had not been most forunately stopped short, he might have managed to murder as many melodramas as he did patients." The anecdote is related in full by another renowned French actor, Constant Coquelin, in *Papers on Acting,* edited by Brander Matthews (New York: Hill & Wang, 1958), pp. 22-24.

15

Romeo and Juliet Are Dead: Melodrama of the Clinical

WYLIE SYPHER

If we define by genre alone, we distinguish melodrama from tragedy by distinctions that may prove ambiguous or even treacherous. These ambiguities may be partially identified when, implausibly, we consider the relations (or disrelations) between *Romeo and Juliet* and Bernardo Bertolucci's problematic film *The Last Tango in Paris*, two dramas of sexuality and death enacted along the margin between so-called tragedy and so-called melodrama.[1]

If melodrama solicits from its audience judgments based upon unequivocal binary codes of good and evil, tragedy provokes double or divided judgments—the good necessarily injured by error or evil. Inherently the melodramatic coding is puritan; inherently the tragic coding is not. The simplistic melodramatic *binary* coding is not the tragic *bifocal* coding, which is provided not only by the audience but also within the paradoxical experience of the characters and, more important, *within the action itself* by appraisals of character as seen by those who surround that character. The tragic situation is viewed and assessed in multiple contexts.

Whereas Romeo and Juliet are seen by others in Verona who pass conflicting judgments on them, the sexual experiments performed by Paul and Jeanne in their apartment are insulated: only the audience observes and appraises their behavior. So the raw behaviorism in *The Tango* tends to efface the differences between the action and the experiences controlling that action. Even the introspections of Paul and Jeanne are not so much divided judgments as rhetorical confessions read by the audience as clinical symptoms. Of course, Romeo and Juliet are equally rhetorical, equally confessional, but they are redeemed from clinical estimates by those who are juxtaposed to them inside the drama, thus enforcing a bifocal (or polyfocal) view of their situation and behavior. In their isolation Paul and Jeanne are like cases whom we are invited to regard by a code as definitive as the melodramatic coding by good and evil.

Indeed, *The Tango* suggests that melodrama is impoverished or reductive tragedy—tragedy deprived of its bifocal or polyfocal contexts. The psychiatric implications of behavior in the apartment promote verdicts all-too-legibly inscribed in the form of diagnosis. In short, *The Tango* illustrates a melodrama of the clinical, which in turn reveals a puritan disturbance about sex.

Just as Tom Stoppard in *Rosencrantz and Guildenstern Are Dead* rewrote *Hamlet* from a behavioristic angle (the Prince appearing as simply mad and dangerous) so Bertolucci has rewritten *Romeo and Juliet* as if it were recast by Troilus after Cressida has betrayed him, or by Iago, for whom love is making the beast with two backs in a lust of the blood and permission of the will. T. S. Eliot complained that *Hamlet* lacks a "formula" or "objective correlative" for the Prince's excessive emotional experience. In its behavioristic coding *The Tango* quickly finds its objective formula when Paul (Marlon Brando) goes down on Jeanne (Maria Schneider) in the bleak apartment. Stoppard's play is amusing. *The Tango* is sinister, for as Jack Fisher remarks, it is not a skin flick but "a study that probes nerves, sinews, and essences," looking into the womb of fear and making sex a prelude to death.[2] Paul teaches Jeanne that "sacred and profane are the same thing" and that "sex is of the body and nothing else."

David R. Slavitt finds that the trouble with the film is the trouble in many contemporary novels: "the study of sexuality *in isolation*," which is "a strategic and procedural disaster."[3] He calls *The Tango* "a serious film, but wrong"—wrong, we may add, through its narrow premises, which are at last antierotic and puritan. Contrasting *The Tango* with eroticism in Bergman and Antonioni, Slavitt deems that "the exclusions of Bertolucci seem absurd and diminished," leaving only "the quivering genitals."

In her audacious review of the film Pauline Kael grants that its basis is biology, yet she believes it is "the most powerfully erotic movie ever made, and it may turn out to be the most liberating movie ever made."[4] Obviously, she is not using criteria that apply to eroticism in legends of Tristram and Iseult, Paolo and Francesca, Heloise and Abelard, Antony and Cleopatra—or Romeo and Juliet, who liberate sexuality by sublimating it. Modern literature has often been a commentary on sublimating, and desublimating, sexuality. In Shakespeare, Mercutio greets the Nurse by noting that the bawdy hand of the dial is on the prick of noon. Brando's hand is soon on the prick and remains there in much of what follows. Like any therapist, Mercutio knows that Romeo is obsessed by the dribbling dart of love, wishing that Rosaline were an open-arse and he a poperin pear. In his lewd conjuring by Rosaline's bright thigh and its adjacent demesnes, Mercutio would raise up Romeo; yet, Romeo is raised up in another mode when he sees Juliet burning bright on the balcony. So there comes a response beyond biology.

Kael says that *The Tango* "centers on a man's attempt to separate sex from everything else," using Paul's premise that "romance and rot are one." She too takes the film not as a mere skin flick but as a study in the torment of eroticism. Kael's admiration for the acting, directing, and filming does not obscure her own grim verdict on Brando's *macho* intoxication with power in bed, on the uninhibited sensualism of Maria Schneider as one of the bitches "who defeat men and walk away," and on all the "poisoned sex Strindberg wrote about." Note: the judgment is Kael's, not judgment from anyone within the drama.

This poisoned sexuality is a byproduct of what Kael finds liberating about the film, for Bertolucci seems to her to have "a remarkably unbiased intelligence." Such intelligence is Bertolucci's knowingness about sex as phrased in Paul's supposition that "sex is all that matters." Much depends on what we mean by sex, which here becomes a shriveled eroticism excerpted from larger contexts of the human experience bracketing Hamlet's confused sexuality.

There is plenty of poisoned sexuality in Shakespeare's darker plays, but not in isolation from the sublimations that we must, albeit naively, term love. The sublimations in *Romeo and Juliet* provide a more liberating counterpoint than Bertolucci's clinical treatment can afford. Kael notes how the film brings in our cultural hangups about sex, which has become a warfare, a locus of concern about the orgasm, the couch, male chauvinism, all our puritan dilemmas about the flesh.

Freud, who sensed danger in almost everything, recognized the deceptions in sublimating, but he likewise granted that civilization requires sublimations. In Shakespeare's play there are two versions of sublimating: Romeo's merely postured attraction to Rosaline, then, however rhetorical, his more imperative gravitation to Juliet. Juliet herself—the antitype of Maria Schneider, who raises her wedding-dress to expose her pubic hair—is capable of an extravagant sublimation in her antipuritan invocation to gentle night making true love acted simple modesty. Jeanne is Shakespeare's Cressida reincarnated, except that Cressida is judged by others within the play, and finally explicitly judges herself. And the Romeo-Juliet romance is subjected to the various estimates brought to bear within the action by Friar Laurence, Mercutio, Tybalt, the Nurse, and Shakespeare's own prologue soliciting pity. Shakespeare may have distrusted eroticism, but he did not separate sex from everything else; and he could transvalue it. Having lost such bifocal estimates, Bertolucci leaves us with what Iago calls the fig end—the "smells, filth, and fluids" Fisher mentions.

The parallels in structure and events in these two death-marked actions convey differences in meanings. In *The Tango* Paul is an aging sullied Romeo suffering discord between his glandular impulses and his depleted and depleting sentimentality, as he idly meditates on his plight while he plays the harmonica. Paul recalls his youth in an aimless nerveless lyric, a sullen barnyard pastoral, and when Jeanne returns with Tom (Jean-Paul Léaud) to film the suburban scene of her childhood, she finds that the garden serves as a privy for some small boys. Both dramas are built on improvisation, the recklessness of the impromptu, the response that seems like fatality. In both the unforeseen encounter opens a headlong passage toward death. Voicing her own doubt, Juliet says to Romeo

> I have no joy of this contract tonight.
> It is too rash, too unadvised, too sudden;
> Too like the lightning. . . . (2, 2)

And as the callow Paris stands behind Romeo's gusty passions, so Tom stands behind Paul as an inept, impotent counterfigure to lust. Kael sees Maria Schneider as having a "freshness" endowing the film with a radiance, her outrageous abundance resembling a bouquet from Renoir. Juliet has a more transparent radiance heightened by our awareness that originally she was played by a boy, thus distancing the flesh. Although Romeo has Paul's sense of the macabre (carrion flies feeding on Juliet's white hand), his death is an affirmation. Paul, that middle-aged dullard who runs a flophouse, dies in morbid self-disgust, in paralysis, in dismal alienation.

The isolation of Romeo and Juliet is not the willful isolation of Paul and Jeanne. Shakespeare's lovers cannot alienate themselves from Verona as Paul and Jeanne alienate themselves from Paris. But all four are estranged from their past. If love in Verona is an instantaneous prodigious birth negating the Montague-Capulet feud, the immediate reaction of Paul and Jeanne to each other is also a rupture with their pasts. However compulsively Paul searches his life with his father on the farm and his scalding memory of his wife Rosa, he finds these revivals as irrelevant as Jeanne finds her own past—the sterility of Tom's trying to make her a romantic image for his film. At the end Jeanne discovers that her involvement with Paul himself is as dead as Romeo's involvement with Rosaline, or as Paul's with his dead wife. If the past is discarded in Verona and Paris, there is no future either: death is a terminus. Even Jeanne's future is in question.

In deleting their pasts, all four major characters seek anonymity. Paul keeps insisting that he and Jeanne must not name themselves. After Jeanne shoots Paul, liquidating her transient exploration of the flesh, she closes the film by repeating that she really knew nothing about him, not who he was, not even his name. Juliet wishes Romeo to appear with some other name: "Deny thy father and refuse thy name. I'll no longer be a Capulet." Romeo's name is no part of him: "I know not how to tell thee who I am." Romeo assures the Friar that he has forgotten the name of Rosaline and that name's woe, just as Paul extinguishes, or tries agonizingly to extinguish, his recollection of Rosa.

The new anonymous life of all four is an initiation that could, or should, yield a discovery of selfhood. Instead, Paul and Jeanne are depersonalized by a behavior that presents an analysis—but without any resulting therapy. Jeanne persists in wanting to name herself. Only at the moment before she shoots Paul does he finally wish to know her name, who she *is*. Juliet alone among the four might be said to realize herself through this initiation. For the others—even for Romeo—initiation leads nowhere since there appears no accessible exit from the automation of sexual response.

In fact, both dramas are studies in automation. After the automatism of Romeo's simpering about Rosaline comes the more lyrical automation of sudden devotion to Juliet. The starker physiological automatism of Paul and Jeanne is symbolized by the automation of the trains passing above the couloir of the street outside, and then by the automation of dancers in the tango palace who strike mechanical poses while Paul and Jeanne perform their own last frantic tango in a parody of the automatic, a rebellious drunken acrobatic of disorder. Tybalt is a mechanism of hate who, as Mercutio says, fights by the book of arithmetic, metronomically keeping time, distance, proportion. As if automatically Jeanne pulls the trigger when she kills Paul. In his sentimentality Tom, like Paris, is a clockwork man who when his film is ended must at once begin a new one because he dreads becoming adult by abandoning his romantic dreams. And Marcel, Rosa's former lover, routinely belies his age by chinning himself in his room. Only Juliet by her generosity and Mercutio by his ridicule escape these automations.

In his behaviorism Bertolucci remodels Richardson's novel on Clarissa Harlowe and Lovelace in a design of reactions already sketched in Benvolio's advice to Romeo:

> Tut, man, one fire burns out another's burning;
> One pain is less'nd by another's anguish. (1,2)

Paul and Jeanne are kin to the constructs in recent bionic art, those feats in engineering anonymous mechanisms seemingly endowed with life—systems behaving as if they were human. That is why, whatever traumas are evident, this film is a limited exploration.

Because the psychometrics are so naked, *The Tango* is stripped of the "romance" modulating Shakespeare's play. Yet both dramas derive from an urban, middle-class culture that fostered romance. Like Jeanne, Juliet is a middle-class girl living in the city, and the whole boy-meets-girl theme has its special bourgeois undertone. Both plays are episodes in a melodrama of middle-class social history of which both romance and anti-romance are facets.

The feudal game of courtly love was an elaborate—often a rhetorical—sublimation of adultery in a ritual that intentionally evaded marriage. This medieval ceremonial exercise took on some exalted meanings when Dante met Beatrice in the streets of Florence. There was still no question of marriage, though Dante was able to elevate his encounter to contemplations of new life under the guidance of his lady. The more secular sublimations in Petrarchan and Platonic cults of love became a fashionable academism mocked in Shakespeare's *Love's Labour's Lost*, where wedlock was a postponed and perhaps inconsequential prospect. The devotions of Romeo and Juliet, those middle-class children, should end in a wedding, and do, though one can hardly envision Juliet as *Hausfrau;* they must be dismissed before they enter domesticity. So we accept Romeo's last banal gesture: "Thus with a kiss I die." Montague and Capulet belong in a Verona where love and marriage coexist in equivocal adjustment.

Such uncorrupted romance could not survive the disillusion of Shakespeare's *Troilus and Cressida* or John Donne's distraught sexuality. The destined wrenching cynicism was, however, masked by the dubious sublimating ideal of wedded bliss until, as Charles Frankel noted, romance became prelude to an institution that reversed its premises: marriage seen as fulfillment of a romance that began in the suicidal love of Tristram and Iseult as an escape from marriage.[5] Then, after the dreary scrutiny of matrimony by Flaubert and others, we have *The Last Tango* with its devaluations of romance, love, marriage, and sex itself; derived from a new puritanism and treating the erotic as pathological.

Nevertheless the middle-class sublimation of sexuality in *Romeo and Juliet* guarded some values we have lost. For the time being, there was Juliet's benign eroticism springing, in its urban milieu, from a biology that was more than biology, "My bounty," says Juliet,

> . . . is as boundless as the sea,
> My love as deep; the more I give to thee
> The more I have, for both are infinite. (2, 2)

Her antipuritan surrender marks a height in middle-class culture that was untenable but estimable. Its untarnished abandon is as precious as the more seasoned and voluptuous sublimation of Cleopatra's final surrender to Antony: "Husband, I come."

We have learned to suspect the middle class of every complicity and the myth of domesticity falsified a pristine bourgeois innocence. The penalty for this falsification is exacted in one of the humane instants in *The Tango* that does, indeed, make the film a sort of landmark. When Paul faces the corpse of his wife laid out among flowers after her lurid suicide, he cannot endure the spectacle betokening his failed wedlock; in agony he tries to wipe away the cosmetic mask affixed to the embalmed body. Between Juliet and Paul, psychoanalysis has intervened to prove that domesticated sexuality inflicts its own pathology.

If Juliet eludes the psychometrics animating Paul and Jeanne, Shakespeare was tough-minded enough to set this Juliet-moment within a spectrum of critical assessments. Mercutio defines love as a great idiot running up and down to hide his bauble in a hole. Friar Laurence knows how "These violent delights have violent ends." Tybalt's hate destroys Eros. The Nurse predicts that Juliet will at last fall on her back. Juliet and Romeo are seen circumferentially, by derision, by sobriety, by malice, by pragmatism. But Paul and Jeanne in their spastic coition are alone; they have, like Conrad's Kurtz, kicked the world out from under themselves. They evoke judgment from only the audience. Their introspection is an isolate. Nobody in the film is in a position to comment directly on what happens in the apartment: not the maid who cleans up Rosa's blood, not Rosa's mother who accuses Paul of being mad and who wants to know why Rosa killed herself (a question Paul cannot answer), not even Tom, who smells death in the apartment he refuses to rent.

We see Paul and Jeanne only as victimized by the syndromes assigned by Bertolucci's premises, which doubtless reflect some of our own premises, making the film a version of homily. Paul and Jeanne exist as case histories demonstrative, as in some of O'Neill's plays, to an audience that has learned to distrust sex with a nearly puritan anxiety. *The Tango* does have its own sense of evil arising from a dread that transfers moral to clinical categories.

Above all, *The Tango* lacks the reassuring exuberance of Mercutio's ribaldry, that serves to refocus the melodrama of disaster. To be sure the film has its passages of oblique black comedy: Paul inviting Jeanne to eat the ass of the dead rat, the animal noises emitted by the two as surrogates for their names, Paul's grim lecturing to Jeanne as he bathes her, then his exposing his buttocks to the tango dancers. Some audiences actually laugh at Tom's idiocy in filming Jeanne. These deflecting interludes, however, lack the tolerance of "sick" comedy, which (in the Woody Allen vein) is able to accept the absurdity of human incompetence, bafflement, neurosis, and death itself as elemental in our existence.[6]

The Tango is a serious, even a puritan, film. If melodrama is a puritan art-form in its reductions to good and evil, *The Tango* is puritan in being a version of polemic against the profanity and insolence of the flesh.[7] The melodramatic commitment to binary values induces a "realism" that is monocular, prohibiting sublimation. The Shakespearean realism speaks polyphonically through the many voices of those who encompass the lovers in a montage of meanings. As intimated by Francis Bacon's two savage title-paintings framing the credits preceding the film, *The Tango* in its alarm projects what Pauline Kael calls "the terror of actual experience"—a terror hardly disguising a latent cynicism that the Middle Ages did not phrase in the debate of body and soul.

The loss of the tragic bifocal awareness leaves only a disturbing melodrama of the clinical in a liberation that is suspect. The film indicates that when sex is isolated from everything else, the biology that remains is an affliction. To repeat: if sex is everything, we must ask what we mean by sex. In *Romeo and Juliet* Shakespeare does not mean what Bertolucci means. Bertolucci's intelligence postulates, ironically, a melodramatic simplification in his single, disabused definition of sex. Shakespeare had at least two definitions: profane and, in its own fragile and provisional way, sacred.

Notes

1. A sane and extended analysis of the differences between the two genres is in Robert B. Heilman, *Tragedy and Melodrama*, dealing with many matters also treated in Peter Brooks, *The Melodramatic Imagination*, and in Michael R. Booth, *English Melodrama*. Heilman identifies the contrasts between tragedy and disaster, melodrama's reduction in self-awareness, its simplistic ethic of good and evil in an essentially binary grid, its often topical or polemic address. Heilman wisely recognizes the many hybrid effects suspended between tragedy and melodrama, citing *Romeo and Juliet* in this connection.

2. Jack Fisher, "Last Tango in Paris," in *Sexuality in the Movies*, ed. by Thomas R. Aikins (Bloomington, Ind.: Indiana Univ. Press, 1975), pp. 221-233—a searching examination of the film.

3. David R. Slavitt, "Sexuality in the Film," in *Sexuality*, ed. by Atkins, p. 234.

4. Pauline Kael, "Tango," *Reeling* (Boston: Little, Brown, 1976), pp. 27-34. Originally a review in *The New Yorker*, Oct. 29, 1972.

5. Charles Frankel, "The Family in Context," *The Love of Anxiety and Other Essays* (New York: Harper & Row, 1965), pp. 49 ff.

6. Robert B. Heilman, *The Ways of the World: Comedy and Society* (Seattle: Univ. of Washington Press, 1978), p. 139.

7. On the sense of sin in the sex film see Wayne A. Losano, "The Sex Genre," in *Sexuality*, ed. by Atkins, pp. 143-44.

16

Melodrama, the Movies, and Genre

JOHN L. FELL

If stage melodrama locates its origins in French pantomime, theater, literary romances, and adventure stories, film engorged the proscenium, splinters and all, more than a century later. By Edwardian times, commercial vehicles of public pleasure had split up, refined, and formularized their product to such an extent that audience appetites were differentiated with respect to age, sex, and sometimes geography. As with other forms of industrialized pleasure, investment capital parlayed the provincial movie business into a national network of distribution and exhibition, so that the merchandising challenge became one of reconciling pinpointed appeals (the Saturday afternoon serial) with maximum audiences (the family picture). Typically, a Poverty Row company produced *Flash Gordon's Trip to Mars.* Andy Hardy was M-G-M stuff.

Melodrama's esthetic legitimacy poses a social issue. Unless it has become artifact, melodrama's antipodes must operate within a society's practiced—at least believed-to-be-practiced—ethical norms. How far are moral polarities shared across class-defined boundaries of sensibility in any given society? In melodrama, behavior finds its reward or comeuppance in terms of "justice." We must somehow agree about justice.

Even more basically, melodrama's threadbare origins require it to mediate, usually unseriously and because of that sometimes effectively, among the separate points of a moral constellation. Like its stage progenitor, movie genre, too, hints at allegory. It hinges some connection between tangible and more elusive realms. The implied sphere, the invisible one, rests on metaphysical givens, unspoken agreements floating free of rational limitation, of cause-effect naturalism.

The application of generic notions to film study has been less cosmic than in literary criticism: not dramatic, narrative, or lyric, not epic or novel, but the western, the sci-fi. More starkly: screwball, crime, horror. As with other popular entertainment modes, such vocabulary often suggests a kind of hard-eyed, bottom-line efficiency: jiggle shows on network television, bug-eyed monsters in 1930s pulp.

Thus far at least, film cannot afford broader groupings. Perhaps Stan Brakhage might be lyric, but what about Michael Snow or Paul Sharrits? Comedy excepted, most movie entertainment falls under romance, a world superior to experience, characters beginning and ending in conditions of stasis, harmony dramatically realized by way of death and survival. Optimistic violence.

The basis of *any* generic consideration is likeness, which is to say conventions. Like its melodramatic forebears, film genre displays certain stylistic precedents from oral narrative. These include a formulaic linear design by whose means agreement is established about those patterns within which any unfolding narrative may be understandably advanced. In the world of movie genre, such conventions are insinuated beyond exposition (namely, screen direction, matching action, parallel editing) into iconography (isolated castle, basement laboratory), character (demented scientist), and themes (rational overreach).

> One doesn't have to sit there and say, "Well, I don't know . . . ethically . . . and maybe he meant." That's a lot of crap: to be so artistic that you don't make sense. One shouldn't have time to say anything but "Here comes Randy, and he's alone. What's his problem? Oh, his wife? What happened? Oh, it did? Ooh. Seven fellows? He'll get 'em. He's already got three before the picture starts, so he only has four to go, and they're probably in Silver City, because that's where he's headed."[1]

"Meaning," the connections audiences draw between their fictive experience and private ideological sounding boards, is also inflected by confrontations within any given genre. Such face-offs occur between separate packets of convention. Some codings overlap categoric boundaries (black-garbed cattle rustlers and vampire counts). Others reinforce themes more adaptably. A villain, let us say, enjoys "Art": painting, vases, string quartets. Inhabiting a detective movie, he is corrupt and very probably homosexual: Casper Gutman in *The Maltese Falcon.*

Located in a western, such a character introduces Eastern, which is to say, European, decadence to the utopian garden. Likely, his taste will be reinforced by clothes, smoking habits, and professional affiliations with a bank or railroad.

If villainous, the art lover in science fiction menaces his community with reactionary impulses toward old ways, days when men still fell vulnerable to irrational behavior, to primitive greeds. (If heroine and hero like art, they evidence a longing for emotions that are more genuine than permitted in their sanitized Erewhon).

Attractions to art in horror movies indicate an alarming disposition to meddle in things better untouched: the occult (Egyptian cat statues) or the dead (Gothic portraits). In musicals, an affinity to Mozart or Robert Schumann contrasts with the vulgar vitality of America or democracy or the people, epitomized by jazz or rock, joyfully announced by Busby Berkeley extravaganzas, or disco dancing, or tap numbers. In each instance, "Art" (one might as usefully have chosen villainous attitudes toward the opposite sex or toward subordinates) threatens the social order. Each infringement conforms to a coherent generic verisimilitude. The character of the threat broadly hints at value constellations that are central to each category of film.

Genre study in the movies has rarely been noted for delicacy of touch, western analyses excepted. Genre groupings (films noirs, weepies) facilely conform to personal enthusiasms. The writer risks constant temptations to justify himself as a media junkie (crucifixion motifs in *Dirty Harry*) or slyly to disclose the depth of his sophistication (upended birdcage nesting in the doctor's apparatus in *Bride of Frankenstein).* Most often, film genres are grouped in terms of historical period, costume, and like iconic codings, including those which operate from the sound track. Yet with reference to more basic considerations, these elements may prove to be the least stable.

A foothold on analyses of such movie conventions may be provided by formalist studies of melodrama, provided we caution ourselves. These reductive investigations ought only to be considered preliminary. More involved strategies must necessarily follow. Melodrama lent itself to formalist Russian inquiry[2] not only because of its popular character but because the idiom's formulaic plot sinews, like the Karloff monster never quite cosmetized by "real" epidermises, enforced a kind of structural simplicity. Schemes like Vladimir Propp's *Morphology of the Folk Tale* might suffice.[3] Certainly, plot conventions have a special grasp on narrative exposition at its most popular.

> [Telling two unconnected stories in the film *Targets]* was very tough to do. While we were making it, the nagging worry was would it work to tell the two stories so independently of each other. I always thought it would because audiences have seen

enough movies so that they would just know the two of them would meet. Just because he's Boris Karloff and the boy is the other star of the picture whether they knew it or not they would feel it. It's a sort of unspoken quality of suspense.[4]

Let us compare the construction of a popular movie to Balukhatyi's structuralist itemization of melodramatic elements: its strategy for eliciting spectator response.[5] Randomly, we choose the first version of *The Invasion of the Body Snatchers*, made in 1956.

> *Returning to his small home town, Dr. Miles Bennell finds various indications that things are amiss. An epidemic of paranoid suspicion appears to be running through the citizenry. People are "no longer themselves." Miles meets an old flame, Becky Driscoll. In the basement of a house, an incomplete body is discovered, growing into the likeness of the householder. Later, more pods threaten to reproduce Miles, Becky, and their friends Jack and Teddy. These alien presences have supplanted all the other citizens. Miles and Becky escape, but Becky eventually falls asleep and is herself transformed. Hysterical, Miles finally convinces authorities of his fantastic experiences.*

> *Plot Themes.* Extreme violations of the normal connections among everyday phenomena: desire on the spectator's part to see it put right. ("The look's gone." "There's no emotion.")
> *Facts of Everyday Life and Characters' Actions.* Tragic or joyous shocks connected with sudden recognitions. ("Miles, there was really nothing to fear. Soon you'll realize it yourself.")
> *Unexpected Twists and Sharp Reversals in the Story Line.* One alternative is an uninterruptedly "unhappy" line of development for the chief character until the denouement with its final "happy" reversal.
> *Strikingly Effective Situations.* Situations susceptible to obvious "sentimental" treatment. (Miles and Becky try to impersonate the feelingless pod people, but Becky involuntarily cries out when she sees a dog endangered by a truck.)
> *Characters.* Vivid, expressive emotional relationships, such as a loving couple. (Becky to Miles: "To live without love or pain. I couldn't stand it.")
> *Speeches and Dialogue.* Impassioned speech. (The film is best remembered for Kevin McCarthy's despairing, "They're here already. You're next, . . . " delivered to unheeding motorists and to the audience.)

Submitting the film's plot to another form of scrutiny, we discover that it may be refined into a very few pivotal shifts. Each clarifies or alters relations between the story's central figures and/or a public context.

> *Public Event Involves Protagonist(s).* Dr. Miles Bennell returns home to confront an apparent psychological epidemic. Becky advises him that her cousin Wilma no longer believes that Uncle Ira is her real uncle.
> *Protagonist(s) Become Suspect.* Miles and Becky first hide, then flee from all the town's inhabitants.
> *Love* (sometimes *Love and Misunderstanding*). Early in the film, the couple declare mutual affection.
> *Villainy Disclosed.* Dr. Kauffman, town psychiatrist, finally explains that the seeds arrived from outer space.
> *Protagonist Endangered.* Successively, each person becomes a pod person. Miles' final betrayal occurs when Becky denounces him.
> *Spectacle/Public Climax.* Miles staggers through heavy traffic, his pleas ignored by drivers who think him a maniac or a drunk.
> *Protagonist Exonerated* (sometimes also *Love Triumphs*). Authorities are finally convinced of Miles' veracity.

A like story pattern will be found in detective films, although protagonists (hard-boiled ones excepted) customarily chase rather than flee. (Propp's fairytale study accommodates either design). Minor variations may be enforced by relations between any given detective and the story's women. Wilder and Diamond's *The Private Life of Sherlock Holmes* (1970) plays games with Holmes's libido, but early detectives tend to asexuality, a condition that requires boy-girl separations and reunions to operate on the level of a subplot. See also Mr. Moto and Charlie Chan. Where detectives have active wives (The Thin Man series) or enjoy sexual dalliance with clients (Philip Marlowe), the more common hero-heroine pattern applies.

In *Adventures of Sherlock Holmes* (1939), named after but otherwise unrelated to William Gillette's play, we locate pivotal situations as follows.

> *Public Event Involves Protagonist.* Holmes is enlisted to facilitate the delivery of the Star of Delhi to the Tower of London.
> *Protagonist Becomes* (here *Pursues*) *False Suspect.* Professor Moriarty misleads Holmes into investigating a convoluted murder mystery while he plans the theft of the Star of Delhi.
> *Love and Misunderstanding.* Holmes's client Ann Brandon suspects Gerald, her fiancé, of killing her brother Lloyd.

Villain Disclosed. Holmes discovers Moriarty's complicity in the murder and locates his Tower of London plan: the Star of Delhi plot is itself a guise to facilitate the theft of the crown jewels.

Protagonist Endangered. Holmes and Moriarty fight.

Spectacle/Public Climax. Holmes knocks Moriarty off the Tower of London's parapet.

Protagonist Exonerated. Love Triumphs. Holmes proves to be correct about everything. Gerald is cleared of Lloyd's murder and reconciled with Ann.

In this movie, the basis on which hero and villain are differentiated proves interesting to our purposes, for in Moriarty Holmes finds not merely his greatest adversary but also the one most like himself: brilliant, daring, capable of masterful, logical forethought, skilled at disguise. (The last trait is a tradition running back to Hawkshaw in Tom Taylor's *The Ticket of Leave Man,* 1863). Understanding his opponent, Moriarty's challenge is to concoct a mystery that may entrap and waylay the detective by its irreconcilable deluge of clues.

Moriarty's affection for hothouse orchids discloses our earlier connections between art and corruption. Here it denotes ultimate disdain for the moral order itself, a decadence positively Oscar Wildean. To his servant Dawes, whom he believes to have neglected the plants, Moriarty snarls, "You have killed a flower, and to think I was incarcerated for months simply for killing a man. For what you have done you should be drawn and quartered." Holmes uncovers the professor's plan by locating a pressed orchid between the Tower of London pages in a Baedeker.

Moriarty's botanical affections equate to Holmes's violin, except that music in 221B Baker Street evidences gentlemanly eccentricity, a healthy alternative to cocaine, some small basis for the detective's minimal humanity. Disguised at one point, Holmes imitates a music hall entertainer and sings "By the Seaside." Music helps Ann Brandon to identify a mysterious flute piece which always accompanies threats to the lives of her family members. In conclusion, Holmes returns to his violin, playing chromatic scales to a bell jar of flies in order to see, of all things, whether any particular pitch will drive them batty.

Various writers (Raymond Durgnat,[6] Dudley Andrew,[7] Leland Poague[8]) have noted that auteurism, the monomaniacal consideration of movie directors' styles as central to film study, applies a structural system of convention analysis shared with genre research. In truth, patterns of generic design both overlap and diverge from individualized, authored plans. To state the matter otherwise, a writer-director's stylized relation to his work is characteristically ironic, but he also may develop highly individualized superstructures elaborating the generic plot mold.

Such a case may be erected atop Hitchcock's early British sound films. During the latter half of the nineteenth century, stage melodrama placed increasing emphasis on sensation scenes, visually striking climaxes such as battles and rescues, increasingly characterized by elaborate technical resources and ambitious staging, such as horse races, naval engagements, and explosions. The elements of spectacle and public event, just described à propos *The Invasion of the Body Snatchers* and *Adventures of Sherlock Holmes*, allude both to such theatrical conventions and, further back, to vestiges of the epic mode that underlies sensation scenes generally. Commencing with *Blackmail* (1929), Hitchcock's early thrillers incorporate such awesome moments with characteristic imagination while continuing to operate within our earlier story patterns.

In the earliest talkie,

> *a young couple's alliance is threatened when Alice allows herself to be picked up in a restaurant following a quarrel with Frank, her police detective boyfriend. Attacked in the new escort's apartment, Alice kills the man with a knife. She and Frank are threatened by a blackmailer, whom Frank pursues until the villain falls from the dome of the British Museum.*

With the dead blackmailer regarded as the murderer, Alice falls free of suspicion in a Hitchcock ending uncharacteristically frank to acknowledge unresolved moral ambiguities. His first *The Man Who Knew Too Much* (1934) reports a very like plot, this time starting with a married couple whose security is threatened when foreign agents kidnap their daughter.

The last three films cited in Table 1 trace identical plot pivots, with the alternative emphasis emergent, because each protagonist becomes a more literal fugitive; Alice was just a suspect. During each initial situation, a pair of young people is erotically and criminally involved. Soon complications threaten the relationship. The final public spectacle simultaneously resolves moral and sexual tensions, blending rescue, violence, and physical consummation.

It's an updated train-track rescue. A characteristic Hitchcock gesture has the man desperately extending a hand to rescue his girlfriend from falling to her death. The image appears first in *Young and Innocent* and reemerges in *North by Northwest* (1959). A man reaching out to a man doesn't work: *Saboteur* (1943). The hero running the risk of himself falling (*Vertigo*, 1958) results in a sexless conclusion. Obviously, many American Hitchcocks pose identical narratives, but by this time the director has complicated his moral world with doublings and overlays of guilt and innocence. A hero, for example, may himself be guilty of some unacknowledged psychological aberration (*Vertigo; Marnie*, 1964) which amounts to a moral equivalent of murder or theft. At this stage, genre has lost dominance over narrative. A character may no longer be considered identical with the plot functions in which he operates.

Table 1

Plot Elements in Selected Hitchcock Features

	Public Event Involves Protagonist	Protagonist Becomes Suspect	Love and Misunderstanding	Villain Disclosed	Protagonist Endangered	Spectacle or Public Climax	Hero Exonerated; Love Triumphs
Blackmail (1929)	Quarrel; Alice leaves with, stabs stranger	Frank conceals suspicion of Alice	Residue of quarrel	Blackmailer threatens Frank & Alice	Alice almost confesses	Pursuit, death at British Museum	Blackmailer = murderer
The Man Who Knew Too Much (1934)	Agent shot at dance; entrusts secret to Bob	Bob & Jill under espionage surveillance	Marriage = no misunderstanding	Kidnappers on phone	Bob trapped in spiritualist church	Foiled murder at Albert Hall	Lorre shot; Betty safe
The 39 Steps (1935)	Music Hall shooting; agent enjoins Richard	Richard flees from Miss Smith murder	Richard & Pamela at odds	Professor Jordan's admission	Richard shot, chased	Mr. Memory exposed at Music Hall	Jordan captured; Richard gets Pamela
Young and Innocent (1937)	Robert finds corpse on beach	Robert arrested, escapes	Erica believes Robert to be murderer	Drummer's tic betrays him to audience	Robert recaptured	Car lost in coal mine (*note*: precedes disclosure)	Drummer captured; Robert gets Erica
The Lady Vanishes (1938)	Iris, Miss Froy, & Gilbert at Tyrol resort	Iris thought demented by head blow	Iris & Gilbert at odds	Dr. Hartz admits espionage	Couple drugged; fight in baggage car	Train waylaid in forest	Train escape; Gilbert gets Iris

There is no intention to propose that this study's plot pattern fits any broader universe among either theatrical melodramas or movie genres than indicated here. Clearly it is dysfunctional to any horror film in which an evil agent serves as protagonist, for this requires a contrary kind of moral resolution. A vengeance story takes different turns: *Seven Men From Now* (1965). The form might accommodate various musicals—Astaire and Rogers RKOs, for example—but one would have to dispense with physical danger and annex suspicion and misunderstanding in order to enlist comic conventions. A like pattern may be extrapolated from the little stories behind early Busby Berkeley production numbers, but again the design has been reduced to situation/complication/resolution: "Shanghai Lil" in *Footlight Parade* (1933), "Lullaby of Broadway" in *Gold Diggers of 1935* (1935).

More interesting for our purposes is the suspicion that modified formal analyses may provide a means to overlay seemingly different genres, the better to disclose congruities. It should follow that relationships between other sorts of evidence—character and setting, for instance—are susceptible to similar kinds of juxtapositioning. This done, we could begin to ferret out rules by which the different systems interpenetrate and modulate one another.

Notes

1. Boetticher quoted in Eric Sherman and Martin Rubin, *The Director's Event* (New York: Atheneum, 1970).
2. Daniel Gerould, "Russian Formalist Theories of Melodrama," *Journal of American Culture* (Spring, 1978), 1(1):152-68.
3. Vladimir Propp, *Morphology of the Folktale*, 2d ed. (Austin, Tex.: Univ. of Texas Press, 1976).
4. Bogdanovich quoted in Sherman and Rubin, *The Director's Event.*
5. The material appears in Gerould, "Russian Formalist Theories," pp. 154-62.
6. Raymond Durgnat, "Genre: Populism and Social Realism," *Film Comment*, July-August, 1975.
7. J. Dudley Andrew, *The Major Film Theories* (New York: Oxford Univ. Press, 1976).
8. Leland A. Poague, "The Problem of Film Genre: A Mentalistic Approach," *Film/Literature Quarterly*, Spring, 1978.

17

The Moral Ecology of Melodrama: The Family Plot and *Magnificent Obsession*

NOËL CARROLL

In the late 1970s, Hollywood film production is increasingly reliant on traditional genres. The exhumation of old formulas—from the 1950s especially but also from the 1930s and 1940s—is becoming more and more pronounced. Programmatic, albeit often high-budget, horror, sci-fi, war, and sports films dominate the current fare of domestic releases. To a certain extent this is a result of Hollywood's innate business conservatism: Nothing succeeds like something that succeeded before; old genres never die, they merely await rebirth in another decade. But Hollywood had been more daring in the range and types of films it experimented with from the late 1960s to the mid-1970s. The retreat to genres is not completely an industry initiative; it is also a response to the growing conservatism of the period, which, in turn, is reflected in the films.

Melodrama is among the genres presently being recycled. Two 1978 releases—*International Velvet* and *Uncle Joe Shannon*—are particularly interesting because of the similarities of their structures. Both concern the symbolic reconstitutions of families; lost parents are replaced by loving parental figures who, concomitantly, gain surrogate children. In certain respects, these films can be seen as in the lineage of the melodramas of kidnap and restoration that are so important in Griffith's Biograph work. They also recall the Dickensesque ploy of an orphan who is rediscovered by a relative. Of course, in Griffith and Dickens, a family is literally reunited, whereas in *International Velvet* and *Uncle Joe Shannon* the reconstitution is symbolic. Nevertheless, the narrative structures in all these examples are predicated on the "rightness" of the nuclear family. Indeed, that "rightness" underlies the esthetic "fitness" of the plot; i.e., narrative closure is achieved through the restoration of nuclear family relations.

International Velvet is a belated sequel to *National Velvet.* In it, Velvet, who is now in her forties, has a niece whose parents have died in some unmentionably gruesome accident. The resentful orphan is shipped from Arizona to England to stay with her aunt who has a writer boyfriend. The child is sullen not only because of her parents' death and her abrupt resettlement, but, more importantly, because she has never felt loved. We ruefully note that the only reason the child did not die with her parents was that, because they always ignored her, they did not take her on their last, fateful trip. The child is described in the film as lacking an identity, as living a cardboard, cut-out existence with no depth of feeling. And this is associated with the lack of parental affection.

The child's lack of a real family (in both a literal and psychological sense) is paralleled by a similar lack on Velvet's part. We learn that Velvet tragically lost her own child as the result of a miscarriage during a riding accident. Both Velvet and her niece are depicted as psychologically "incomplete"; they both need families to make them "whole."

The niece's alienation first begins to ease when riding and caring for Velvet's legendary stallion, Pie. Her eyes glow while she watches the birth of Pie's last foal. As the colt gambols with its mother, the editing connects the maternal scene with the niece, symbolically defining the child's yearning as not just for the horse but, more broadly, for a family. When Velvet buys the niece the horse, the girl rides it day in and day out, becoming even more obsessive about riding than Velvet had been in the earlier film. Years pass as the child, now a teenager, evolves into Velvet Junior. However, she is so preoccupied with the perfection of her equestrian art that she forgoes boyfriends and a social life. Thus, though somewhat fuller, the character is not yet complete. For that we wait until the final reel when as a member of the British Olympic riding team she "miraculously" wins a Gold Medal while also learning the meaning of teamwork. With the medal comes the sense of personal identity she lacked all along and this is connected with her marriage to the captain of the American riding team. Returning to England, the niece introduces her new husband to "her parents," finally acknowledging the family bond whose denial has caused all the emotional tensions in the film. The act is further commemorated when the niece gives Velvet her Gold Medal; this compensates for the award that Velvet didn't receive, for technical reasons, in the earlier film. Thus, from one horse race, we get two generations of families whose constitution neatly solves all the emotional problems presupposed by the rest of the plot.

The melodramatic elements of *International Velvet*—including the emotional extremes, coincidences, and improbable complementary plot symmetries—are even more exaggerated in *Uncle Joe Shannon*. Released as a "Christmas" film, it underscores its use of the "family plot" with all the imagery of the Yuletide season. Christmas is the day on which our culture celebrates the completion of its mythic first family. Because Christmas exists in large measure as a mass fantasy—inextricably bound up with childhood associations of the warmth, generosity, and security of the family—the holiday is one of the most potent symbols in Hollywood's arsenal. In the hands of a master propagandist like Frank Capra, a Christmas carol at the right moment becomes a veritable national anthem, instilling a wave of irrational fellow-feeling that makes Capra's nebulous populism seem almost plausible. The mechanics of this effect are simple—Christmas imagery induces regression, rekindling childlike beliefs in social stability and community that grow out of idealizations of the family. In *Uncle Joe Shannon*, the ideological use to which Christmas is put is not in the service of a broad political stance like populism but as a reaffirmation of the family and its role as the central and natural form of human relation.

The film opens with the eponymous Joe playing his trumpet at a recording studio. The camera pans around him, the circular movement suggesting that he is complete as well as at the center of his harmonious universe. It is his son's birthday and Joe gives the boy a trumpet like his, only smaller. Joe is at the height of his career, but the film makes it clear that fame is less important to him than family. Joe is unremittingly uxorious, touching and kissing his wife at every turn. He ignores triumphant curtain calls after his concert at the Hollywood Bowl in order to be home in time for his son's birthday party. But disaster strikes; his home is aflame as he pulls into his neighborhood. The film dissolves, and seven years later we see Joe—a skid row wino desperately clutching his horn. He has lost both his family and his art. These are the two losses the plot must recuperate.

Joe visits a prostitute, but she is out. Her son, Robbie, who calls all her clients "uncle," demands that Joe tell him a story. Joe and Robbie fall asleep. Next morning, the police awaken them at gunpoint. Robbie's mother has run away and the boy must go to an orphanage. He revolts and hides in Joe's car, convinced he can make something (namely, a father) out of this bum.

In the tradition of Chaplin's *The Kid* (a particularly interesting film in terms of the family plot), Robbie comes to idolize Joe. Christmas is approaching so Robbie steals a Santa Claus outfit from a department store, and the duo plays street-corner renditions of "Jingle Bells" to earn their keep. At this point Joe does not yet understand that Robbie is his salvation. He slaps the boy for playing with his own dead son's trumpet, tries to send Robbie away, and finally puts the boy in the orphanage. Joe's inability or, perhaps more aptly, his refusal to acknowledge Robbie as his symbolic son is an example of a key device of melodrama for engendering suspense. We know the boy is exactly what Joe wants; when will he realize it?

Joe attempts to commit suicide after he puts Robbie in the orphanage. This is the symbolic turning point in the film. Director Joseph Hanwright floods the scene with metaphors. As Joe sinks to the bottom of the bay, he looks up and sees a ball of light shimmering on the surface. Having "seen the light," he struggles upward, no longer "drowning in self-pity." He kidnaps Robbie from the orphanage. In subsequent scenes, his music begins to improve. The opening symbol of "harmony" continues; each station in Joe's progress is reflected in his playing. Insofar as the etymology of "melodrama" is drama plus music, *Uncle Joe Shannon* is at least notable for making Joe's solos an explicit index of each phase of his moral growth.

Though Joe acknowledges his paternal affection for Robbie, a catastrophe (the favorite type of plot complication in melodrama) erupts. Robbie has cancer. Joe convinces him to undergo surgery. But when Robbie's leg is amputated, the boy feels Joe has betrayed him. He refuses to talk to his surrogate father. He won't practice using his wheelchair or his crutches. The doctors fear that he has lost the will to live.

The plot becomes perfectly symmetrical. Now Joe must redeem Robbie. He gives Robbie his son's trumpet, a gesture whose phallic significance is no harder to decipher than the horse symbolism in *International Velvet*. But Robbie still won't budge. Joe tries to infuriate him back to life. Joe plays his horn at a Christmas party for the other hospitalized children. He has never played better. Hearing the music, Robbie struggles downstairs to reclaim his "father." Unsteady on his crutches, he glowers at Joe; but hatred and pride give way to love. The boy hangs on Joe's neck while Joe plays mellifluously with one hand. The camera circles them, echoing the opening shot. Both have become complete again. The father has a son, and the son, a father. The music, the camera movement, and the Christmas iconography heighten the effect of this "family reunion." The esthetic "unity" and integration of elements here not only correspond to but mirror the theme of emotional symbiosis between father and son.

Coming on the heels of a decade of radical and/or feminist criticism of the nuclear family, melodramas like *International Velvet* and *Uncle Joe Shannon* are somewhat surprising. In their particular use of the family plot, they project and unquestioningly endorse the family as the right structure for human relations. Parent-children relations are posed as inevitable—something characters are irresistibly drawn toward (for their own good). Emotion is engendered in the audience by means of characters who, for a given period of time, fail to see or refuse to acknowledge the rightness of the symbolically reconstituted family proposed by the plot. The idea of the family, as it is shared with the audience, makes these stories possible. But, at the same time, the existence of these stories reinforces prevailing beliefs in the idea by symbolically rehearsing a faith in the family through fictions that train, or, at least, further inculcate audiences in this particular way of ordering everyday human events.

A sense of *déjà vu* accompanied my encounters with *International Velvet* and *Uncle Joe Shannon.* I knew I had seen their basic plot structures in operation before, and I set about trying to remember where. The answer came quickly; it was *Magnificent Obsession,* a 1953 adaptation of a Lloyd Douglas novel of the same title, directed by Douglas Sirk. Sirk was, among other things, a highly successful director of film melodrama whose critical currency shot sky-high in the early 1970s. Part of the reason behind this reevaluation is the fact that new German directors, like Rainer Werner Fassbinder, who are interested in parodying or extending the melodramatic form, honor Sirk as a major forebear, including, for example, homages to his style in their films. Sirk is now considered a central exemplar of film melodrama. In some cases, especially with reference to *All That Heaven Allows* and *Written on the Wind,* favorably disposed critics argue that Sirk uses melodramatic formats in order to subvert regnant values and preconceptions. Historically, melodrama has at times provided a vehicle for social criticism. Yet, though I am not sure whether *All That Heaven Allows* and *Written on the Wind* merely appear subversive, I am certain that *Magnificent Obsession* is conformist in terms of form and content, and form as content.

Whereas in previous examples, the symbolic transformations of the family plot involve the replacement of parents and children with surrogates, in *Magnificent Obsession* the plot works to substitute a lost husband with a new one. Like many melodramas, the film begins with a tragic accident. Millionaire playboy Bob Merrick overturns his speedboat; an ambulance rushes to the scene with Dr. Wayne Phillips's resuscitator. At the same time, the venerable Doctor Phillips has had a stroke, but without his resuscitator, he dies. His young wife, Helen, is informed. Several characters pointedly remark on the irony of the situation. A great humanitarian and surgeon has been lost so that a wastrel like Merrick can live. They presuppose an injustice or imbalance in the way Wayne Phillips died, something that will in fact be rectified in the way the plot unravels.

Merrick is introduced as reckless, arrogant, brash, discourteous and selfish— the very opposite of the saintly, always thoughtful-to-others Helen Phillips. Merrick, hospitalized in Wayne Phillips's clinic, barks at the doctors, diagnoses himself, and lectures on medicine; he announces that he once was a medical student—a fact that will become important shortly. The clinic staff treats Merrick aloofly and he sneaks out of the hospital. In the tradition of melodramatic coincidences, he hitchhikes a ride with none other than Helen Phillips. He tries to make a pass at her until he learns that she is Mrs. Phillips and that he is connected with her husband's death. He gets out of the car but faints. She returns him to the hospital, learns who he is, and vows to avoid him. Yet their fates have already been intertwined. His desire for her continually grows while she resists each of his advances.

Another story line develops parallel to the romantic interplay between Merrick and Helen. Just as these two characters "discover" each other's identities, so Helen gradually "discovers" who her husband, Wayne Phillips, really was. People write to, and visit, her with stories of mysterious debts owed to Dr. Phillips. At crucial points in their lives, Phillips helped them with money, advice, and influence. In each case, he swore them to secrecy. When they attempted to repay him, he said it was already "all used up." We learn, primarily through a painter named Randolph, that Phillips practiced a bizarre, quasi-religious faith. He believed that helping others gives the benefactor access to "power." One could achieve whatever one wanted through this cosmic power. Strained analogies with electricity are offered to explain how this moral-metaphysical mechanism works. For example, the secrecy is like insulation. Great men "ground" themselves in this power. In fact, their greatness "flows" from this power. Christ is cited as one of the founders of this system of self-interested altruism. Randolph's career as a painter floundered until he mastered the method under Phillips's tutelage.

Randolph explains Phillips's religion, his "magnificent obsession," to Merrick who, despite warnings against trying to "feather one's own nest" with it, attempts to apply the power in his pursuit of Helen. He helps a parking attendant whose family is in trouble and suddenly he sees Helen. He rushes to tell her about this "miracle" and about his allegiance to her husband's faith. She grows increasingly annoyed and, in her efforts to escape from him, is hit by an oncoming car. As a result of the accident, she is blinded. Along with her widowhood, this is another tragedy the plot will commutate.

Merrick, moved by the consequences of his actions, begins to practice Phillips's doctrines in earnest. He secretly helps the Phillips's family by buying their house at an exorbitant price. He also enrolls in medical school again as the best means to help others, and predictably he specializes in surgery. Quite clearly, he is becoming Wayne Phillips. Helen refuses to allow him to see her, but he takes advantage of her blindness and visits her at the beach daily. He tells her that his name is Robbie Robinson. His whole manner is changed. He is no longer brash but humble, self-effacing, other-directed, and reassuring. He emotes all the cultural cues of being a "concerned" person—a visible altruism has supplanted his earlier selfishness. He secretly pays for Helen to travel to Switzerland where she is examined by a battery of the world's most renowned specialists. When they tell her that a cure is impossible, he flies to her side to lend support. He takes her to a peasant festival to distract her, and after they dance all evening he confesses his love as well as his real name. She says that she knew he was Merrick (the theme of identity again) and that she loves him. But the obvious denouement is blocked, enhancing melodramatic suspense. She runs away; she is afraid that he will marry her out of pity.

He goes on to become an internationally famous doctor. His side-burns turn grey. He repairs patients' private lives, demanding secrecy and refusing future repayment on the grounds that by that time "it (the power) will be all used up." As he rushes about the hospital corridors, we assume that this is what Wayne Phillips must have looked like. In short, during this interlude, both Merrick and Helen prove they are "good," which, in this context, means "self-sacrificing." They are ready to reap their rewards.

Randolph tells Merrick that Helen is ill in New Mexico. He arrives and the local surgeon asks Merrick to perform the operation. Merrick is afraid he is not skilled enough, though we realize he has stored up a sur-feit of "power." After some reluctance he operates, hoping to restore Helen's eyesight. He spends an all-night vigil at her bedside. She awak-ens; she can see; they will marry. The injustices and imbalances, the dis-equilibriums in Helen's life, introduced earlier in the plot, are adjusted by means of the practice of Wayne Phillips's "magnificent obsession," and homeostasis returns. Helen regains her husband in the form of Mer-rick who has been molded according to the Phillips prototype. The origi-nal family has been reconstituted with a kind of narrative symmetry that portends "destiny."

Sirk's *Magnificent Obsession* differs from Lloyd Douglas's novel in many respects; a large number of plot details have been changed, dropped, or added including Randolph's occupation, Merrick's age, Helen's blindness, etc. Also, Sirk's film avoids Douglas's banking meta-phors for the power, relying only on the electrical one, while also delet-ing Douglas's notion that religion is a science. According to Sirk, his script, which was prepared by Robert Blees, was primarily based on the screenplay for the 1935 adaptation of *Magnificent Obsession*, directed by John Stahl. Nevertheless, the Sirk film remains true to the essential tenets of Douglas's mysticism. As in Douglas's *Disputed Passage* and *Green Light* (also films directed by Frank Borzage in 1939 and 1937 respectively), *Magnificent Obsession* promotes an ethic of service and sacrifice, devoted to systematic selflessness which is connected to imper-sonal, moral powers that have causal efficacy in the world of everyday events. That is, Douglas and Sirk present a viewpoint where morality is treated as part of the basic structure of the universe. Facts and values are not strongly demarcated; moral disequilibriums are reflected in events.

In the film, Merrick's wasteful existence and arrogant manner "cause" Phillips's death and, later, Helen's blindness. His melodramatic regenera-tion, through a hodgepodge of metaphysics and popular mechanics, results in redressing these tragedies. In this sense, what I call a moral ecology is presupposed by the plot. That is, the plot is structured as if there were a strong causal interdependency between a fundamental moral order (which is geared toward producing self-sacrifice) and every-day events. A violation of the moral order, an imbalance like Merrick's selfishness, causes a repercussion which, in turn, causes further events until the imbalance in the system is adjusted and equilibrium again obtains in the relationship between the moral order and human affairs. Melodrama, in general, emphasizes strong dichotomies of good and evil as well as exact correspondences between moral conflicts and dramatic ones. In *Magnificent Obsession*, the metaphor of "the power" is a device that conflates the moral order and everyday events into one synchronised (ecological) structure.

The values and virtues in all variants of *Magnificent Obsession* are "other-regarding." They include some elements that are not normally thought of as "moral," but more as matters of etiquette. In Sirk's film Merrick is initially marked as "bad" because he is rude, impatient, and domineering. Politeness and courtesy-to-all rather than the proverbial white hat is the most important sign of the good guy in American film. Merrick is the villain until he learns the power—a form of cosmic sensitivity (and good manners) to others—at which point he is virtually a demigod.

Stoicism, both in terms of physical and emotional sufferance, is also lauded. Both Helen (vis-à-vis her blindness) and Merrick (in his love of Helen) evince it and are duly rewarded. This stoicism, especially in Helen's case, is other-regarding; she does not want to burden her friends and companions. Humility and generosity, of course, are the prime ingredients of "the power." Thus, the film projects a seductive fantasy, cathecizing receptive audiences in courtesy, stoicism, humility, and charity. A constellation of values is ideologically reinforced by promising that that precise ethos is connected with, is even constitutive of, "the source of infinite power."

The moral order, or at least the moral order being valorized, is presented as part and parcel of the nature of things as a causal force or as a regulatory force with causal efficacy. In this respect, the particular moral order is represented as natural, namely, as part of the nature of things. The nuclear family—the favored form of human relationship in this ethos—is also part of the cosmic order. If damaged, it restores itself. This process is given as natural in a context where to be natural is right and vice versa. The family plot in melodramatic fiction structures human events in a way that exemplifies and endorses the ideology or ethos it presents as natural.

In *Magnificent Obsession*, the family is not only associated with the structure of the universe (unfolding itself), but also it has connotations of being curative, both psychologically and physically. By the end of the film, Helen is no longer alone and she is no longer blind. Both the sicknesses of the heart and those of the body have been cured by Bob Merrick's becoming Dr. Phillips. This notion of the curative power of the family is implicit in the family plot. Though *International Velvet* and *Uncle Joe Shannon* lack the metaphysical trappings of *Magnificent Obsession*, they too rely on the idea that the (figurative) restoration of the family is "restorative" in a broad sense, namely, a remedy for existential maladies. The family plot is a narrative structure with strident ideological implications; it portrays the family as part of some underlying order and as having naturally revivifying powers.

Sirk develops the theme of order in *Magnificent Obsession* visually in a way that buttresses the family plot with consistent metaphorical imagery. Throughout the film, there is a recurring motif of nature. Large windows look out over landscapes; one of the many examples is the forestry outside Randolph's house which we see when he opens the blinds. The Phillips's home is surrounded by compositionally emphatic, well-kept lawns and trees. We see many tranquil, picture-postcard vistas around the lake. Nature is presented as quiet, serene, and harmonious. That these specific connotations are the relevant ones for the imagery in *Magnificent Obsession* is established in the opening shots. Merrick's white speedboat with its red stripe plows through the placid lake. Sirk stresses its speed and its intrusiveness as it cuts a high, vertical wave through the water. Merrick's recklessness, symbolized by the boat crash (and later the car crash outside Randolph's house), is set against the order and calm of nature. When nature reappears, as it does often, it stands not only for beauty but for organic unity. Though the idea that the natural order is providential or divinely appointed is never made explicit, it hovers in the background. The "harmony" of the landscapes functions as a visual correlative to the moral ecology of the plot.

Another major motif is that of floral arrangements. There are flowers of all kinds everywhere in the film. Sometimes these flowers satisfy a simple compositional need, drawing the audience's attention to what will be a dramatically pertinent sector of the screen. Sometimes the flowers play a symbolic role; when a despairing Helen, who believes she is incurably blind, accidentally knocks a pot with a rose in it off her Swiss balcony, we remember an earlier rose, associated with Dr. Phillips's death, and the pathos of the scene is magnified by correlating her blindness with her other major tragedy. But over and above the local effects of flowers in a given shot or scene, the sheer statistical volume of floral arrangements in the film as a whole is expressive. They connote beauty, nature and design, a cluster of attributes that summarize the sentimental order of the family plot.

Of course, the use of color throughout the film serves a similar end. Image after image can only be described as color coordinated. The compositions resemble those of a department store catalogue. Everything is new and matches everything else in the most balanced and symmetrical way. For example, in the first beach scene there is a green and white striped tent in the background and a matching chair in the foreground. As the camera pulls back when Helen arrives in her pink dress we see two matching, low, symmetrically disposed, red beach chairs. Later she has a green beach blanket to go with her green swimsuit. These color coincidences can be quite insistent. Helen hands a lilac bouquet with a white spray to a companion wearing a lilac-colored suit with a white collar. We see a close-up of Helen's farewell letter to Merrick; it is written in lilac-colored ink and it is held in front of a floral arrangement with lilacs visible in the background. Not all of the color coordination is as aggressive as some of these examples but it is never understated either. We feel that both the manmade and natural environments are incredibly designed. That sense of design is educed through visual cliches of harmony and order that associatively bolster the concept of design and destiny (the inevitability of the family) in the narrative.

The concurrence of the style of composition and choice of iconography with the narrative theme in *Magnificent Obsession* is an example of a variation of the pathetic fallacy, though the technique is really more of a donnée than a fallacy when it comes to film melodrama. Sirk began his artistic career (in theater and film) in Germany in the 1920s. In certain respects, the stylization of *Magnificent Obsession* recalls some tendencies of the expressionist-neoromantic films of the Weimar period. His color symmetries, for example, are reminiscent of the black and white, architectural symmetries of Fritz Lang's *Siegfried's Death*, where the composition also has connotations of "design" and "destiny." Another expressionist device—the use of height to signal authority—comes into play in one of the key scenes in the film. Just before Merrick operates on Helen, he has a crisis of nerve. He looks up; there is a cut to a low-angle shot of Randolph standing behind a plate of glass and observing Merrick from the gallery of the operating theater. The soundtrack blares the "Ode to Joy" theme from Beethoven's *Ninth Symphony* (which has been the leitmotif of the "magnificent obsession" throughout the film). The low camera angulation plus the "celestial choir" render Randolph as a fatherly, godlike figure suddenly come to earth to dispense courage, strength, and assurance. This notion of (secret) providential intervention inflects the significance of the stylization throughout the film—all the various visual orders and designs are ciphers of a supranatural system which works through characters, casting them in terms of a specific ensemble of "other-regarding" virtues and quite literally "sanctifying" the family. Stylization functions as a virtual hierophany in *Magnificent Obsession*, expressing a religious faith in the subservience of the visible world to deeper principles.

Neither *International Velvet* nor *Uncle Joe Shannon* traffic in theology as overtly or as systematically as *Magnificent Obsession*. Their idiom or rhetoric is psychology rather than religion. Both assume an extremely broad notion of a psychological economy that has the capacity to adjust to the loss of beloved objects through processes of symbolic replacement. This somewhat general principle is then put in the service of the nuclear family. The psychologically wounded characters find replacements for lost relatives who actually play the social (not merely the psychological) role of their lost family. The films begin with a valid enough (though vague) psychological principle but employ it to construct plots that celebrate the inevitability of the nuclear family. Undoubtedly, the use of psychology is more palatable to audiences of the 1970s than the theology of *Magnificent Obsession*. But the effect is the same.

PART 5

TEXTS
AND
DOCUMENTS

The Forest of Bondy; or The Dog of Montargis

GUILBERT DE PIXÉRÉCOURT

Editor's Note

Although horses had already appeared in theatrical performances at the Cirque Olympique (including the celebrated *Accusing Horse* who solved a crime by producing a piece of the culprit's jacket), Guilbert de Pixérécourt's *The Forest of Bondy, or The Dog of Montargis* was the first and most famous of a long line of French plays with a dog hero. In an enthusiastic review of the premiere at the Théâtre de la Gaité in 1814, the novelist and short story writer Charles Nodier urged his readers to hurry to see *The Forest of Bondy* before its canine star was hired away by some clever provincial manager. According to Nodier, *The Dog of Montargis* enjoyed great success with fashionable society as well as with the usual followers of melodrama. For many weeks, after the conventional greeting, "How are you today?" the question asked by all Parisians was, "Have you seen the Dog?"

At the first performance, Pixérécourt's "Historical Note," giving the authentic biography of the dog hero, was distributed to members of the

MR CONY AS LANDRI

A theatrical print, published by. W. C. Webb of London in 1843, showing the famous American dog Hamlet with Barkham Cony (1802-1858) as Landri in Pixérécourt's *The Forest of Bondy.* In such plays the trained dog would jump at the villain's throat and tear open a concealed bag of red ochre to creat a bloddy and horrifying effect.
Courtesy Harvard Theatre Collection

audience. The story of the Chevalier d'Aubri was well known at the time, and historians debated whether his dog was a barbet or a greyhound; the Théâtre de la Gaité opted for the former. The lead in *The Forest of Bondy* was actually split between Dragon (who is onstage in only a few scenes) and the mute boy Eloi, originally played by beautiful dancer and mime Mlle Dumouchel. In both the London and New York productions of the 1816 English adaptation, this character (called Florio) was played by actresses, but in the original 1814 Covent Garden version, the role was acted by the famous equestrian, tightrope artist, and pantomimist, Andrew Ducrow.

The Dog of Montargis was considered by Nodier as Pixérécourt's masterpiece. The original French Dragon was signed to a long contract and became a celebrity, along with such other animal stars of melodrama as the stags Coco and Azor and the elephants Baba and Kiouny.

THE FOREST OF BONDY

OR

THE DOG OF MONTARGIS

by

René Charles Guilbert de Pixérécourt

(text prepared by David Nicholson)

Historical Note

Aubri de Mont-didier, traveling alone through the forest of Bondy, is murdered and buried at the foot of a tree. His dog remains for several days on his grave and leaves it only when compelled to do so by hunger. He comes to Paris, to the house of a close friend of the unfortunate Aubri and, by his mournful howling, seems to announce to him the loss that they have both suffered. After eating, the dog starts his moaning again, goes to the door, turns his head around to see if he is being followed, comes back to his master's friend, and pulls him by his coat to tell him to come with him. The strangeness of all the moves made by this dog—his coming without his master whom he never left, this master who suddenly disappeared, and this apportionment of justice and events which scarcely allows crimes to remain undetected for very long—all of these things cause Aubri's friend to follow the dog. As soon as he reaches the foot of the tree, the dog redoubles his wailing, scratching the ground to tell him to search in this spot: the friend digs there, and finds the body of the unfortunate Aubri.

Some time thereafter, the dog sees, quite by chance, the murderer, whom all the historians call the chevalier Macaire; he jumps at his throat, and it is exceedingly difficult to make him let go. Whenever the dog meets Macaire, he attacks him and chases him with the same fury. The animosity of this dog, directed only against this man, begins to strike people as something extraordinary; they recall the affection he had for his master, and at the same time several occasions where this chevalier Macaire had given proofs of his hatred and envy toward Aubri de Mont-didier. A few other circumstances augment these suspicions. The king, informed of all the things that people are saying, sends for the dog, who appears calm until the moment, when seeing Macaire in the middle of a score of courtiers, he turns around, barks, and tries to jump at him.

In those days, single combat between the accuser and the accused was decreed when the proofs of the crime were not sufficient. These sorts of combats were called *God's judgment*, because people were persuaded that the heavens would have performed a miracle rather than let innocence go down to defeat.

The king, struck by all the evidence that was mounting against Macaire, judged that it was high time for the testimony of battle, that is say, he decreed a duel between the chevalier and the dog. The lists were marked in the Ile Saint-Louis, which at that time was only an uninhabited wasteland. Macaire was armed with a heavy club; the dog had an opened cask where he could retreat and from which to make his forays. The dog is let loose; immediately he runs out, circles around his adversary, dodges his blows, threatens him first on one side, then on the other, wears him down, and finally springs up, seizes him by the throat, knocks him down and forces him to confess to his crime in the presence of the king and of all his court. The memory of this dog has been thought worthy of being preserved by a statue that can still be seen, within the last few years, on the mantelpiece in the great hall of the Chateau of Montargis.

It is this fact, unbelievable no doubt if it were not recorded in our old chronicles and reported by historians worthy of credit, who place it in the reign of Charles V, nicknamed *the Wise*, that I have attempted to put on the stage.

Such temerity finds its justification in the moral goal that the author has set himself. Indeed, how can we help but admire such a prodigy and not recognize in this the all-powerful hand of the deity? How could we not be touched by an example of loyalty so rare among men, above all if the author has been able to embody it with some skill and encase it with forms ever so slightly dramatic. This task presented great difficulties, but the author receives for his labor very sweet recompense every night in the flattering eagerness with which the public comes in throngs to the performances of this work, in the enthusiastic applause that it receives, and above all in the tears that his work causes to be shed.

Authors who report this anecdote and upon whose authority it was thought fit to draw include:

Olivier de la Marche, *Traité des Duels*. (He lived in 1437.)
Jules Scaliger, *de Exercitatione*. f^0. 272, edition of 1557.
Belleforest, in his book *Histoires prodigieuses*.
Claude Expilly, in his *Plaidoyer sur l'Édit des Duels*, p. 343.
Bernard de Mont Faucon, *Monumens de la Monarchie française*, vol. 3, p. 70.
De la Colombière, in *le vrai Théâtre d'honneur et de chevalerie*, edition of 1648, vol. 2, p. 300.
St.-Foix, *Essais historiques sur Paris*, edition of 1778, vol. 3, p. 181.
Sainte Palaye, *Mémoires sur l'ancienne Chevalerie*, vol. 3, p. 397.

Translated by Daniel Gerould

Characters

Dragon, Capt. Aubri's dog	Blaise
Col. Gontram	Florio
Aubri de Mont-didier	Dame Gertrude
Macaire	Lucille
Landry	Guards, Peasants, Servants, etc.
Seneschal	

ACT I

Scene: a large Gothic hall, which is used for the county meetings and public ceremonies. The back is quite open to the country. Music. Dame GERTRUDE, *without.*

GERTRUDE. Stop a bit! Stop a bit! Don't be in such a hurry!
[The three peasants and WILLIAM *enter, bowing to Dame* GERTRUDE.]
So, the Seneschal is to give me the meeting here. What can he want with me? Something of prodigious importance, I dare say.
WILLIAM. Yes, I dare say it is, for I heard him say it was summit about the great lodger-folk, as are returning from the wars. But here is the Seneschal. He'll tell you better than I can.
[Enter SENESCHAL *and four servants.]*
SENESCHAL. Well, Dame Gertrude, every hour I am in expectation of the arrival of the regiment of the guards, commanded by Colonel Gontram, at our village of Bondy. Heroes with their brows encircled with laurels ever receive our heartiest welcome. It is for that purpose I have consulted with you, landlady of the first inn of the village, how we might show them the greatest respect. This hall will be decorated with the trophies of my armory, and with the embellishments of your tasteful fancy, it will, I think, in every respect answer our purpose.
GERTRUDE. I am sure, Mr. Seneschal, Dame Gertrude is always proud to obey your honor's commands. My inn, though I say it, is a capital inn. It is the only inn in the place, to be sure, but it has excellent accommodations, and all that it contains is not too good for those veterans, who have fought so bravely for their country.
SENESCHAL. Nobly spoken, Mrs. Gertrude. Have you provided a repast, to be brought here, to refresh the soldiers after their weary march?
GERTRUDE. I have, Mr. Seneschal, and the lads and lasses, with garlands and streamers, are ready to meet and welcome them.
*[*BLAISE *enters, making a great noise with his sabots, and crying—]*
BLAISE. Missus! Missus! *(Aside.)* Dash me! If there bean't Mr. Seneschal himself. I must off with my stumpers. *(Takes off his sabots).* I ax a thousand stumps—pardons, I do mean, sir, but I have got a little private business with missus here.

GERTRUDE. Private business with me, dolt! Speak out directly, I insist upon it. I've no private business with anybody.

BLAISE. Don't you be angry, missus, but that chap as slept last night in our loft, that little wee pockfretten man, with a hump on one shoulder—he brought his donkey with 'un, you do know—no offence to you, I do hope, sir, but it was his donkey for all that.

SENESCHAL. Go on, friend.

BLAISE. Patience, sir, patience. Well, then, dang me, missus, if I can get either of them 'ere two beasts to pay their reckoning.

GERTRUDE. You can't?

BLAISE. No, neither stumpy nor donkey. And when I told 'em that warn't manners, he as could speak best of the two, called I a baboon. Now missus, if that be genteel, I know nought of good breeding.

GERTRUDE. Booby, let the fellow go, and do you run to my granddaughter, Lucille, and to her cousin, Florio, and tell them to come here directly—here in the town hall.

BLAISE. What for?

GERTRUDE. What's that to you? Tell them to bring our carpets and garlands, that were trimmed up so smart.

BLAISE. Carpets and garlands! Now what the dickens can you want with them there?

GERTRUDE. Hoity, toity! Do as you're bid, and hold your tongue, Mr. Impertinence.

BLAISE. I wool—she's mad wi' I. I be always timbersome when she do say hoity toity.

SENESCHAL. Go, and take these men with you, and bring hither some of the coats of mail. I shall give a feast tonight.

BLAISE. No, shall ye though? I'll go directly. A feast tonight! His armory! I'll comparison myself up like King Pepping. Come along, Gregory, come, Peter, come, Jonathan. (*Exit, with four peasants.*)

SENESCHAL. While I give the necessary directions to my people, you will see to the decorations of the hall. We have no time to lose, for young Captain Aubri tells me the regiment may be hourly expected.

GERTRUDE. Aye, that young Captain Aubri knows all about it. He was born in this village, and has been waiting here some days to join this very regiment on his return from Paris, where he has been to present the colors taken from the enemy, to the king.

SENESCHAL. Which preference, they say, has caused much jealousy among some of the officers of the regiment.

GERTRUDE. Psha! Jealousy! Merit always makes jealousy. That is the reason Dame Growley is always so jealous of me.

LUCILLE (*without*). Come, cousin Florio, come along.

GERTRUDE. But see, our young folks are coming already with some of the fine crinkum crankums.

SENESCHAL. Farewell then, Mrs. Gertrude. I know I may depend on you.

GERTRUDE. That you may, Mr. Seneschal. Your servant.

[Exit SENESCHAL *and four Servants. Music. Enter* LUCILLE, *carrying a basket.]*

LUCILLE. Come along, Florio.

GERTRUDE. Well done, my child. Lucille, here is a job you will like. Arrange these garlands, and dispose of these carpets to the best advantage. There will be a festival this evening in the hall.

LUCILLE. Yes, grandmama. A festival! Florio! Florio!

[Enter FLORIO. *Music.]*

GERTRUDE. I shall leave it all to you and your cousin Florio.

LUCILLE. Oh, yes! Florio will be of great assistance to me.

GERTRUDE. Aye, aye, I know how it is. Florio is a prodigious favorite.

LUCILLE. He is good, and he's unfortunate.

GERTRUDE. Yes, he's unfortunate. He lost his parents when young, and his speech by an accident. Though dumb, he is not deaf, I'm sure, for he obeys every word you say.

LUCILLE. Yes, we understand each other, don't we, Florio?

[Music. FLORIO *nods assent.]*

GERTRUDE. Well, well, be always a good boy, Florio, and I will never forsake you.

[Music. FLORIO *kisses* GERTRUDE'S *hand.]*

I must now go and give orders for a good supper for our glorious defenders. Children, make the best use of your time in my absence.

LUCILLE. We will, grandmama.

[Exit GERTRUDE. *Enter two* GIRLS *with the decorations. Music.]*

Come, my dear Florio, help me to arrange this.

[Exeunt girls. FLORIO *signifies he will do it willingly.]*

How beautiful it will be! There, twine these garlands round the windows. Place these carpets and flowers on the balustrades. What think you, Florio?

*[*FLORIO *makes signs that he approves, takes the garlands, forms festoons round the windows and doors, places the carpets and flowers, etc. Music.]*

Is not that pretty, my dear Florio?

*[*FLORIO *signifies that everything must be pretty that comes from her her mouth. Music.]*

Flatterer! You say that I am pretty. But it is not me, but my age that is pretty. Who is not pretty at sixteen? I am good, too, good as well as I can be. But that's nothing—all women are so.

*[*FLORIO *signifies not all. Music.]*

Or ought to be.

*[*FLORIO *consents. Music.]*

I love you, Florio, as my brother, and Florio loves Lucille as his sister.

*[*FLORIO *signifies not so. Music.]*

He feels such gratitude toward her.

*[*FLORIO *signifies not so. Music.]*

How, Mr. Florio? You do not love me as your sister? You do not feel gratitude towards Lucille, who so much pities your misfortune, and

---

who takes such lively interest in all that concerns you? Fie, Florio, fie! I did not think you could be so ungrateful.

[FLORIO *answers by the most expressive pantomime that it is not grati-tude, but love, the most passionate, he feels for* LUCILLE. *Music.*]
Don't talk to me of love, but mind your work.

[FLORIO, *attentive to the last wish of* LUCILLE, *runs to the other win-dow, jumps on the balustrade, and begins to decorate it, like the first, when he loses his balance and is near falling, but is saved by* LUCILLE, *who gives a loud shriek. While* LUCILLE *is supporting* FLORIO, *their faces are quite close to each other, and* FLORIO *snatches a kiss.* LUCILLE *immediately disengages herself and retires a short distance with a pouting air, wiping her cheek with her apron.*]
That is very wrong, Florio, indeed! I don't like it.

[FLORIO *follows and sues for pardon. Music.*]
No, sir, I will not forgive you, ever. [FLORIO *kneels.*] No, sir, I won't. I am very angry, very angry indeed! To dare to rob me of a kiss.

[FLORIO *assures her that he is in despair for having displeased her, and that he is ready to return the kiss he has stolen. Music.*]
Restore the kiss you have stolen! A likely matter!

[FLORIO *protests he could put it back in the same place. Music.*]
You could put it back in the same place! That I defy you.

[FLORIO *insists that he could. Music.*]
Well, now, just for curiosity, let's see how you could manage that.

[FLORIO *approaches her with much timidity and kisses her again. Music.*]
I declare he has hit it. The same place exactly.

[*Enter* BLAISE, *in a coat of mail, a breastplate, a helmet with plumes, his visor down, and a truncheon.*]
BLAISE. Caitiffs! Desist.

LUCILLE (*runs away and screams*). Oh, Lord! What's that?

BLAISE. King Pepping. (*Lifts up his visor when* FLORIO *catches hold of him.*) Why, don't you know me? I'm Blaise.

LUCILLE. No . . . yes . . . why, it is that fool, Blaise, sure enough. And how came you trussed up in that fashion?

BLAISE. Seneschal sent I to the armory. All the headpieces, and breast-platters, and jeon pairs of breeches to be stuck up here for a merry-making. Ecod, it puzzled I, at first, how to put 'em on. I run my left leg into King Pepping's right arm, and rammed my head so tight down a field marshal's stomach, it stripped the skin off my ears to get 'em out again. Here do come t'other lads. Somehow they weren't so awkward-like at it as I was.

[PEASANTS *enter with pieces of armor, which* LUCILLE *makes them arrange about the room. Music.*]
LUCILLE (*instructing the peasants*). There now, one here, another there. Well done! That's mighty tasty. Come, Florio, let's you and I go and ask grandmother what's next to be done.

[*Music. Exeunt* FLORIO *and peasants.*]

BLAISE (*detaining* LUCILLE). Stay, miss, stay a bit. Now, just tell me if it bean't a burning shame for a pretty girl like you to look so sweet upon Dumby there, when there's such a nice young fellow as I stands at your elbow?

LUCILLE. You!

BLAISE. Yes. I have all my senses about me, and that's more nor he can say for himself.

LUCILLE. But he has common sense, and that's more than you can say for yourself.

BLAISE. There now! That's the way you be always snubbing a body.

LUCILLE. 'Tis your own fault. Why don't you leave me alone? I have told you a thousand times, I love Florio, because he is unfortunate, because my grandmother loves him—because everybody loves him—because, poor fellow, he has nothing in the world, and I have nothing either.

BLAISE. Put nought and nought together, and what does that make?

LUCILLE. Why, something, perhaps. In six years hence, what with industry and good managing, we may have saved up a little money. Then I shall be twenty-two and Florio twenty-five, and that's a nice age for us both to be married, you know.

BLAISE. Yes, Dumby will make a right proper husband for you, I do take it.

LUCILLE. You take it so, do you?

BLAISE. Yes, I do take it.

LUCILLE. Then take that along with it. (*Gives him a sound box on the ear.*) And never speak to me again, you ugly monkey, you!

BLAISE. Dang her little fistesses. But here be Captain Aubri coming. He be the Seneschal's favorite, and your grandmother's favorite, too, and—

LUCILLE. Yes, he's everybody's favorite in this place.

BLAISE. Well, then, I have a great mind to tell he of you, that's what I have.

[*Enter* AUBRI.]

AUBRI. Ah! My pretty Lucille, where is the Seneschal?

LUCILLE. Not here, captain. But if you'll have the goodness to wait a little bit, he'll not be long, I dare say.

BLAISE (*mimicking her*). "He'll not be long, I dare say." She be soft now as mother's milk. Who'd think the little toad could hit so plaguey hard?

AUBRI. Why, Blaise, Lucille! My pretty girl, you were quarreling when I came in.

BLAISE. Noa, captain, noa. She was only just pummacking me a little bit.

AUBRI. Why, one would think you had both been married for a year at least.

LUCILLE. I married to him! I'm sure, I'd rather . . . yes, I'd rather never be married.

BLAISE. Aye, that be always the way. Now, sir, be that treating I like a
christian? (AUBRI *smiles.*) By the by, captain, talking of christians,
how do your dog do? This is the first time I ever see'd you without
him. He do ne'er pop his snout in the village, but folks do say, "There
be Captain Aubri coming."

AUBRI. I have just let him range about the forest for a time. He'll pick
up something to eat there, I warrant.

BLAISE. I be glad he do pick up there, 'cause most days he do pick it
off my plate. Sartain your dog Dragon be a beast of uncommon satigasity.

LUCILLE. That be more than you are, though you do both dine off the
same plate.

[Military band heard at a distance.]

AUBRI. Hark! My regiment is arrived. Now, then, to put on my sword
and belt, and present myself to my commander.

LUCILLE. The soldiers coming in! Oh, captain! Captain! Do take me
with you, to see them march into the village.

AUBRI. Allons, then, my little Lucille. *(Exeunt, arm in arm.)*

BLAISE. To see the soldiers! Ah, she be true woman, fond of all sorts,
silent and noisy. Dang me if I do know which she'd follow soonest, the
dumb or the drum, for my part.

*[Exit. To a grand military march, the regiment of guards is seen to defile
down the mountains. They come forward, preceded by peasants, male
and female, with streamers. GERTRUDE, LUCILLE, BLAISE, and
FLORIO mix with the group. When the guards are all drawn up by
MACAIRE and LANDRY, the SENESCHAL enters with Colonel
GONTRAM.]*

SENESCHAL. Colonel Gontram, I esteem it the most honorable and
agreeable part of my office to receive and welcome, in the name of the
whole country, an officer the fame of whose exploits has been borne
even to the extremities of the empire.

GONTRAM. For my brave companions in arms, I thank you, Mr.
Seneschal. Your flattering tribute of praise is theirs, and I hasten to
restore it. To the general may belong the merit of the plan, but the
soldiers' is the hard task of its execution. Let them then share the full
measure of glory whose valor has insured the success.

*[Loud flourish of drums and trumpets. Branches of palm are raised,
which form an avenue for the tables, which are arranged at the bottom
of the stage—GERTRUDE, LUCILLE, FLORIO, etc., busy in preparing
them. Music.]*

BLAISE. There! Now, what does your generalship think of that? All
my doings.

GERTRUDE. Hold your fool's tongue, do. *(She stops his mouth and
puts him out.)*

[Enter AUBRI.]

GONTRAM. Ha! My dear Aubri!

MACAIRE *(aside, and spitefully to LANDRY).* His dear Aubri!

GONTRAM (*to* AUBRI). Has your mission proved favorable?

AUBRI. More so than I dared to hope, my colonel. Admitted to an audience, I presented to the king the colors our regiment took from the enemy. His Majesty, having read your letter, addressed me in these obliging terms: "Aubri, we are satisfied with the account Colonel Gontram gives of your valor. We nominate you captain of the company now vacant, and give our consent to your marriage with his daughter."

MACAIRE (*low to* LANDRY). Landry, did you hear? Captain of a company, and husband to Clotilde!

LANDRY. Too well I heard.

GONTRAM. I suppose you did not long delay carrying this pleasing intelligence to your good mother, and to my daughter, Clotilde.

AUBRI. Profiting by your permission to join you here, I flew to offer to my lovely Clotilde the homage of a heart whose love was sanctioned by the sovereign and approved by her father, and before my departure from Paris I had the happiness of passing two days with my mother.

GONTRAM. I congratulate you, my dear friend, in having made such good use of your absence, and I am certain there is not one of your comrades who is not pleased with your good fortune.

LANDRY. Certainly. (*aside to* MACAIRE) Why don't you speak?

MACAIRE (*with suppressed jealousy*). You interpret well our sentiments, Colonel. We know that the reward granted by the king to an individual in the regiment is an honor done to us all. Perhaps, however, we may each be allowed to feel some portion of regret that he himself was not the fortunate person.

[*The* SENESCHAL *approaches.*]

SENESCHAL. Will Colonel Gontram and his brave companions deign to partake of our rural cheer?

GONTRAM. Willingly.

[*The trumpets sound, and the whole party disperse themselves, the officers at a circular table in front, the soldiers at the back. Music.*]

BALLET

[*After the ballet the whole party rise from table.*]

SENESCHAL. Will Colonel Gontram permit me to show him the apartments which are prepared for him?

GONTRAM. I am ready to attend you. But before I seek repose, some confidential person must bear this letter to the governor at Laigny. It is of the utmost importance and requires an immediate answer.

MACAIRE (*comes forward*). Colonel, I am at your service.

GONTRAM. No, Macaire, you must be fatigued with your long march. It is fair that Aubri, who has rested while he waited for us, should have the preference.

MACAIRE (*aside to* LANDRY). The preference! How that cursed word torments me!

AUBRI. Colonel, I was about to observe the same. *(Taking the letter.)* Tomorrow, at your hour of rising, I will bring you an answer.

[Drum rolls, a march. Exeunt all but MACAIRE, LANDRY, AUBRI, and GERTRUDE.]

GERTRUDE *(advances)*. Gentlemen—Lieutenants Macaire and Landry, I hear you called—your beds are prepared at my house. Captain Aubri will show you the way.

[MACAIRE and LANDRY retire up.]

AUBRI. No, dame, I shall not be your lodger for tonight. I have business at Laigny.

GERTRUDE. What? Pass through our forest of Bondy so late! St. Denis forbid! Why, there's hardly a week but we hear of some horrid murder.

AUBRI. Fear not! My dog, Dragon, will be my companion.

GERTRUDE. He might be of some service to warn you of danger, but Dragon is not strong enough to defend you from assassins.

AUBRI. Such fears affright not a soldier.

GERTRUDE. Well, heaven protect thee! You soldiers will have your own way. Gentlemen, shall I show you my house?

MACAIRE. We will follow you anon, dame.

GERTRUDE. You'll easily find it, it's the only inn in the place. And such accommodation! But I'm not given to boasting, so I'll say no more till you come. Farewell, Captain Aubri. I wish you was safe back again with all my heart.

AUBRI. Never fear. Goodnight, dame. I shall take an early breakfast with you.

[Exit Dame GERTRUDE.]

Farewell comrades, till we meet again.

MACAIRE *(stops him)*. Aubri, ere we part, I must have some discourse with you. Before you came into the regiment, I was happy. I was honored. Happy in the possession of the confidence of my colonel, I looked forward to a marriage with his daughter, and the expectation of the next vacant company. You have blasted all my hopes, supplanted me in my love and my ambition. My hate, therefore, my most deadly hate, is yours.

AUBRI. I have long seen with regret, Macaire, that the most unjust suspicions have excited your animosity against me, and I have carefully refrained from provoking a temper naturally violent. I cannot but pity you.

MACAIRE. Pity me! Heavens! Do I live to be an object of pity to Aubri?

AUBRI. He must ever be an object of pity who is a prey to his unruly passions.

MACAIRE. Spare morality, and answer me at once. Will you give up your pretensions to Clotilde and resign your commission in this regiment?

AUBRI. When did you ever know me guilty of a base and dishonorable action? Give up a distinction conferred upon me by my sovereign? Resign the hand of Clotilde, the stimulus to all my actions, the sweet reward of all my labors? Never but with life.

MACAIRE. With life then defend them. Will you accept my challenge?

AUBRI. My courage is as well known as my abhorrence of dueling.

MACAIRE. You have your choice.

LANDRY. Why should two valuable lives be sacrificed? Surely one should suffice. You are both so skilled in arms that to have the first fire is to have the other's life at command. Let fortune, then, the soldier's fate, decide in his favor, who throws the highest.

MACAIRE. I consent.

AUBRI. I cannot turn assassin, or impiously throw away that life which belongs not to me.

LANDRY. If you agree not to these conditions, Captain Aubri, your courage must be suspected.

AUBRI. He who dares suspect shall have sufficient proofs.

MACAIRE. *I* dare! Give *me* your proofs.

AUBRI. Thus urged, the laws of honor must be obeyed.

LANDRY. You consent, then?

AUBRI. I do.

LANDRY. The lot shall then be Macaire's.

MACAIRE. Soon we will return with the means of vengeance. Till then, farewell.

[Exeunt MACAIRE and LANDRY.]

AUBRI *(alone).* To what a dreadful extremity am I reduced! Renounce the dearest object of my wishes, at the moment I have attained them, or commit an act my soul abhors! Become a duelist! Yet should I refuse, to have my fair name disgraced! To be branded as a coward! How shall I decide?

[Enter LUCILLE.]

LUCILLE. Oh, Captain Aubri, I'm so glad I've found you! My grandmother is so uneasy at your passing the forest with no arms but your saber, and no companion but your dog, poor Dragon, that she has sent your pistols. Not by me, but by Florio, for I could not touch them for the world.

AUBRI. Thanks, my pretty Lucille. Wear this ring for my sake.

LUCILLE. That I will, but there is no occasion for a keepsake to make me remember Captain Aubri. Here is Florio with the pistols. So goodnight, and a safe return. *(Exit LUCILLE.)*

[FLORIO enters and gives the pistols to AUBRI. Music.]

AUBRI. The kindness of these peasants quite overpowers me. *(To*
LUCILLE.*)* Goodnight. *(To* FLORIO.*)* Florio, you appear faithful and discreet. Can I entrust you with a commission?

[Music. FLORIO signifies that he would do anything for him.]

The journey I am about to take may be longer than I expect. Should I not return by tomorrow morning at eight o'clock, will you promise to bear this purse and pocket book to my mother? You know the street where she lives.

[*Music.* FLORIO *expresses surprise, but promises to obey his orders.*]
And take these pieces of gold for yourself.
[FLORIO *refuses.*]
Nay, take them. Aubri requests you will.
[FLORIO *takes them. Aside.*]
It may be his last request. They are here. (*To* FLORIO.) Florio, good-night. Remember.
[*Exit* FLORIO. *Music.* MACAIRE *and* LANDRY *enter.* LANDRY *places a table in the center.*]
MACAIRE. There is a pistol, well loaded. (*Putting it on the table.*) Landry is our mutual friend.
LANDRY. And there is a dice-box. Now, whoever throws the highest is to have the first fire, at eight paces. Macaire, I'll throw for you. (*Aside.*) I'm sure of my throw. (*He throws twelve.*) Twelve! (*Showing the dice.*) That's an unlucky throw for you, Captain Aubri. Here, Macaire. (*Giving him the pistol from the table.*)
MACAIRE. Not yet. 'Tis Captain Aubri's turn.
LANDRY. He has no great chance. (*He changes the dice.* AUBRI *throws twelve.*) Twelve! 'Tis wonderful! We must begin again. (*He is about to throw.*)
MACAIRE (*snatches the box*). Let me throw.
LANDRY (*aside*). Imprudent man! He has got the wrong dice. (MACAIRE *throws ten.*) Ten! Come, not so bad. (AUBRI *throws eleven.*) Eleven! (*Aside.*) Nay, then, Macaire is lost! His own rashness has destroyed him.
MACAIRE (*gives the pistol to* AUBRI). My life is in your hands. I am ready to follow you.
AUBRI. Not a step! Here, on this spot, will I take my revenge.
[MACAIRE *places himself to receive the fire of* AUBRI, *who seems to take aim at him.*]
MACAIRE. I am ready. Take your ground.
AUBRI. Now, Macaire, 'tis thus that Aubri is revenged. (*Turning suddenly, he fires the pistol through the window.*) Comrade! Comrade! I had the courage to expose my own life, but not to take yours. Henceforth let us be friends.
MACAIRE (*gloomy, aside*). Again! In every way my conqueror!
VOICES (*calling without*). Follow! Follow!
LANDRY. Ah! The report of the pistol has alarmed the village. The colonel is here. What excuse can be found?
AUBRI. I will answer for all.
[*Enter the* SENESCHAL, *Colonel* GONTRAM, GERTRUDE, LUCILLE, *and* FLORIO, *etc. Music.*]
GONTRAM. What means this tumult?
AUBRI. I am in fault, my colonel. Dame Gertrude, in her careful attention to my safety, sent me my pistols to guard me through the forest. Thinking that the loading might be damp, I discharged this through the

casement, and humbly crave your pardon for my disturbance.

SENESCHAL. I am glad it is nothing worse. I am often awakened by the noise of firearms in the forest which do not end so peaceably.

GONTRAM. Aubri, again farewell. Tomorrow morning I shall expect you. Let the watch be set.

AUBRI. Tomorrow, colonel, at an early hour.

MACAIRE *(aside)*. That morrow you shall never see.

[They separate according to their different quarters, MACAIRE threatening AUBRI as MACAIRE passes through arch.]

Curtain

ACT II

Scene: the portico of the inn, supported by rustic pillars. On the left is the door and two windows; the windows are on the first and second wings, the door is on the third. Farther on the same side is the stable. On the right is a staircase which leads to the chamber of LUCILLE, under which FLORIO is discovered asleep. At the back is seen a yard with a palisade, the forest in the distance. A lamp is suspended from the roof. The entrance to the yard is supposed to be at the back to the right.

The clock strikes four. The dog, Dragon, is heard to bark at the back for some time. At length he comes on and scratches at the door of the inn. Finding it not open, he tries to get in by putting his paws upon the latch. At last he jumps up and seizes the handle of the bell, and keeps pulling and ringing till Dame GERTRUDE opens the window.

GERTRUDE. Hey-day! Who is this ringing so early in the morning? *(The dog barks.)* What, Dragon, is it you? And all alone! Oh, heaven defend us! Something dreadful has happened to your master, Captain Aubri. I'll come down and open the door. *(She comes out with a lantern. Dragon barks and pulls her by the gown, as if to invite her to follow him.)* He seems to try to draw me from the house. Ah, poor Captain Aubri, some accident has surely befallen him. He may be close to the house, may-hap. *(The dog barks.)* Well, Dragon, I will follow you. If I find him hurt, I can return for assistance. *(She places the lantern on the stage while she shuts the door. Dragon takes it up in his mouth and runs off with it, looking behind to invite her to follow him.)* Well, Dragon, I'm coming! I'm coming!

[Exeunt. Apposite music at intervals. Enter MACAIRE and LANDRY by an opening which they make by removing some of the paling, and which they replace. LANDRY puts a spade which he has brought with him against the paling. Music agitated.]

LANDRY. There. The spade is replaced on the spot whence we took it.

MACAIRE *(wild and distracted)*. Did no one perceive us? Are you sure? No one?

LANDRY (this sangfroid contrasted with the agitation of MACAIRE). The owl or the raven might have looked on. What other witness could have been abroad such a night as this?

MACAIRE. Has every precaution been taken for concealment?

LANDRY. The thicket and the earth are sufficient concealment of the body, and we went out and returned without a soul's perceiving us.

MACAIRE. Hush! Landry, hush!

LANDRY. What now?

MACAIRE. Did you hear no footsteps?

LANDRY. All silent as the grave.

MACAIRE. I thought we were pursued.

LANDRY. Vain terrors!

MACAIRE. Oh, they are too real! First and dreadful terrors of conscious guilt.

LANDRY. Let us retire to rest.

MACAIRE. To rest! Rest for me! Ha, no, no!

LANDRY. Have you not rid yourself of a hateful object? One who, like your evil genius, seemed to mar all your happiness?

MACAIRE. True. Yet had I a right to take his life?

LANDRY. Yes, the right of hatred and thy interest. But useless now are these reflections. Let us retire. We have already stayed too long. (Seeing FLORIO.) Some one lies there.

MACAIRE (all agitation). How! Where!

LANDRY. Beneath that staircase.

MACAIRE. Wh—at? Who?

LANDRY (approaches the staircase). 'Tis a boy asleep.

MACAIRE (a little reassured). Or feigns to sleep.

LANDRY. If I thought that . . . (puts his hand on his dagger).

MACAIRE. Another murder! Oh, no, no. (Restraining LANDRY.) Landry, you shall not! No more, I conjure thee! Come, let us go in! Ah, when again will these eyes be closed in peaceful rest?

[Music. LANDRY goes to FLORIO to see if he is really asleep, and signifies to MACAIRE that it would be more prudent to put him out of the way, and draws his dagger. MACAIRE holds his arm and forces him into the chamber by a window on the ground floor, which they had left open. BLAISE is heard in the stable speaking to the horses.]

BLAISE. So ho, there, Smiter! Whoy ho, Captain! (He enters with a quarter-sieve in his hand.) Dang the horses! How they do whinney for their breakfast. They do know what it be o'clock, just like I, and they do always ha' their corn at 4 o'clock i' th' morning. (He fills a small basket at the corn bin with the quarter measure, singing while he does it:)

> Oh, Bondy's forest's dark with leaves.
> Oh, Bondy's forest's full of thieves!
> They hold your bridle, take your cash,
> And then they give your throat a gash.
> Ira lara la (et cetera)!
> All in the forest of Bondy!

LUCILLE *(looking out at the casement)*. Aren't you ashamed, Blaise, to be making such a noise? Why, 'tis but four o'clock, and you'll wake every guest in the house.

BLAISE. Wake 'em! How can that be, foolish? It be what I sings every night to put myself to sleep. Ira lara la *(singing the burthen)*.

LUCILLE. Hush, I tell you! Remember who's here—officers, gentle-folks, that belong to no less than the king!

BLAISE. Hee, hee! It bean't about them, missy, that you be in such a fantigue. It be for your own dear dumby, young Mr. Mumchance, who be asnooring there under the staircase, to be nearer your chamber.

LUCILLE. Well, suppose he is. What then?

BLAISE. What then! Why, he might sleep in the stable, as I do. I gave him an invitation, for stable bean't a single bedded room. There be snug lodging for single men under every manger. But no, he mun quarter here, forsooth. As house be full of military, Mr. Dumby be your advanced guard, I do suppose.

LUCILLE. Well, and suppose that too. It is no reason why you should keep plaguing him.

BLAISE. I don't plague 'un, not I. I do sing because I ha' got it in my natur, just like a nightingirl. *(Sings.)*

> A duke did through the forest push,
> A robber jumped out of a bush;
> Your money quick, lord duke, he said,
> Or, please your grace, I'll shoot you dead.
>   Ira lara la *(et cetera)!*
> All in the forest of Bondy.

(He goes into the stable with the corn.)

LUCILLE *(coming out of the chamber)*. He does it on purpose to spite me. But I'll be quits with you, Mr. Grumps. I'll teach you to be a spy upon people, that's what I will. *(She hides behind the pillars on seeing BLAISE.)*

BLAISE. The poor beastesses be munching away for dear life! Why, Louis! I say, odd rot it, awake man! Awake! It be peep o' day, so I'll put out the lamp. *(He lets down the lamp, which is fastened by a string cord to the roof on a pulley.)* Miss be gone in again. She do fancy I can see nought, but I can see pretty plain what she be ater. *(Blows out lamp.)* Yes, yes, I can see clear enow how she ha' made up her mind. *(He puts the lamp near the staircase.)*

[LUCILLE *appears at the back and seems to be watching for some opportunity to play him a trick.*]

Dumby do sleep plaguey sound. I can't rouse 'un yet, though I ha' tried hard. It's my notion he don't care much for miss ater all, else he'd never snore. Your true lovers, I ha' heard, do never snore. I'll ha' tother touch at him. *(Going nearer to FLORIO and increasing his voice.)*

Fat Friar John the forest paced;
A cord was tied about his waist.

[While BLAISE *is singing,* LUCILLE *comes gently behind and hooks the cord, which has suspended the lamp, to his girdle. She then beckons LOUIS from the stable, and they pull the cord with all their force, and BLAISE is taken off his legs.]*

BLAISE *(crying out violently).* Murder! Help! Help! Murder!

*[*FLORIO, *who is awakened by the noise, comes up to him and releases him.* MACAIRE *rushes in, followed by* LANDRY. *Music.]*

MACAIRE *(his looks distracted).* Who calls me? What would you?

LANDRY. Silence, silence, my friend!

BLAISE. Lawk, sir, I do want nought of you, not I. But, when folks will hang up in the air, I must bawl out.

LUCILLE. It was only a little trick of mine, sir. I am very sorry it has disturbed you.

BLAISE. A trick of yours, was it? Now, I'll tell your grandmother of you, that's what I will. She shall give it you for hanging up I by the hips, for all the world like a haunch of venison.

LUCILLE. Well, go and tell, do now. And I'll go with you, and so shall Florio. So, come along.

BLAISE. Ah! Do take Dumby now with you, to bear false witness. But he can't speak nought against I, that be one comfort.

[Exit LUCILLE, FLORIO, *and* BLAISE.*]*

LANDRY. It was fortunate for us that we had not to encounter more penetration. You would have discovered all. What could you be thinking of?

MACAIRE. Exhausted by fatigue, I had fallen into a restless slumber. The most horrible dreams tormented me. I saw my victim, heard his groans and his last heart-rending words. "Can you murder me, Macaire?" Tortured by remorse, I thought I was flying through the forest, when I was awakened by the dreadful cry of "Murder!" Without knowing what I did, I rushed, as I thought, to meet my accuser.

[Dame GERTRUDE *without.]*

GERTRUDE. Holloo! Blaise! Florio! Lucille!

MACAIRE *(violently agitated).* Hark! What noise is that? Someone called from without!

GERTRUDE *(without).* Quick! Rise! Get up!

MACAIRE. We are discovered!

LANDRY. 'Tis impossible!

[They exeunt into chamber. Enter Dame GERTRUDE, *speaking as she enters.]*

GERTRUDE. Blaise! Florio! William! Rise! Rise!

*[*LUCILLE, BLAISE, FLORIO, *and six other domestics come out of the inn, the* SENESCHAL *and Colonel* GONTRAM *from their apartments,*

MACAIRE *and* LANDRY *from theirs. The* SENESCHAL *and* COLO-
NEL *are attended by servants.]*

GERTRUDE. Oh, run, run to the entrance of the forest! There you will
find the body of the unfortunate Captain Aubri! The moaning of his
dog will guide you to the spot.

MACAIRE *(aside to* LANDRY). What, did you not dispose of the dog?

LANDRY. I thought I had done it effectually.

SENESCHAL *(to servants).* Come, follow!

[Exit with BLAISE, FLORIO, LUCILLE, *and two servants and four
peasants.]*

LANDRY *(aside to* MACAIRE). Now, Macaire, be firm, or we are lost.
(Aloud, with a confident manner and apparent solicitude.) How, Dame
Gertrude, what said you? Our companion Aubri!

GERTRUDE. Has fallen by the hand of an assassin.

GONTRAM. How came you to the knowledge of this dreadful calamity?

GERTRUDE. I will tell you, Colonel. I'll tell you, if my fright will permit. I had risen very early to make preparations—it was just four
o'clock—when I heard a noise at the door. The bell rang violently. I
opened the casement, looked out, and saw Captain Aubri's dog, Dragon.
On my opening the door, he barked and drew me by the gown, as if he
meant to say his master was in danger. Trembling and astonished, I followed him to the entrance of the forest, where he stopped, and, plung-
ing into a thicket, he began to scratch the earth, which had been freshly
turned up. He never rested till he had exposed to my view—oh, piteous
sight!—the body of his murdered master!

GONTRAM. Dear unfortunate Aubri! I was then the innocent cause of
your death. Let us now avenge it, comrades! Let us search the forest.
The murderer shall not escape. *(Takes the hand of* MACAIRE.) To
you, Macaire, to you in particular I entrust this charge. I know you
loved not Aubri in his life, but I see grief depicted on your countenance
at his death.

MACAIRE *(confused).* You cannot imagine—

GONTRAM. Yes, I can guess what passes in your mind. You now feel
the injustices of your conduct towards that youth. This does you
honor, Macaire.

MACAIRE *(still confused).* Oh, Colonel!

GONTRAM. Your own feelings will prompt you to seek and bring to
condign punishment the author of this horrid murder.

LANDRY *(to* GERTRUDE). But where is the faithful and attached
companion of our lamented Aubri?

GERTRUDE. Lying upon the body of his master. Neither by caresses
nor menaces could he be induced to quit it.

[Enter BLAISE, *flurried and out of breath.]*

BLAISE. Well, if it bean't the most surprisingest, most unaccountablest!
Who would ha' thought that . . .

GERTRUDE. Speak! Thought what?

BLAISE. Thought that—I'm quite out of breath—oh, missus!

GERTRUDE. What has happened?

BLAISE. E'en a'most an impossibility. They ha' gotten wicked wretch as ha' swassinated Mister Aubri.

GERTRUDE. What, in custody?

BLAISE. Yes, nabbed. Taken up.

GERTRUDE. So much the better.

LANDRY (aside to MACAIRE). For us it is.

BLAISE. They ha' nabbed 'un, that be a sure thing, for they ha' found both cash and pocketbook as belonged to the dead body, on parson o' barbarous malefactor.

GERTRUDE. How?

BLAISE. How? Why, all through Dragon. Dang me if that 'ere dog bean't a magicianer.

GERTRUDE. Did the poor, faithful dog then . . .

BLAISE. Lord love you! He be as sensible . . . aye, as sensible as I. We had scarce gotten to the thicket where 'a lay, then he began to sniff, sniff, sniff at murderer's pocket, and by and by 'a pops snout right into 't.

GERTRUDE. Well?

BLAISE. Says Seneschal, who be almost as deep as Dragon hissel, says he, sarch that 'ere young fellow, when ecod, out comed poor Mr. Aubri's purse and pocket book. Now that, as Seneschal did say, was strong proof consumptive.

GONTRAM. 'Tis most extraordinary.

GERTRUDE. And who is this wretch? Do you know him?

BLAISE. Know 'un! Would be odd if I didn't. Why, it be Dumby.

GERTRUDE. Florio!

BLAISE. Yes, yours and Miss Lucille's darling.

GERTRUDE. It can't be. You must be out of your senses to say so.

MACAIRE (apart to LANDRY). This mistake is most fortunate.

GERTRUDE (to GONTRAM). Oh, sir, it is impossible! Florio is a poor orphan, deprived of speech. I have sheltered him, brought him up in innocence—I have, poor boy! Everybody that knows him, pities him, loves him, and . . .

BLAISE. What I do tell thee be true, though, and here Seneschal do come wi' 'un. How innocent he do look i' the face! Oh, there be no trusting to the phizmahogony. (Retires up, talking with GERTRUDE.)

LANDRY (apart to MACAIRE). Let us go away as soon as possible.

MACAIRE. Colonel, our presence here is useless. We hasten to execute your orders.

GONTRAM. Nay, now your search is unnecessary. The culprit is in custody.

MACAIRE. Let me hope, then, you will honor me with the dispatches entrusted to the unhappy Aubri.

GONTRAM. True, to the governor at Laigny. In this confusion they had escaped me. Wait in my apartment, and I will bring you your instructions.

[*Exeunt* MACAIRE *and* LANDRY. *Music. The* SENESCHAL *enters with* FLORIO, LUCILLE, *guards, peasants, etc.*]

LUCILLE (*in great distress*). Oh, Seneschal! Grandmother! Good gentle folks! Pray, do not put my poor dear Florio in prison.

GONTRAM. Who has a right to stay the cause of justice? The judge must be as impartial as the law of which he is the organ.

GERTRUDE. That youth, Mr. Seneschal, is innocent.

SENESCHAL. I wish he may prove so.

GERTRUDE. With my life I'll answer for it.

LUCILLE. See how he weeps. (FLORIO *in tears.*) My dear Florio, do not take on so! They cannot be so wicked as to harm you.

SENESCHAL. Can he write?

GERTRUDE. No, Mr. Seneschal.

SENESCHAL (*to* LUCILLE). Then you, who seem so familiar with his language, you must interpret from his actions the answers I cannot understand.

[*Music.* FLORIO *throws himself on his knees to the* SENESCHAL *and weeps.*]

SENESCHAL. Your tears are interesting. Your age, your misfortune, and the seeming goodness of your life, till now, plead strongly in your favor. But the heavy charge now brought against you can only be refuted by your innocence.

[FLORIO *calls heaven to witness his innocence. Music.*]

LUCILLE. He relies on providence and the equity of his judge for his preservation.

SENESCHAL. Florio, have you so soon forgotten the instructions of your youth, and the virtuous examples around you, as to take away the life of a fellow creature?

(*Music.* FLORIO, *in despair, shrinks with horror at the idea, and throws himself into the arms of* LUCILLE.]

LUCILLE. He says his soul shrinks with horror at such a thought.

SENESCHAL. Is there therefore any proof that this purse and pocket-book belonged to Captain Aubri?

GONTRAM. There is. The one was the work of my daughter, the other a present from me.

SENESCHAL. That is strong proof indeed!

GERTRUDE. Florio, do you acknowledge that these belonged to Captain Aubri? (FLORIO *assents.*) Unhappy boy! He is his own accuser!

SENESCHAL. How came they in your possession?

[FLORIO *endeavors to explain that* AUBRI *gave them to him to carry to Paris. Music.*]

LUCILLE. He says that they were given to him by Captain Aubri to carry to . . .

SENESCHAL. Whither?

[*Music.* FLORIO *points to the side of Paris.*]

LUCILLE. To Paris.

SENESCHAL. And for whom?

[FLORIO *makes every effort to explain but is unable.]*
  Was it for a friend?

[FLORIO *shakes his head.]*

GONTRAM. For my daughter, perhaps?

[FLORIO *again shakes his head.]*

LUCILLE. Was it for his mother?

[FLORIO *signifies that it was.]*

GONTRAM. For his mother! That is most improbable! Aubri had
  passed two days with his mother in this very week. And, far from re-
  ceiving pecuniary aid from her son, she, on the contrary, added to his
  income. Besides, why deprive himself of his pocketbook? Every circumstance but adds proof—alas! too positive—that Florio is the perpe-
  trator of this most horrid deed.

SENESCHAL. How did you reenter the inn?

[FLORIO *assures him he never went out. Music.]*

LUCILLE. He assures you that he never went out.

SENESCHAL. Where does he, in general, sleep?

GERTRUDE. In a room upstairs. But last night I was obliged to remove
  him for the accommodation of my customers.

SENESCHAL. Where did he lie last night?

GERTRUDE. In the stable with Blaise.

BLAISE. I axes a thousand pardons, missus, for gainsaying you. It be
  true, he was to ha' slept in that stable, and I had put two bundles of
  nice clean straw under manger for 'un, but he did not like it and chuse
  to turn in there all alone underneath the staircase.

GONTRAM. This is most material, Mr. Seneschal. Why should he
  choose that uncomfortable situation, but for the facility it affords of
  going out and coming in without noise, by passing over that paling?

LUCILLE. No indeed, Mr. Seneschal, that was not his motive. If I must
  speak the truth, it was out of love for me that he lay there. He was so
  happy to watch over me and be my guard! Ah, my poor, dear Florio!
  Who could have thought that your love for me would have put your life
  in danger?

GERTRUDE. He is innocent. Dame Gertrude pledges herself he is innocent. Appearances are against him, but appearances are often deceitful.
  The principles of honesty and religion I have taught him since his childhood could not in any instant be destroyed. No, the first crime a youth
  commits is never murder. Look at his calm and open countenance. Is
  that like guilt? Let full time be granted, I'll to the village and seek
  some clue to find the real assassin! Courage, my dear child. Heaven
  will never abandon the innocent. *(Music. She rushes out. All go up
  the stage to look at Dame* GERTRUDE *as she goes out.)*

GONTRAM *(perceiving the spade against the paling).* Whose spade is this?

[*Music.* FLORIO *signifies that it is his.]*

SENESCHAL. Did you place it here?

[*Music.* FLORIO *assents.*]

LUCILLE. He did.

GONTRAM. This is the strongest evidence of all. The spade is his. He placed it here, he owns it. Look, Mr. Seneschal. See? It is covered with fresh earth.

[*All the spectators come forward to look at it, and express conviction. Music.*]

SENESCHAL. Florio, what answer can you make to that?

[FLORIO *appears confounded.*]

GONTRAM. Mr. Seneschal, what need there further proof? Either pass judgment on this wretched youth, or at the foot of the throne I will seek that justice you refuse.

SENESCHAL. Florio, every circumstance conspires to convince of your guilt. Your crime is but too evident. Let him be conducted to the court. There before the assembled people I must pronounce the dreadful sentence of the law!

[*All in the utmost consternation.* LUCILLE *utters a piercing cry.* FLORIO, *with his hands crossed upon his breast and his eyes raised to heaven, seems to meet his fate with resignation. The soldiers advance to bear him away;* LUCILLE *throws herself on her knees to prevent them. The spectators, the* COLONEL, *and the* SENESCHAL *appear much affected. Music agitated.*]

Curtain

ACT III

Scene I

A large hall of the inn. It is opened at the back and terminated by a balcony which projects on the outside and looks upon a garden, at the end of which is a woody eminence. This balcony extends to the whole breadth of the stage. There is a window on the left and a door on the right. LUCILLE is looking out on the balcony.

LUCILLE. Blaise returns not. I sent him to the prison to see my dear unhappy Florio, to give him all the consolation in his power. Alas! They cruelly refused to admit *me* to him. This barbarous judgment is another murder. Could my Florio, ever so kind, so gentle, become at once . . . oh, never, never! Soon they will find out his innocence, but perhaps too late. *(Weeps.)*

[BLAISE *is seen at the back. He enters crying.*]

BLAISE. Oh, miss! 'Twill soon be all over! Already I seed all from up yonder. Poor Dumby and I didn't well agree—*(sobbing)*—but now he is going to be hanged, I . . . oh! *(Roars.)*

LUCILLE. Oh, Blaise, have you then seen my poor Florio?

BLAISE *(blubbering at intervals).* Yes, miss, they let I bid 'un good-bye. I handed to 'un bottle o' wine you sent to comfort 'un. He took but one tiny sup, so I drank the rest to comfort *me*. He do send his complim . . . I do mean his long last, last love to 'ee. He do vow he be innocent. And, poor soul, 'a lifted up his two hands to clouds, and—oh! But come, miss—*(wiping his eyes)*—while there be life, there be a little hope still. Where be Seneschal?

LUCILLE. In the next room writing to the king an account of the whole affair.

BLAISE. To the king! Dang it, if the king do take it in hands, who knows? I do think now he'll say, "This here affair, my lords, be but a blindish-like business, and it be my notion, my lords, that when I come to sift the bottom on 't, things mought seem to be what they mought be, my lords. And, if 't be as how . . ." Yes, I'd lay ten to one, the king will say just so, in my very words. So, cheer up a bit, do 'ee now.

[Drum rolls. A mournful march.]

LUCILLE. What do I hear?

BLAISE *(looking out)*. Mercy on us! They be a-taking 'un to the place o' execution! They be to pass under this very balcony! What can I say to poor miss? *(To* LUCILLE.) Oh, I . . . I'll go see, miss . . . oh, dang it! I can stand it no longer. *(Exit* BLAISE.)

LUCILLE *(alone)*. The noise approaches this way. Oh, should it be him! *(Goes upon the balcony.)* 'Tis he, my Florio! My poor Florio! They are dragging him to execution.

[The procession, leading FLORIO *to execution, is seen to pass over the eminence at the back. He casts the most piteous looks toward* LUCILLE, *who faints at the sight of him. The door at the right opens with a sudden noise, and* BLAISE *and Dame* GERTRUDE *enter. Music.]*

GERTRUDE *(with violent agitation)*. Lucille! Revive! Look up! Look up!

LUCILLE *(revives)*. Is it you, grandmother? Have they killed him?

GERTRUDE. Killed him! No. I hope to save him.

LUCILLE. Do you, grandmother? Do you indeed? *(Throws herself on* GERTRUDE's *neck.)*

GERTRUDE. Is the Seneschal at home?

LUCILLE. I believe he is, grandmother.

GERTRUDE *(knocks at door)*. Mr. Seneschal! Mr. Colonel!

[Music. The SENESCHAL *and* COLONEL, *and servants, come out of chamber.]*

Give instant orders that the execution may be stopped.

SENESCHAL. On what grounds?

GERTRUDE. First, stop the execution. The unhappy culprit is on the scaffold. The information that I bring may lead to his acquittal.

SENESCHAL. Go, and from me direct . . .

LUCILLE. Oh, let me fly! But will they believe . . . *(going)*.

SENESCHAL *(to a servant)*. Do you follow her.

LUCILLE. Dearest Florio! Oh, that I may arrive in time! Stop! Stop! Oh, stop! *(Exit, followed by servant and* BLAISE.)

SENESCHAL. Now, Dame Gertrude, what information have you to give?

GERTRUDE. As Florio has been condemned by circumstances, fresh evidence may perhaps preserve him. Mr. Macaire, in going to Laigny, was obliged to pass near the cottage where lay the body of the unfortunate Aubri. His dog, Dragon, who had never quitted it for a moment, no sooner perceived him than with the most frightful howl he rushed upon Macaire. His comrades surrounded him, but in vain they opposed their resistance. Dragon, with his eye flashing fire and his mouth foaming with rage, seemed to point out the murderer and to long to revenge the death of his master.

GONTRAM. And so you think that this slight accusation . . . ?

GERTRUDE. It is not slight. Remember how Mr. Macaire hated the young Aubri. This passion . . .

SENESCHAL. Hold! Such groundless assertion is offensive to justice.

GERTRUDE. Forgive me, Mr. Seneschal, if my anxious zeal to save an orphan's life should make me speak too free. But look! See!

[MACAIRE is seen running from the eminence at the back, pursued by Dragon. The SENESCHAL and the COLONEL go up the stage with GERTRUDE. Music. MACAIRE, pale, with his hair disheveled and in the greatest disorder, enters from the right. He shuts the door with every sign of fear, then crosses the stage and goes into the apartment on the left without observing those who are at the back.]

GERTRUDE. Now with your own eyes you have seen the truth of what I told you.

SENESCHAL. It is very extraordinary.

GONTRAM. But it proves nothing but that Macaire, otherwise very brave, dares not expose himself to the fury of this animal.

GERTRUDE. Hear me to the end! You know how Dragon discovered by his scent his master's purse and pocketbook on the person of Florio. But you know not what the bystanders are ready to declare upon oath, that he afterwards fawned upon this poor Florio and repeatedly licked his hands. Now, let me ask you, would he have fawned upon the assassin of his master? Oppose these marks of kindness to the rage and fury he shows on seeing Macaire, and say who is most likely to have been the murderer.

SENESCHAL. Colonel Gontram, this evidence is strong and cannot be dismissed without further examination.

GONTRAM. Vengeance on the murderer of my friend is all that I desire. Should Macaire be guilty, let his punishment be equal to his crime. I will give instant orders for his company to be drawn up; meanwhile, do you assemble the villagers. His accusation will be public, and his defense unprepared. The secret workings of his soul will be seen upon his countenance.

SENESCHAL. They will. Your instructions shall be punctually obeyed. Dame Gertrude, follow me.

[Exeunt. MACAIRE comes out of his apartment. Music.]

MACAIRE. Did I not hear the sound of voices in this hall, and my name pronounced aloud? No person was here when I came in. I must have deceived myself. No, no, it was another phantom of my troubled brain. Am I in a frightful dream, or is it real? Has this arm, which till now was terrible only to my country's foes, been raised to murder my companion, my friend? Torn by anguish and remorse, life's a burthen! Oh, Aubri! Oh, my friend! *(He falls upon a bench quite overcome.)*

[LANDRY *is seen on the eminence. He endeavors to draw the attention of* MACAIRE, *who is too much absorbed to observe his signs.* LANDRY, *having first seen that he is not observed, draws from his belt a roll of parchment, undoes the belt and makes a packet of it, then throws them over the balcony.* MACAIRE, *roused by the noise, sees* LANDRY, *who motions him to pick up the packet, and disappears.* MACAIRE *rises, picks up the packet, and reads.]*

MACAIRE. "You shall be freed from the danger that threatens you. The animal whose sagacity was so much to be dreaded shall be disposed of." Ah! Then I breathe again! *(Reads.)* "I have given you *my* belt, which wear instead of yours that was left in the forest. I have got leave of absence and shall not require it. Be collected! And above all, heed not the scruples of your conscience, then all will go well." How easy to give such advice, how difficult to follow it. Landry is in the right. My belt wanting, that alone might have convicted me. In my terror I had forgotten it. *(Puts on the belt.)* Someone approaches. Now, Macaire, be firm! Your life depends on your conquering your feelings.

[*Enter the* SENESCHAL *and the* COLONEL, *followed by* GERTRUDE, *who stands apart.]*

SENESCHAL. Well, Lieutenant Macaire, have you recovered from your alarm?

MACAIRE. Alarm! What alarm?

SENESCHAL. Why, the alarm occasioned by . . .

MACAIRE *(with forced gaiety)*. True, true! I have, Mr. Seneschal, and trust that the valor or the honor of a soldier is not compromised by avoiding the attack of a furious animal, whose master had taught it to be gentle only to himself—as the colonel knows.

GONTRAM. I do, and am perfectly ready to think, Macaire, that what happened proceeds from that natural cause. There are some, however, who think otherwise, and upon such a trifling circumstance dare to suspect that you are no stranger to the murder of Aubri.

MACAIRE. I, my colonel! I! Who dares? I am ready to submit any proof, sir, you may require.

SENESCHAL. The execution of Florio has been respited, and the whole village demands that both you and he should be confronted.

MACAIRE. This proposal is strange, but if it be your wish, sir, I am ready.

GONTRAM. Go, Macaire. Return hither at the head of your company, and with the bold front of conscious innocence, confound the malice of your accusers.

MACAIRE. I go, my colonel. *(Aside.)* May my courage support me in this most dreadful trial! *(Exit.)*

SENESCHAL. Now, Dame Gertrude, were not your suspicions of Macaire unfounded?

GERTRUDE. Well, I say nothing, but . . .

[BLAISE, *at the threshold of the door, beckons and makes signs to* GERTRUDE.]

BLAISE. Missus! Hist! Only a couple of words!

GERTRUDE. Presently, presently.

BLAISE. Nay, it mun be directly, else 't won't do.

GERTRUDE. Well, be quick. *(Bringing him forward.)*

BLAISE *(whispering).* I ha' gotten th' murderer this time in good earnest.

GERTRUDE. Where?

BLAISE. I' my pocket.

GERTRUDE. Idiot!

BLAISE. If 't bean't himsel, it be what will find him out. His belt! Mum! Nought more nor less. Hush!

GERTRUDE. Hush indeed! No, no. Come forward and tell these gentlemen all you know directly. *(Puts BLAISE over to COLONEL.)*

BLAISE. Why, mun I though?

GERTRUDE. Yes, everything.

BLAISE. Hem! Well then, missus, you do know little Annette, blacksmith's daughter, o' our village here? She were out making a faggots i' th' forest this morning, when she came to a thicket, as mought be three foot high like.

GERTRUDE. Well?

BLAISE. Patience! Well, what should be in middle of thicket but this here belt, all smeared with blood? She makes me but three hops to skirt o' wood and fell a-bawling for her dear life. When we came up, she had th' belt in her hand. Now, you mun observe that thicket where she found un ware but twenty paces from where Mr. Aubri, poor soul, ware killed.

SENESCHAL. Indeed! Well, proceed in your story.

BLAISE. I ha' nigh done 't, sir. Well, we all began a-putting this and that together, and, says I—I ware spokesman, sir—that belt ha' been used to assassinating purpose, 'cause there be blood on 't, and, says I, belt do belong to one o' the guards as marched yesterday into our village, so, it be one o' guards who ha' done the job, so Dumby be no guard, so it can't be Dumby. So I brought th' belt here. So, when I came to missus, I said, I—oh, you do know that, so that is all.

SENESCHAL. All the guards have belts alike. We cannot then discern to which of them it belongs.

BLAISE. Axing your pardon, sir, they ha' but one belt apiece, and any blockhead that is not blind may see one o' them han't gotten his own.

GERTRUDE. Hold your tongue. *(Putting him across.)*

GONTRAM. Thy reflection is just, my friend. At length I hope to hit

---

upon a method of discovering the real assassin. Give me the belt.

BLAISE. There 'a be, and much good it may do you, sir.

[Music. Enter LUCILLE with FLORIO in haste.]

LUCILLE. But a few minutes later, and this poor sufferer would have been no more.

SENESCHAL. He is not yet acquitted, but strong circumstances have lately arisen in his favor.

[FLORIO expresses his thanks to the SENESCHAL. From the rising ground the company of guards, with MACAIRE at their head, march down and are drawn up in the hall. The COLONEL passes in review the whole company, examining their accoutrements minutely. He finds nothing wanting, and all stand unconcerned. At length he says with a solemn voice:]

GONTRAM. The murderer of Aubri is amongst you! The stain of blood upon his belt has discovered him.

[The soldiers look at each other—all but MACAIRE, who by an impulse quickly bends his head and looks with terror on his belt.]

MACAIRE *(forgetting himself).* On the belt!

GONTRAM. Macaire! Why such terror? Is there any stain of blood on you?

MACAIRE *(violently agitated).* On me, my colonel?

GONTRAM. Give me your belt!

[MACAIRE trembles so he can scarcely unclasp it.]

How! This is not yours. 'Tis Landry's. Here is his name! *(Showing it written on in the inside.)* Where is yours?

MACAIRE *(in the deepest confusion).* My belt, Colonel? I've lost it in the forest. No! Not in the forest . . .

GONTRAM *(coming closer to him and holding the belt before his eyes).* No, 'tis here! Stained with the blood of the murdered Aubri!

MACAIRE *(shudders and puts his hands before his eyes).* Aubri's blood! Oh, hide it from my sight! It calls for vengeance! I can bear it no longer. I confess my crime! That youth is innocent!

[FLORIO utters an exclamation of joy.]

I murdered Aubri in the forest of Bondy.

GONTRAM. Horrible confession! Bear him hence! And let the most ignominious death . . .

MACAIRE *(drawing a pistol).* No, this shall prevent . . . *(He is about to shoot himself when two guards wrest the pistol from him.)*

GONTRAM. Bear him to instant execution!

[Exeunt all but MACAIRE and two guards. They are leading him away when, in a frenzy of despair, he breaks from his guards, and, seeing no other way to escape, he leaps through the window. One of the guards fires his pistol after him.]

GUARD. Curse on the pistol! He has escaped unhurt!

[Reenter Colonel GONTRAM.]

GONTRAM. Now, what's the matter?

GUARD. Macaire has escaped!
GONTRAM. Escaped!
GUARD. He will reach the waterfalls.
GONTRAM. He must not! Go round by the bridge! There you may intercept his flight! Sound the alarm!
[Exeunt COLONEL and guards. Alarm bell, drums, etc.]

Scene II

Extensive view of rocks and waterfalls. Across the stream, from rock to rock, an alpine bridge. Music. MACAIRE is seen to cross it, followed by Dragon. MACAIRE then descends a sloping rock and comes on the stage.

MACAIRE. Why should I fly? 'Tis not to preserve this wretched life, but to avoid a base and ignominious death!
BLAISE (without). Holloo! Holloo!
GUARD (without). Holloo! Holloo!
MACAIRE (starts). They are here! On every side I am beset! Then for my last and desperate attempt!
[GUARD enters.]
GUARD (to MACAIRE). Wretch! Yield your forfeit life!
MACAIRE. Never will I surrender to those I have been accustomed to command!
[The GUARD rushes on MACAIRE. They struggle. MACAIRE overcomes him and exits. The dog is heard, without, and MACAIRE is seen to fly up the rocks, and appears on a high one that overhangs the waterfall. GUARD sounds his bugle, and all the hills are covered with soldiers and peasants.]
GUARD (to soldiers). Present! Fire!
[The soldiers point their muskets and are about to fire when MACAIRE leaps from the point of the rock into the stream, and the curtain drops amidst the huzzahs of the peasantry that the murderer has at length met with his merited fate.]

The End of The Forest of Bondy.

Dumas Père's *Tour de Nesle*

ALEXANDRE DUMAS
VLADIMIR VOL'KENSHTEIN

Dumas Père on *Tour de Nesle* **(from** *Mes mèmoires,* **1852–54)**

What struck me as the essence of the drama was the struggle between Buridan and Marguerite de Bourgogne, between an adventurer and a queen, the one armed with all the resources of his genius, the other with all the powers of her rank.

It goes without saying that genius was naturally destined to triumph over power.

And then, I had had an idea in my head for a long time that seemed to me highly dramatic; I wanted to try to put the following situation before the public:

A man arrested, sentenced, thrown in the depths of a dungeon, without resources or hope; a man who will be lost if his enemy has the courage not to come and rejoice in his humiliation, but rather has him poisoned, strangled, or stabbed in his corner; this man will be saved if this enemy of his yields to the desire to come and insult him for one last time; because, with speech, the sole weapon that is left him, he will so frighten his enemy that she will remove one by one the chains from his arms and the iron collar from his neck, and will open for him the door which she so carefully had closed upon him and will lead forth in triumph the man who expected that, if he ever left his living tomb at all, it would only be to mount the scaffold.

The struggle between Marguerite de Bourgogne and Buridan gave me this situation. As you can well imagine, I did not let it slip away from me. It is what has since become known as *the prison scene*.

Once that was settled, I did not worry any more about the rest of the play. I wrote Harel that I was his man for the *Tour de Nesle* and asked him to come see me so that we could arrange the terms under which this new drama would be undertaken . . . .

The day of the first performance came: it was 29 May 1832. . . . We arrived halfway through the second scene of act 1, just in time to hear Buridan's speech about the *great ladies*.

The auditorium was at the boiling point. You could sense that it would be a big success; it was in the air; everyone could feel it.

The end of the second scene had a tremendous impact. Buridan leaping out the window into the Seine, Marguerite disclosing her bleeding cheek and exclaiming: " 'See your face and then die,' did you say? Let it be as you wish . . . Look, and die!' "; all this had a thrilling and terrifying effect! And, when, after this orgy, this flight, this murder, this laughter extinguished in groans, this man hurled into the river, this lover of one night pitilessly murdered,—the nonchalant and monotonous voice of the night watchman is heard calling: "Three o'clock, and all is well; Parisians, sleep!" the audience burst into applause. . . .

Never have I seen an effect comparable to that of the prison scene, which, moreover, was marvelously played by the two actors between whom it takes place and who carry its entire weight. . . .

After the prison scene (act 3, scene 2), the rest of the play could be good or bad, without its making any difference; success was assured. . . .

Finally, there came the fifth act, which had so frightened Harel. It was divided into two scenes, the eighth, of a diabolic humor, and the ninth, which, for dramatic horror, could be compared to the second. Something about it reminded one of the ancient fatalism of Sophocles, blended with the scenic terrors of Shakespeare. Thus the success was enormous, and the name of Monsieur Frédéric Gaillardet was proclaimed amidst the applause.

Translated by Daniel Gerould

Vol'kenshtein on Dumas Père's *Tour de Nesle:*
A Russian Formalist Analysis*

There is a whole series of works with a strongly pronounced single action and counteraction, which develop, however, not in the form of complexes of the type AKO—that is, with contrastive beginning and ending moments, but in the form of a second type of complexes, namely— let us retain the designation of the single action as O and the counteraction as K—according to the schema OK or KO, with mounting intensity. As we shall see, some absolutely outstanding works have been constructed according to such a schema.

In works fashioned by complexes of the type AKO, there is portrayed not only the struggle of the hero of the drama with the counteraction (K), but also the struggle of the hero with himself; in works fashioned by the repeated complexes of the type OK or KO, there is portrayed a struggle without such inner dissension, although sometimes it is accompanied by extraordinary suffering and emotion.

In the schema OK (KO), O signifies the strong onset, the predominance of the single main action; K signifies the upsurge, the thrust of the counteraction. Here we have the alternation of pressure and resistance, the "change of good fortune and bad fortune," to use Aristotle's language.

The simplest genre of this type is adventure drama and, in large part, so-called melodrama (for example, many plays by Alexandre Dumas, père).

To this category, for example, belong plays portraying the struggle between the detective and the criminal, Sherlock Holmes and the villain Moriarty. In this case the entire interest lies in those incredible stratagems and tricks to which the adversaries have recourse in extricating themselves from the most difficult predicaments. Both are animated by total and unshakeable passion, the one by noble professionalism, the other by ignoble professionalism.

It is evident that for such characters, there can only be misfortunes; there can never be doubts. The dramatic situations in such plays are built on alternation of the different thrusts of one single action and counteraction according to the schema OK or KO, while the separate acts tend sometimes to O, sometimes to K—depending on diverse considerations of the dramatic architectonics.

More complex in its composition—in its particular esthetic and emotional details—but in essence of the same constructional type, is the type melodrama, for example, Alexandre Dumas's *Tour de Nesle.*

Here in the first act in the scenes with Marguerite de Bourgogne we find the dramatic complex AKO: Queen Marguerite is infatuated with the

*from *The Law of the Drama*, by Vladimir Mikhailovich Vol'kenshtein. Moscow and Leningrad: Izdatel'stvo Moskovskoye Obshchestvo Dramaticheskikh Pisatelei i Kompozitorov, 1925.

courtier, Philippe d'Aulnay, with whom she has spent the night in the Tour de Nesle. Usually she kills the young courtiers whom she and her sisters have invited to the Tour de Nesle, but she does not wish to kill Philippe d'Aulnay. However, after he scars her face—through her mask—with a pin (in order to recognize her later), she orders him to be killed. This complex *AKO* is not repeated. All the rest of the play develops according to the schema *OK*. This takes the form of a series of duels between Captain Buridan, the defender of the murdered man and the witness of his death, and Marguerite de Bourgogne.

Now Buridan succeeds in terrorizing the queen; now the queen cleverly extorts an accusatory letter entrusted by Buridan to the murdered man's brother, Gaultier d'Aulnay, with whom Marguerite has an amorous liaison and to whom Buridan threatens to disclose her secret—the secret of the Tour de Nesle. When Buridan is arrested, he says, "Not a bad move, but all is not lost!"[1] Such is the invariable motto of the melodramatic hero-adventurer. Buridan succeeds in getting out of the godforsaken tower; the jailer turns out to be his former servant. The jailer promises to expose the queen and to deliver to her royal spouse, Louis, at the moment of his arrival in Paris, a case containing a paper in which is proved her frightful crime of bygone days—incest.

The struggle takes on a particularly intriguing character: it turns out that Buridan and Marguerite were lovers, and that twenty years ago, with his aid, she killed her father, Robert II of Bourgogne.

Marguerite fears these frightful disclosures; she yields, frees Buridan from prison, appoints him prime minister, but plots secret revenge and so forth.

At the end of the melodrama Buridan and Marguerite arrange a rendezvous at the Tour de Nesle, each perfidiously feigning to be in love with the other. Knowing that death awaits him, Buridan sends Gaultier d'Aulnay to the staircase where murder is being hatched, and he himself bursts into the tower by another way. Gaultier d'Aulnay is killed, but at this moment Buridan and Marguerite discover that Philippe and Gaultier are their children.

If this revelation had occurred earlier, we must assume that the combatants either would have brought their struggle to an end or would have experienced a moment of doubt and hesitation—complexes of the type *AKO* would have arisen in the play. The revelation crowns the play; it is frightful, but now it is impossible to rectify anything; the struggle is finished. The revelation at the end of the melodrama creates a spectacular situation and a moment akin to katharsis in tragedy; herein lies its significance.

During the entire play, both Buridan and Marguerite, not knowing how closely they are related, act without hesitating—in the manner of Sherlock Holmes and Moriarty. The acts are built according to the schema *OK* or *KO*. We shall designate Buridan's striving for power and revenge *O*, and the villainous strivings of Marguerite *K*.

We shall come up with the following schemas:

Act I. Here there are two scenes:
In the first, Buridan saves Philippe d'Aulnay in the tavern. Both are invited by love letters to the Tour de Nesle.
OK
In the second scene, Marguerite murders Philippe d'Aulnay (after some hesitation); Buridan escapes by jumping out the window.

$$\overbrace{\underset{A1\quad K1\quad O1}{KO}}$$

Schema of the act: *OK—KO.*

Act II. Here there are two scenes:
In the first, there is a meeting between Marguerite and the courtiers about the corpses of murdered noblemen floating to the surface of the Seine. Then Buridan appears disguised as a gypsy and staggers the queen with his riddle: he knows everything that has taken place in the Tour de Nesle.
KO
In the second scene, Buridan extracts from Marguerite the promise to appoint him prime minister. But Marguerite extorts from Gaultier the memorandum book that accuses her.
OK
The schema of the act: *KO—OK.*

Act III. Two scenes:
In the first, Buridan comes to arrest the prime minister, intending to take his place; but Gaultier arrests Buridan.
OK
In the second scene, Buridan languishes in prison. All, it would seem, is lost. But, thanks to the jailer, he succeeds in getting free; the queen herself frees him.
KO
Schema of the act: *OK—KO.*

Act IV. One scene:
Buridan is appointed prime minister *(O)*. But Marguerite has incited Gaultier against him; she names Buridan as the murderer of Philippe d'Aulnay *(K)*. Wishing to crush her, Buridan, pretending to be in love, invites her to the tower *(O)*; but she arranges with the executioner Orsini to murder Buridan *(K)*.
OKOK

Act V. Two scenes:
In the first, Buridan discloses to Gaultier that Marguerite killed his

brother, and invites Gaultier to the tower *(O)*. Afterwards, he accident-ally discovers that both d'Aulnays are his and Marguerite's children, and he experiences something like katharsis.

Oh, God! What have I done? What have I done?
A curse! Oh, my children, my poor children! . . .
God, how cruel is your punishment![2]
        OB (B—the moment of purification)

In the second scene, Marguerite waits in the tower with the execu-tioner for Buridan, but he comes in through another entrance. He discloses to Marguerite that Philippe and Gaultier are their children. Marguerite is deeply shaken; he infects her with his moral fervor; but at this moment— to their horror—Gaultier is killed as he ascends the stairs where the assas-sins were lying in wait for Buridan.

                KOB

Schema of the act: *OB—KOB.*

We see the regular alternation of moments *O* and *K* only in the fourth act, consisting of a single scene.

In the acts divided into two scenes, the construction is either *OK— KO* or *KO—OK;* in poetics, such a schema is called "junction."[3]

The final moment of each scene in these acts is carried over to the beginning of the following scene.

In the fifth act, there is an incursion of moments of *katharsis* (not very convincingly executed).

The struggle is waged with sharply mounting intensity.

As opposed to the crude adventure play, melodrama can be imbued with high emotionality; in melodrama there can arise (as we have seen) complexes of the first type *AKO;* in the finale there appear moments characteristic of tragedy. But to the extent that the struggle in melo-drama usually takes place among adventurers of various dispositions—the villains against one another, or the virtuous in conflict with the villains, both sides implementing their desires without any hesitations whatso-ever—it is a primitive type of drama. Its contrasts are contrasts of victo-ries and defeats, and not contrasts of an internal dialectic, united in a single, repeating complex. It is also characteristic (I already pointed this out in my *Dramaturgy)* that a reversal for the better sometimes occurs in melodrama not as a consequence of the resourcefulness of the combat-ants, but owing to a fortunate conjunction of circumstances. Thus, for example, Buridan succeeds in escaping from the prison owing to the fact that the jailer turns out by chance to be his former comrade-in-arms. Now this links melodrama with the chronicle play where (as will be shown in the following chapter) all kinds of coincidences are to be found; here is an obviously epic device for constructing a dramatic action.

As in the *Tour de Nesle,* in many adventure dramas or melodramas we find secondary plots of the type *AKO.*

Translated by Daniel Gerould

Translator's Notes

1. In the original, "Bien joué, Marguerite. A toi la première partie, mais à moi la revanche, je l'espère!" (act 3, scene 5). Vol'kenshtein's citations come from a Russian adaptation called *The Mystery of the Tour de Nesle*, which is partially in verse, although Dumas's play is entirely in prose.

2. In the original, "Oh, malheur! malheur! mes enfants! . . . justice de Dieu!" (act 5, scene 5).

3. In Russian, *styk*. A term introduced by Osip Brik in 1919 and used by the Russian formalists. It refers to patterns of repeated sounds (and by extension, the repetition of a word or phrase) linking the end of one line of poetry with the beginning of the following line. It occurs in folk songs and popular lyrics as well as in the verse of major poets. See *Two Essays on Poetic Language by Osip Maksimovič Brik, postscript by Roman Jakobson*, Michigan Slavic Materials (Ann Arbor: Department of Slavic Languages and Literatures, February 1964), pp. 29 ff. Brik's essay, "Zvukovye povtory," originally appeared in *Sbornik po teorii poeticheskogo jazyka*, 2 (Petrograd, 1917).

20

Fear in Literature

ANDRÉ DE LORDE

An entire literature of Fear exists.

Why should this be astonishing? Each one of us has in his innermost being a secret longing for violent emotions. At all times, in all parts of the globe, horror shows have drawn large audiences. The huge amphitheaters in Rome were too small to hold the citizens eager to see the gladiators slaughter one another and the Christians thrown to the lions. If the Inquisition had made public its interrogations conducted on the rack, they would have had to turn people away. To witness the hideous torture of Damiens, the crowd surged towards the square as though to holiday festivities.

"Bah!" you will say, "Times have changed; in our days, the progress of civilization has made such barbarous pastimes unthinkable." True enough. Still, set men, bulls, and horses at one another in an arena, and excited spectators will shriek with joy; at break of day guillotine some human wreck half-dead with fright, and there won't be enough soldiers, their bayonets fixed, to hold back the pushing throng of those who want to *see*. And don't those tender hearts, who are revolted by such spectacles, seek out at fairs the most violent and horrific "attractions"? Don't they derive acute pleasure at the circus or music hall from watching the most dangerous feats? If I perspire with anxiety as I follow the movements of the dancer along the tightrope, if my breathing stops with the music when this young person in pink tights is about to attempt what she herself calls *the death leap*, it is because I actually imagine an atrocious death for her, her battered corpse bloodying the sand in the ring. No doubt, if I were sure that the accident was going to happen, I would be the first to rush forward to prevent it; but if, on the other hand, I was certain that it would not happen, I would lose interest in the show. A most curious compromise on the part of our conscience is at work here. If my sensibility steps forth to reproach me for the odious satisfaction that I find in thus anticipating a calamity, I immediately assuage these scruples by involving the law of probabilities. There is only one chance in a thousand that the accident will happen precisely today; but as soon as this reassuring thought runs the risk of dulling my pleasure, I revive it again by calling up in my mind's eye the image of the fall, despite what seems possible. I would not be as ferocious as that Englishman who went to every show of a wild animal act in order to be present when the lion tamer would get eaten; but, by going once quite by chance, I have a slight hope, without admitting it to myself, that today will be the day, more or less in the same way that I dream—without daring to believe it—that my lottery ticket will be the winning one. . . .

Fear has always existed, and each century has stamped upon its literature the mark of the fears that tormented it, but the primitive caveman and the contemporary businessman have not shuddered for the same reasons. The sources of fear have varied, but not fear itself, which is eternal and immutable. . . .

Feeble as they are, the Gothic novels had a real vogue; not only were Anne Radcliffe and Monk Lewis imitated by a host of minor writers, they also had the honor of inspiring two of England's greatest authors, Walter Scott and Lord Byron, to write many a picturesque descriptive passage. In France, *The Monk* and *The Mysteries of Udolpho*, translated in 1797, were read, appreciated, and plagiarized; the novelists, from Ducray-Duminil to Eugène Sue, went to them for stirring subjects for many, many years, and the playwrights along the Boulevard of Crime brought to the stage the principal episodes of these works.

As early as 1799, Guilbert de Pixérécourt, the father of melodrama, stages at the Ambigu his *Château des Apennins*, borrowed from Anne Radcliffe's novel, but where the horror is considerably attenuated. This astute dramatist knew how to turn a famous novel to good profit in the theater; he neglected no "effect" capable of moving or astounding the spectators: *Victor, ou l'enfant de la forêt, l'Homme à trois visages, Le Monastère abandonné*, quite like *Le Château des Apennins*, are full of ingenious situations. In one of his plays, *Christophe Colomb, ou la découverte du Nouveau Monde* (1814), whose action in part unfolds in the

Antilles, Pixérécourt, on the look-out for novelties, was even convinced that he should, "for the sake of greater verisimilitude," have his savages speak the language of the Antilles taken from Father Breton's Caribbean dictionary. The results are not without savor, as witness this piece of dialogue between King Oranko and his subject Kavaka:

> ORANKO. Cati louma.
> KAVAKA. Amouliaca azackia Kereber *(Oranko hestitates)*.
> ORANKO. Inolaki . . . Chicalama . . .
> KAVAKA. Hava a moutou Koulé Ouékelli.
> ORANKO. Areskoui, azakia, kavaïti avou.
> ALL. Anakilika!
> ORANKO. Ouallou hougousou!

And so it goes on and on . . . for whole scenes the actors carry on the dialogue in Caribbean. . . .

The true genius of fear is, in actual fact, incarnated in Edgar Poe, and his work brings together all the seeds of terror that can blossom in the human soul: physical horrors, moral anxieties, painful apprehensions of the other world and even this sensation previously unrecorded in literature, *the fear of being afraid*, that tortures the unfortunate Roderick Usher. The dominant trait of this exceptional talent is the conjunction of unbridled imagination and imperturbable logic, the fusion of nightmare and truth. In the midst of his most hallucinatory dreams, Poe always keeps one foot firmly planted in reality. In his work, macabre fantasy and meticulous precision conducive to verisimilitude become intertwined, overlap, and grow inseparable. There results from this union an impression of dread that no one else, not even Dante, has ever produced. As the reader enters into contact with Poe, a secret terror softly steals and glides into his soul, then takes possession of him, clasps him tightly, makes him shudder. The strongest nerves can offer no resistance; willy-nilly, we follow Poe into a hell, to which his art has been able to lend a semblance of life. First he rocks us on the waves of a raging sea, and then he suspends us on the edge of a bottomless abyss; vertigo seizes us, anguish makes our throat contract. . . . "Panic-stricken" genius is the phrase that Barbey d'Aurevilly has used in speaking of Poe: no epithet could be more fitting. . . .

Poe's literary influence has been immense. Strangely enough, it was felt in France before showing any signs in his own native country. In the second half of the nineteenth century, while Charles Nodier, Gérard de Nerval, Théophile Gautier, and Erckmann-Chatrian continue the Hoffmann tradition and write fantastic rather than terrifying works, we see the example of the American master inspire numerous disciples. . . .

His influence can be seen on many writers, including some of the greatest: above all on Baudelaire, who translated almost all of Poe and who is indelibly marked by his work; there are many poems in *Les Fleurs du mal* where we catch reminiscences of Edgar Poe, and it can be asserted that without him, Baudelaire would not have realized all his capabilities.

Poe's mark is no less visible on Barbey d'Aurevilly and Villiers de l'Isle-Adam. Both read Poe (Barbey has even devoted some magnificent pages to him), both have been subject to his authority; but *Les Diaboliques* and the *Contes cruels* are very far removed from Poe's *Tales of the Grotesque and Arabesque*. That is because Barbey and especially Villiers are unrepentant romantics. They can only conceive fear with a stately train of situations and antitheses in the style of Victor Hugo; the veiled figures, the funeral processions, the cloistered leper in Villiers's *Duke of Portland* are scarcely more believable than the coffins in Hugo's *Lucrèce Borgia* or the drowned bodies in Dumas père's *Tour de Nesle*. All of this literary satanism is hardly frightening; it has a musty smell of old bric-a-brac and the property room.

Much more realistic in their sober precision, Mérimée's novellas achieve effects of terror that strike you with unexpected rapidity like a gypsy girl's dagger. *Colomba*, *Lokis*, and *La Vénus d'Ille* surpass by far in emotional intensity the best of the *Contes cruels*. The true spiritual heir of Edgar Poe is uncontestably Marcel Schwob—with the difference that separates talent from genius. Strange affinities exist between these two spirits: the same sarcastic and terrifying imagination is characteristic of each of them; they both possess the same "meditative faculty" which Poe bestows upon his Egaeus in the tale "Berenice." The painful anxiety of the one, and the Jewish sensibility of the other, reach by different routes the same goal. There is in Schwob's *Sur les dents* a ferocious irony that closely connects this tale to Poe's "Loss of Breath" or "The Man Who Was Used Up," and *L'Homme voilé* equals in phlegmatic horror *"The Cask of Amontillado"*. . . .

Writers could not simply go on imitating Poe indefinitely, still less could they outdo him. They were obliged to renew the genre. This is what has been attempted by the creators of the *scientific-marvelous*, a rich source of terror and delight. The progress of the sciences, the quasi-fabulous discoveries of the past thirty years, and the publicity given to research accomplished by inventors have contributed to arousing our minds to new objects of curiosity. Science has gone from the laboratory to the novel.

Jules Verne confined himself to considering as accomplished certain discoveries that already exist to all intents and purposes. Wells, Rosny the elder, and Maurice Renard go much further still: they are not concerned with what *will be*, but with what *could be*, and, boldly wielding the hypothesis, they venture out into the vast expanses of the unknown. Here, it should be observed, there is no question of the supernatural, which for science does not exist. At most, they propose for our scrutiny facts susceptible of a dual interpretation, the one miraculous, the other rational (Wells's *Pollock and the Porroh Man* and Maurice Renard's *Le Singe*); the true domain of these storytellers remains the uncertain and the not yet known. That is how Wells imagines perilous journeys through time, that is how Rosny supposes the intrusion onto our planet of one of those invisible worlds that fill the emptiness of infinite space, that is how Maurice Renard makes us perceive the diabolical experiments conducted by the magician Lerne who understands human cross-breeding as well as Dr. Alexis Carrel. Pure imagination? No, certainly, not, since such tales offer us, as applied to the study of imaginary phenomena or of monsters, the most rigorous methods of investigation. We find in Wells the study pursued with a perfect logic—except in one point—of what would happen *if* a man succeeded in making himself invisible by the discoloration of his blood. Thus these authors create new subjects of terror, which are addressed less to the nerves than to the understanding and which answer to our desire for the truth while at the same time giving sustenance to the need for shudders which is a part of our nature.

Translated by Daniel Gerould
from *La Revue Mondiale* (15 March 1927).

The Orphan's Dowry

PIERRE-HENRI CAMI

ACT I
"The Heart of a Rag-Picker"

The scene is a rag-picker's hut.

THE OLD RAG-PICKER *(to his son).* The poor girl who we found unconscious in the snow and who we've just brought to our modest hut is regaining consciousness.

THE ORPHAN. Where am I? Oh! Let me guess, worthy rag-pickers! You picked me up in the dark deserted street where the Viscount Stonybroke chloroformed me!

THE RAG-PICKER'S SON. Chloroformed you?

THE ORPHAN. Yes. The wretch seized the little cloth bag that I wore on a string around my neck and that contains the oyster bequeathed to me by father on his deathbed.

BOTH THE RAG-PICKERS *(in unison).* The oyster?

THE ORPHAN. Yes. A pearl-bearing oyster. It is a strange story. Lis-

ten! A long, long time before that, one of my father's ancestors was
getting ready to swallow an oyster when he noticed a magnificent pearl
inside the shells. Now his feverish hand was just about to grasp the precious jewel when the oyster suddenly closed. All his efforts to open
this oyster again proved futile. It was useless to think of breaking it
open, because the pearl would have been pulverized by the blow. My
father's ancestor lived out his whole miserable existence beside that
oyster, which contained a fortune, but which he was not able to open.
The poor devil died a pauper and, in his will, bequeathed his pearl-bearing oyster to my father's grandfather, who was equally unsuccessful in
opening it, and left it on his deathbed to his son, that is, to my father's
father. And he was hardly any more fortunate than the others. He
died in abject poverty and my father became the inheritor of the fatal
oyster. It was then that the Viscount Stonybroke, who had heard the
story of the pearl-bearing oyster, asked for my hand in marriage, in the
hope of getting possession of the accursed oyster. I refused to give myself to this avaricious nobleman. The Viscount Stonybroke left in a
terrible rage, swearing that he would have the oyster by fair means or
foul. My poor father died a short time thereafter. On his deathbed, he
gave me the pearl-bearing oyster. "Here is your dowry, my dear child,"
he said to me; "now I can die in peace." After I had buried my poor
father and sewn the oyster into a little cloth bag that I wore on a string
around my neck, I left the paternal garret. Without a sou, I wandered
through the city, where, that very night, the Viscount Stonybroke, who
was lying in wait for me, chloroformed me in the dark deserted street
and stole the pearl-bearing oyster from me. Thanks to you, worthy rag-
pickers, I did not die of cold in the snow. Thank you, oh! Thank you!
(She bursts into sobs.)
THE RAG-PICKER'S SON. Don't weep, mademoiselle. If the heart of
an aristocrat was cowardly enough to rob a defenseless orphan, here
you will find, I swear it to you, the heart of a rag-picker noble enough
to bring back the oyster stolen from the orphan!

ACT II
"Face to Face"

The scene is an underground vault.

THE VISCOUNT STONYBROKE. Three years have passed since I stole
the oyster from the orphan. And I still have not been able to open this
fatal oyster. Every night I descend into this underground vault and, far
from inquisitive eyes, I make frightful efforts to pry open the two
halves of this bivalvular mollusc. But there is no time to lose: back to
our arduous work.
THE RAG-PICKER'S SON *(appearing out of nowhere)*. There is a score

to be settled, monsieur le vicomte, between the two of us! At last! After three years of patient searching, I have discovered your mysterious hide-away! Between the two of us!

THE VISCOUNT STONYBROKE *(arrogantly)*. Do you know with whom you are speaking, churl?

THE RAG-PICKER'S SON. Oh! No insults, monsieur le vicomte! At this hour, all social distinctions have been abolished and, in this underground vault, there are only two men face to face: an honest rag-picker and a wretch! And, mark it well, monsieur le vicomte, the honest rag-picker would not exchange his basket that he carries on his back for your dishonored coat-of-arms! Come, no more useless words; give me back the orphan's oyster!

THE VISCOUNT STONYBROKE *(trying to brazen it out)*. This oyster belongs to me!

THE RAG-PICKER'S SON. You have lied, monsieur le vicomte! That precious mollusc contains the orphan's dowry. Besides, this photograph will confound you once and for all. *(He shows him a photograph.)*

THE VISCOUNT STONYBROKE. Death and destruction! A photograph of the oyster! I am undone!

THE RAG-PICKER'S SON. Yes, a photograph of the oyster that the orphan entrusted to me to guide my search.

THE VISCOUNT STONYBROKE. Come then, the game is up. Let us commit suicide. *(He commits suicide.)*

THE RAG-PICKER'S SON *(carrying off the oyster)*. And now, let us hasten to bring back her dowry to the orphan!

ACT III
"Happiness Regained"

The scene is the rag-picker's hut.

THE RAG-PICKER'S SON. Poor dear orphan! The day I brought you back the pearl-bearing oyster, you promised to become my wife once I succeeded in opening its accursed shells.

THE ORPHAN. Yes. On that day, we will be happy! But the oyster has already been here for six months, and you still have not succeeded. It is enough to make one despair.

THE RAG-PICKER'S SON. Alas! My poor father died as a result of the frightful efforts he made trying to open the homicidal oyster! As for me, I vainly seek a way, but I see none. For ten days I have not slept, racking my brains for an idea. I give up. I cannot go on like this any longer! *(Looking at the oyster lying on the table.)* Oh! The accursed oyster! You bring misfortune to all those who come near you!

THE ORPHAN. Oh! A miracle! Look: the oyster is opening wide! The precious pearl appears between the two valves! We are rich! But how has this miracle come to pass?

THE RAG-PICKER'S SON. It is no miracle. I understand everything.
Overcome by insomnia, I have just, with all due respect to you, yawned
repeatedly. Yawning, with all due respect to you, is contagious. The
oyster could not resist, and its valves opened in a providential yawn.

Curtain

Translated by Daniel Gerould

Forum Reviews

During the past decade melodrama has become a respectable, even fashionable subject for critical and scholarly investigation. Long neglected works of nineteenth-century popular fiction and drama have been found to offer a rewarding field for research. The impact of low upon high culture, as seen in the infiltration of melodrama into superior genres, can prove to be a fascinating study for the literary critic and theater historian. Books and collections of articles on melodrama and melodramatists now appear with greater frequency but are often elusive, inaccessible, or hard to identify. Our reviews of four recent studies by Hassan El Nouty, Gilbert B. Cross, Peter Haining, and Sven Eric Molin and Robin Goodefellowe call attention to useful works which may have escaped the notice of those interested in melodrama and the popular arts. Two collections of essays, which could not be reviewed because copies were not available in time, are also worthy of mention. *Cahiers de la Cinémathèque*, No. 28, 1979, coordinated by Maurice Roelens, is entitled "Pour une histoire du mélodrame du cinéma" and contains articles on "Melodrame, cinéma, histoire," "Le mélodrame, le mot, et la chose," "Le mélo maternel dans le cinéma américain 1930–39," "Ida Lupino," "Les Enfants du Paradis," and other subjects. *Performance and Politics in Popular Drama: Aspects of Popular Entertainment in Theatre, Film, and Television, 1800–1976*, edited by David Bradby, Louis James, and Bernard Sharrat (Cambridge: Cambridge University Press, 1980) contains five essays dealing with melodrama.

Hassan El Nouty. Théâtre et Pré-cinéma: Essai sur la problèmatique de spectacle au XIXe siècle. A.-G. Nizet, 1978

Positing the opposition between *dire* (speak) and *montrer* (show) that dominated seventeenth-century French theater as a result of the anti-spectacle bias inherent in classicist poetics, Professor El Nouty sets out to examine those nineteenth-century dramatic works, both popular and literary, which, in their attempts to reinstate the visual, anticipate the technically superior means of presentation found later in cinema. Part 1 of the study traces the revenge taken by spectacle during the early nineteenth-century revolt against literary theater. Derived, in spirit, from the revolutionary shows and imperial ceremonies and addressed to a broad public, the dioramas and panoramas of Daguerre, the lumino-cinetic sets of Cicéri, and the epic mimodramas at the Cirque Olympique (such as Laloue's *Jerusalem Delivered* and *The Fall of the Bastille*) represent the truly innovative *spectacles oculaires* (visual performances) of the period that Professor El Nouty feels are precursors of a popular theater for the masses, as later evolved in the outdoor pageants of Firmin Gémier at the Festival de Vaud.

Using a wide range of first-hand documents, almanacs, and reviews, Professor El Nouty constructs a highly partisan and polemic argument, defending visual theater as politically and artistically progressive and asking the reader to re-assess the received hierarchy of literary values. In this perspective, Théophile Gautier as a critic and theoretician who declared, "Le temps des spectacles oculaires est venu" ("The time for visual performances has come"), becomes a prophetic figure for the history of nineteenth-century theater, although Professor El Nouty points out that the bourgeoisie was quick to take over visual performance for its own purposes of imperialism and colonialism.

The *spectacles oculaires* are not precinema simply because they contain a multiplicity of rapidly shifting scenes but rather because they share film's aim of integral spatial realism and reveal the supremacy of image over word. Accordingly, Shakespeare is not precinema; in his plays the words themselves evoke the setting, producing a verbal scenography that is quite distinct from visual performance.

Part 2 of *Théâtre et Pré-cinéma* offers analyses of a number of dramatic works judged unstageable in their own time, for which existing theatrical forms and techniques proved inadequate. Because of the problems of material execution, plays or pseudoplays, such as Musset's *Lorenzaccio*, Mérimée's *La Jacquerie*, and Gobineau's *La Renaissance*, were forced to remain ideal theater waiting for a medium that had not yet been discovered. Disputing official literary history, Professor El Nouty finds the contributions of the great French romantics to the development of a new popular theater to be slight and timid. Stendhal's *Racine et Shakespeare* is not a major critical statement, because it is directed to the liberal bourgeoisie, not to the mass audience, who, after all, preferred Pixérécourt and visual performance. The supposedly revolutionary *Hernani* is actually the old-fashioned theater of words poured into the conservative five-act mold and a pillar of the established order that it pretended to overthrow. As a defeatist tragedy, Hugo's play was the very type of pessimistic art used by the ruling classes to hold back the rebellion and undermine belief in the future. "The popular theater at the time of *Hernani*," Professor El Nouty writes, "whether it was melodrama or mimodrama—and the genres became mixed in various proportions—was resolutely optimistic."

Although *Lorenzaccio* and *La Jacquerie* can both be seen as prefilmic in their handling of stage space, they like all the French romantic dramas are simply inverted melodramas with unhappy endings *(anti-mélodrames)* because of the "prevalence of the nocturnal" in their fatalistic, obsolescent ideologies. The problem of history in drama becomes the crucial test for successful artistic revolution. Here the romantic poet-playwrights fail in that they are unable to incorporate historical action in their dramas, except marginally as masquerade or anecdote. On the other hand, Louis Vitet and his followers in their *Scènes Historiques* reject conventional forms and create a new dramaturgy capable of dealing with the collective reality of history and its mass heroes. Such an archeological theater leads directly to Ariane Mnouchkine's *1793* at Le Théâtre du Soleil in our own day.

Gobineau's multidrama *La Renaissance* can best be realized in television which permits drama *à grand spectacle* and at the same time preserves the primacy of the word. Flaubert's psychodrama *La Tentation de Saint Antoine* lies beyond spectacle because it integrates into the text itself everything that performance could accomplish; it is a fully enregistered *théâtre du livre* (theater of the book). For Professor El Nouty artistic and technical questions are always closely linked. Theater, cinema, and television are stages of a quest for unforeseeable media. The metamorphoses of spectacle are not yet over.

Daniel Gerould

Gilbert B. Cross. Next Week—East Lynne: Domestic Drama in Performance 1820-1874. Associated University Presses, 1977.

Gilbert Cross begins his critical survey of English domestic drama in 1820, the date of Moncrieff's *The Lear of Private Life*, the first such play with an English setting, and concludes it in 1874, the date of T. A. Palmer's dramatization of *East Lynne*. Neither the title nor the dates limits the investigation, however, as the author refers to earlier and later examples and has much to say about melodrama in general. After a look at the monopoly and its effects, he sets out to explore the genre with special reference to the influence of its patrons, its conventional nature, and its equivocal use of social problems.

Professor Cross thinks of melodrama as a kind of folk literature in which the dominance of the audience so thoroughly conventionalized both themes and treatment that playwrights had to drop the role of creative artist and take up that of folk narrator. "It became as foolish to look for the individuality of the average melodramatist as it would be to seek out the author of a traditional ballad or folk tale" (p. 70). His chapter on "Visual and Aural Signals" describes the stereotypical qualities of the genre as the effects of anonymous traditional laws, like those of true folklore, ruthlessly enforced by patrons who after the O. P. Riots of 1809 found themselves in total control of their entertainments, if not of much else in life.

The tyranny of the audience extended to the content of the plays as well. In Chapter 4, "The World of Domestic Drama," Cross points out that the genre was both realistic and romantic: it portrayed the life of the people but subtly idealized that life, giving it color, excitement, and point. On the stage the urban working class could see its fragmented, alienated existence reflected in a world-view, that gave life meaning.

This world view, says Cross, was deeply conservative. Despite the revolutionary note heard occasionally in plays like Walker's *The Factory Lad* (1832), melodrama called not for a new social order, but nostalgically for the restoration of the old order in which master and peasant had lived together on the land, their interests bound by mutual obligation. Furthermore, the people went to the theater not for analysis or social protest, but for entertainment. Strong anxieties evoked by images of injustice had to be allayed in the happy ending. By simplifying complex issues and focusing indignation on scapegoat-villains who could be defeated with the help of Providence, successful melodramatists satisfied their audience's hunger for compensatory images with which to nourish a harmonious view of their lives.

These images were necessarily utopian and idealistic, like those of the fairy tale. They affirmed values of family life, freedom from want, and the virtue of hard work. Cross reminds us that conventional morality itself, as opposed to its abuse, was not challenged in the theater until the realistic plays of Robertson, Gilbert, Pinero, and Shaw began to supersede the domestic drama.

The author draws widely upon the available texts for his examples and takes full account of the scholarly work on melodrama. An extensive bibliography contains many useful items not mentioned elsewhere.

David Nicholson

Peter Haining. The Mystery and Horrible Murders of Sweeney Todd, The Demon Barber of Fleet Street. Frederick Muller, 1979.

A decidedly popular work by the author of many books and anthologies dealing with the bizarre and macabre, Haining's *Mystery and Horrible Murders* is chiefly valuable for its full summary of, and extensive quotations from, the first known version of Sweeney Todd, an inaccessible penny dreadful in 18 issues by Thomas Prest, as well as for the numerous rare illustrations that are included. Most of the book is devoted to inconclusive speculation about the historicity of the demon barber. Without a bibliography or reliable notes or references, Haining's explorations of the great question: did Todd really exist? meander off into journalistic hokum about fascinating journeys of discovery and gossipy crime lore, such as the chapter on the underworld of Fleet Street and the appendix on the man-eating monster of Scotland. Students and amateurs of popular culture can enjoy *The Mystery and Horrible Murders of Sweeney*

Todd as a representative instance of modern popular culture, not so very different in spirit and execution from the penny dreadfuls of an earlier era, although addressed to a supposedly more sophisticated audience.

Daniel Gerould

Sven Eric Molin and Robin Goodefellowe. "Dion Boucicault, The Shaughraun: A Documentary Life, Letters, and Selected Works. Part One: The Early years." George Spelvin's Theatre Book, 2, No. 1 (Spring 1979), 3-108.

The life and career of Dion Boucicault, master melodramatist, has attracted the interest of various admirers,* including Boucicault himself, who in his old age published several autobiographical articles in the third person. These reminiscences form the core of Molin and Goodefellowe's documentary account of Boucicault's youth and formative experiences in the theater. This is the first of about eight parts. The second part, which will follow Boucicault's life up to his first trip to America, will appear in early 1981.

Quoting also from letters, memoirs, and the like (much of it already familiar to the Boucicault buff), the authors consider first Boucicault's parentage and birth. Though the evidence is inconclusive, they believe his father was Dr. Dionysius Lardner, for whom he was named, and not the man his mother married. The puzzle of whether he was born in 1820 or 1822, and thus had his first great success at age 18 or 20, remains unsolved.

Molin and Goodefellowe devote about 30 pages to the production of *London Assurance* (1841), quoting Boucicault's own account, "Debut of a Dramatist" (*North American Review*, April 1889, pp. 454-63), his published preface, reminiscences by James Wallack and John Coleman, an excerpt from Macready's diary, and the young dramatist's exultant letter to his mother inviting her to join him in London. Also reprinted here is his essay, "Early Days of a Dramatist" (*North American Review*, May 1889, pp. 584-93). Most of the rest of the article consists of quoted reviews of the 15 or 16 plays (some of them lost) that Boucicault wrote, rewrote, or adapted between 1841 and 1844, the date of his second big success, *Old Heads and Young Hearts.*

During this period Boucicault mastered his craft by seeing what worked in the theater. He learned to be facile and prolific, and he learned how to please. As the authors point out, these early experiences were

---

*   Works about Boucicault include Robert Hogan's *Dion Boucicault* (New York: Twayne, 1969); Albert E. Johnson's "The Birth of Dion Boucicault," *Modern Drama*, 11 (September 1968), 157-63; Julius H. Tolson's "Dion Boucicault" (Ph. D. Diss., University of Pennsylvania, 1951); and Townsend Walsh's *The Career of Dion Boucicault* (New York: The Dunlop Society, 1915). Charles Lamb Kenney's *The Career of Dion Boucicault* (New York: The Graphic Co., n. d.) is thought to have been written by Boucicault himself.

crucial. Only in his Irish melodramas did Boucicault become something more than the "engaging and craftsmanlike hack" (p. 106) that his training made him.

David Nicholson

Bibliography

1. General and Theatrical

a. Books

Birdoff, Harry. *The World's Greatest Hit: Uncle Tom's Cabin.* New York: S. F. Vanni, 1947.

Booth, Michael R. *English Melodrama.* London: Herbert Jenkins, 1965.

Charlemagne, Armand [Placide le Vieux]. *Le Mélodrame aux boulevards: facétie littéraire, historique, et dramatique.* Paris, 1809.

Cross, Gilbert B. *Next Week—East Lynne: Domestic Drama in Performance, 1820-1874.* London: Associated University Presses, 1977.

Disher, Maurice W. *Blood and Thunder: Mid-Victorian Melodrama and Its Origins.* London: Frederick Muller, 1949.

——. *Melodrama: Plots That Thrilled.* New York: Macmillan, 1954.

Ginisty, Paul. *Le Mélodrame.* Paris: L. Michaud, 1910.

Grimsted, David. *Melodrama Unveiled: American Theatre and Culture 1800-1850.* Chicago: University of Chicago Press, 1968.

Hartog, Willie C. *Guilbert de Pixérécourt: sa vie, son mélodrame, sa technique et son influence.* Paris: Honoré Champion, 1913.

Heilman, Robert Bechtold. *Tragedy and Melodrama.* Seattle: University of Washington Press, 1968.

Istel, Edgar. *Die Entstehung des deutschen Melodramas.* Berlin and Leipzig: Schuster & Loeffler, 1906.

Lacey, Alexander. *Pixérécourt and the French Romantic Drama.* Toronto: University of Toronto Press, 1928.

Mason, F. J. *The Melodrama in France: From the Revolution to the Beginning of Romantic Drama, 1791-1830.* Baltimore: J. H. Furst, 1912.

Rahill, Frank. *The World of Melodrama.* University Park, Pa.: Pennsylvania State University Press, 1967.

Sacher, Herbert. *Die Melodramatik und das romantische Dramen in Frankreich.* Leipzig: R. Noske, 1936.

Saxon, A. H. *Enter Foot and Horse: A History of Hippodrama in England and France.* New Haven: Yale University Press, 1968.

Smith, James L. *Melodrama.* London: Methuen, 1973.

Steele, William Paul. *The Character of Melodrama.* Orono, Me.: University of Maine Press, 1968.

Thomasseau, Jean-Marie. *Le Mélodrame sur les scènes parisiennes de Coelina (1800), à l'Auberge des Adrets (1823).* Lille: Université de Lille, 1974.

Vahland, Barbara. *Der Held als Opfer: Aspekte des Melodramatischen bei Tennessee Williams.* Bern: Herbert Lang, 1976.

Van Bellen, Else Carel. *Les Origines du mélodrame.* Utrecht: Kemink & Zoon, 1927.

Virely, André. *René Charles Guilbert de Pixérécourt.* Paris, 1909.

Winkler, Burchard. *Wirkstrategische Verwendung popularliterarischer Elemente in Sean O'Caseys dramatischen Werk unter besonderer Berücksichtigung des Melodramas.* Göppingen, 1977.

b. Articles and Chapters in Books

Altick, Richard. "Dion Boucicault Stages *Mary Barton.*" *Nineteenth-Century Fiction,* (June 1959), 14(1):129-41.

Anderson, J. "The New Drama of Creeps and Chills." *Theatre* (August 1927), 46:14.

——. "The Stage Villain on the Run." *Theatre* (September 1926), 44: 383-92.

Armato, Philip M. " 'Good and Evil' in Lillian Hellman's *The Children's Hour.* " *Educational Theatre Journal* (December 1973), 25 (4):443-47.

Armstrong, William. "The Art of the Minor Theatres in 1860." *Theatre Notebook* (April-June 1966), 10(3):89-94.

Axton, William. "Modes of the Popular Victorian Theatre." *Circle of Fire: Dickens' Vision & Style & the Popular Victorian Theatre,* pp. 16-34. Lexington, Ky.: University of Kentucky Press, 1966.

Bachellier, Jean-Louis. "Les Combles du mélodrame—*Les Mystères de Paris:* Roman-feuilleton et mélodrame." *Revue des sciences humaines* (April-June 1976), no. 162, pp. 205-18.

Bailey, J. O. "Melodrama." *British Plays of the Nineteenth Century,* pp. 30-34. New York: Odessey, 1966.

Baker, Henry B. "The Old Melodrama." *Belgravia* (May 1883), 50: 331-39.

Balukhatyi, Sergei. "K Poetike Melodramy" (Poetics of Melodrama). *Poetika* (1927), 3:63-86. Reprinted Munich: Wilhelm Fink, 1970.

Bank, Rosemarie K. "Melodrama as a Social Document: Social Factors in the American Frontier Play." *Theatre Studies* (1975-76), no. 22, pp. 42-48.

Bargainnier, Earl F. "Melodrama as Formula." *Journal of Popular Culture* (Winter 1975), 9(3):726-33.

Bentley, Eric. "Melodrama." *The Life of the Drama,* pp. 195-218. New York: Atheneum, 1967.

Billaz, André. "Mélodrame et littérature: le cas de Pixérécourt." *Revue des sciences humaines* (April-June 1976), no. 162, pp. 231-45.

Bispham, David. "Melodrama, or Recitation with Music." *Harper's Bazaar* (January 1909), 43(1):21-25.

Bluestone, Max. "The Imagery of Tragic Melodrama in 'Arden of Feversham.' " *Drama Survey* (Summer 1966), 5(2):171-81.

Booth, John. "Pantomime; Shakespeare; Melodrama." *A Century of*

Theatre History. 1816-1916: The 'Old Vic,' pp. 19-27. London: Stead's, 1917.

Booth, Michael R. "The Acting of Melodrama." *University of Toronto Quarterly* (October 1964), 34:31-48.

——. "A Defense of 19th-Century English Drama." *Educational Theatre Journal* (March 1974), 26(1):5-13.

——. "The Drunkard's Progress—Nineteenth-Century Temperance Melodrama." *Dalhousie Review* (Summer 1964), 44:205-12.

——. "Introduction." *Hiss the Villain*, pp. 9-40. New York: Benjamin Blom, 1964.

——. "The Metropolis on Stage." In H. J. Dyos and Michael Wolff, eds., *The Victorian City: Images and Realities*, 1:211-24. London: Routledge & Kegan Paul, 1973.

Borione, Elizabeth. "Naissance et mort de la tragicomédie." *Nos Spectacles: Revue technique d'expression* (June-July 1966), no. 118, pp. 5-7.

Brady, W. A. "Melodrama: What It Is and How to Make It." *Green Book Magazine* (August 1915), 14:310-13.

Brockett, O. G. "The Function of the Dance in the Melodramas of Guilbert de Pixérécourt." *Modern Philology* (February 1959), 56(3):164-61.

Brooks, Peter. "Une Esthétique de l'étonnement: le mélodrame." *Poétique* (1974), 19:340-56.

Browne, Porter Emerson. "The Mellowdrammer." *Everybody's Magazine* (September 1909), 21(3):347-54.

Brunetière, Ferdinand. "Mélodrame ou tragédie: à propos du *Dédale* (de Paul Hervieu)." *Revue des deux mondes*, 15 January 1904, pp. 305-21.

Bryden, Ronald. "Melodrama." *London Observer*, 19 May 1968, p. 20.

Burns, Wayne. "Artistic Development 1849-1852: Melodrama with a Difference." *Charles Reade: A Study in Victorian Authorship*, pp. 86-112. New York: Bookman Associates, 1961.

Carpenter, Bruce. "Melodrama." *Way of the Drama: A Study of Dramatic Forms and Moods*, pp. 122-28. New York: Prentice-Hall, 1929.

Christout, Marie-Françoise. "La Mise-en-scène: des mélodrames et des drames d'adventures." *Nos Spectacles: Revue technique d'expression.* (June-July 1966) no. 118, pp. 13-16.

Chute, M. "Meal-o-dramas." *Graphic* (1 November 1913), 88:808.

Corrigan, Robert W. "Melodrama: The Drama of Disaster." *The World of the Theatre*, pp. 103-15. Glenview, Ill.: Scott, Foresman, 1979.

Craig, Edward G. "Melodrama." *Yale Review* (12 November 1930), pp. 212-16.

Culler, Dwight A. "Melodrama and the Dramatic Monologue." *PMLA* (May 1975), 90(3):366-85.

Davis, J. F. "Tom Shows." *Scribner's Magazine* (April 1925), 77:350-60.

Davis, Owen. "Why I Quit Writing Melodramas." *American Magazine* (September 1914), 78(3):28.

Davoine, Jean-Paul. "L'Épithète mélodramatique." *Revue des sciences humaines* (April-June 1976), no. 162, pp. 183–92.

"Decay of Melodrama." *Living Age* (16 April 1910), 265:182–84.

Dell, Floyd. "Melodrama Then and Now." *Stage* (March 1929), 6:27.

Dent, A. "Boost for Melodrama." *Drama* (Winter 1964), no. 75, pp. 40–42.

Descotes, Maurice. "Coelina ou l'enfant du mystère de Pixérécourt (1800). Le Public renouvelé." *Le Public de théâtre et son histoire*, pp. 209–43. Paris: Presses Universitaires de France, 1964.

Disher, M. Willson. "Melodrama." In Phyllis Hartnoll, ed., *Oxford Companion to the Theatre*, 3d ed., pp. 631–34. London: Oxford University Press, 1967.

———. "Melodrama and the Modern Mind." *Theatre World* (April 1939), 30:152.

———. "Nineteenth Century Melodrama." *Pilot Papers* (London), July 1946, p. 36.

Donohue, Joseph. "The Plays of the Early Nineteenth Century: The Rise of Melodrama." *Theatre in the Age of Kean*, pp.105–26. Oxford: Blackwell, 1975.

Doumic, René. "Le Mélodrame et le théâtre romantique." In Louis Petit de Julleville, ed., *Histoire de la langue et de la littérature de France*, 8:369–91. Paris: A. Colin, 1899.

Downer, Alan S. "Melodrama." *The British Drama: A Handbook and Brief Chronicle*, pp. 275–79. New York: Appleton-Century-Crofts, 1950.

———. "Players and the Painted Stage: Nineteenth Century Acting." *PMLA* (1946), 61:522–76.

———. "A Preface to Melodrama." *Players Magazine* (January-May 1945), 21, nos. 4–8.

Drummond, A. M., and Richard Moody. "The Hit of the Century: Uncle Tom's Cabin—1852-1952." *Educational Theatre Journal* (December 1952), 4(4):315–22.

Dullin, Charles. "À l'École du mélodrame." *Souvenirs et notes de travail d'un acteur*, pp. 29–32. Paris: Odette Lieutier, 1946.

Eaton, W. P. "Is 'Melodramatic Rubbish' Increasing?" *American Magazine* (December 1916), 82:34.

———. "Why Do You Fear Me, Nellie? The Melodramas of Forty Years Ago." *Harper's* (July 1941), 182:164–70.

Eisenberg, Emanuel. "The Black Hand of Melodrama." *Theatre Arts* (November 1928), 12:825–32.

Estève, Edmond. "Le Père du mélodrame: René-Charles Guilbert de Pixérécourt." *Études de littérature préromantique*. Bibliothèque de la Revue comparée, 5:139–68. Paris: É. Champion, 1923.

Estill, Robin. *"The Factory Lad:* Melodrama as Propaganda." *Theatre Quarterly* (October-December 1971), 1(4):22–26.

Evans, Bertrand. "Gothic Drama and Melodrama." *Gothic Drama from Walpole to Shelley*, pp. 162–76. Berkeley: University of California Press, 1947.

Fargher, Richard. "Victor Hugo's First Melodrama." In D. G. Charlton, J. Gauden, and Anthony H. Pugh, eds., *Balzac and the Nineteenth Century: Studies in French Literature Presented to Herbert J. Hunt, by Pupils, Colleagues and Friends*, pp. 298–310. Leicester: Leicester University Press, 1972.

Farjeon, Herbert. "An Apology for 'Bad' Plays." *Saturday Review* (London), 27 October 1923, pp. 463–65.

Fergusson, Francis. "Melodramatist." In Oscar Cargill, N. Bryllion Fagin, and William J. Fisher, eds., *O'Neill and His Plays*, pp. 271–82. New York: New York University Press, 1961.

Follain, Jean. "Le Mélodrame." In Noel Arnaud, Francis Lacassin, and Jean Tortel, eds., *Entretiens sur la paralittérature*, pp. 32–52. Paris: Plon, 1970.

Frantz, Pierre. "L'Éspace dramatique de *La Brouette du Vinaigrier* à *Coelina.*" *Revue des sciences humaines* (April–June 1976), no. 162, pp.151–62.

Gallagher, Kent G. "Emotions in Tragedy and Melodrama." *Educational Theatre Journal* (October 1965), 17(3):215-19.

Gassner, John. "Drama Versus Melodrama: An Experience of the Thirties." *Dramatic Soundings: Evaluations and Retractions Culled from 30 Years of Dramatic Criticism*, pp. 411–14. New York: Crown, 1968.

Gerould, Daniel. "Gorky, Melodrama, and the Development of Early Soviet Theatre." *yale/theatre* (Winter 1976), 7(2):33-44.

———. "Russian Formalist Theories of Melodrama." *Journal of American Culture* (Spring 1978), 1(1):151–68.

Gibbs, P. "Revival of Melodrama." *Graphic* (13 September 1913), 88:472.

Goff, Lewin. "The Owen Davis-Al Woods Melodrama Factory." *Educational Theatre Journal* (October 1959), 11(3):200-7.

———. "Stars of the 'Ten-Twent-Thirt.'" *Educational Theatre Journal* (May 1954), 6(2):120–28.

González López, Emilio. "El Melodrama expresionista de Valle-Inclán y el extrañamiento dramático." *Estudios Escénicos* (September 1976), no. 21, pp. 95–110.

Gorchakov, Nikolai M. "Historical Melodrama." *Stanislavsky Directs*, trans. Miriam Golding, pp. 277–350. New York: Funk & Wagnalls, 1950.

"The Great Heart of the British Public and the Morality of Melodrama." *Graphic* (1 October 1910), 82:512.

Griffin, Martin. "Melodrama." *Catholic World* (August 1935), 141: 564-68.

Halliday, E. "Curses, Foiled Again!" *American Heritage* (December 1963), 15(1):12-23.

Hamilton, Clayton. "Melodrama, Old and New." *Bookman* (May 1911), 33:309-14.

———. "Melodramas and Farces." *Forum* (January 1909), 41:23-32.

————. "A New Defense of Melodrama." *The Theory of the Theatre.* Consolidated edition, pp. 86–94. New York: Henry Holt, 1939.

Hanratty, Jerome. "Melodrama Then and Now: Some Possible Lessons from the Nineteenth Century." *Review of English Literature* (1963), 4(2):108–14.

Hartog, Willie G. "Guilbert de Pixérécourt: The Father of the Melodrama." *Fortnightly Review* (1920), 108:130–42.

Heilman, Robert Bechtold. "Tragedy and Melodrama: Alternate Forms." *The Iceman, the Arsonist, and the Troubled Agent,* pp. 22–62. Seattle: University of Washington Press, 1973.

————. "Tragedy and Melodrama: Speculations on Generic Form." *Texas Quarterly* (Summer 1960), 3(1):36–50. Reprinted in James L. Calderwood and Harold E. Toliver, eds., *Perspectives on Drama,* pp. 148–62. New York: Oxford University Press, 1968.

Houghton, Norris. "Catastrophes and Violent Deaths: An Enquiry into the State of Melodrama Today." *Theatre Arts* (March 1947), 31:52–55.

Howarth, W. D. "Word and Image in Pixérécourt's Melodramas: The Dramaturgy of the Strip-Cartoon." In David Bradby, Louis James, and Bernard Sharratt, eds., *Performance and Politics in Popular Drama: Aspects of Popular Entertainment in Theatre, Film, and Television, 1800-1976,* pp. 17–32. Cambridge: Cambridge University Press, 1980.

Hughes, Ernest. "Ten-Twent'-Thirt': A Golden Era of Native American Melodrama." *Variety* (10 January 1962), p. 230.

Hüttner, Johann. "Sensationsstücke und Alt-Wiener Volkstheater: Zum Melodrama in der ersten Hälfte des 19 Jahrhunderts." *Maske und Kothurn* (Graz-Wien, 1975), no. 21, pp. 263–81.

James, Louis. "Is Jerrold's Black-Ey'd Susan More Important than Wordsworth's Lucy? Melodrama, the Popular Ballad, and the Dramaturgy of Emotion." In David Bradby, Louis James, and Bernard Sharratt, eds., *Performance and Politics in Popular Drama: Aspects of Popular Entertainment in Theatre, Film, and Television, 1800-1976,* pp. 3–16. Cambridge: Cambridge University Press, 1980.

Jubin, Georges. "Le Théâtre Populaire et le mélodrame." *Revue d'art dramatique* (November 1897), 2(5):972–76.

Kilgarriff, Michael. "Rise and Fall of Melodrama." In Michael Kilgarriff, ed., *The Golden Age of Melodrama: Twelve 19th Century Melodramas,* pp. 15–26. London: Wolfe Publishing, 1974.

Kitto, H. D. F. "New Tragedy: Euripides' Melodramas." *Greek Tragedy: A Literary Study,* pp. 330–69. 3rd ed. London: Methuen, 1961.

Knight, G. Wilson. "Victorian." *The Golden Labyrinth: A Study of British Drama,* pp. 240–76. London: Phoenix House, 1962.

Knowles, Dorothy. "Melodrama." *French Drama of the Inter-War Years, 1918-39,* pp. 287–90. New York: Barnes & Noble, 1968.

Kowzan, Tadeusz. "Le Mythe de la Dame aux Camélias: du mélodrame au mélodramatisme." *Revue des sciences humaines* (April–June 1976), no. 162, pp. 219–30.

Krutch, Joseph Wood. "What Is Melodrama?" *Nation* (9 May 1943), 138:545-46.

Landa, M. J. "The Grandfather of the Melodrama." *Cornhill Magazine* (1925), 59:476-84.

Lawrence, W. "Sensation Scenes." *Gentleman's Magazine* (October 1886), 261:400-5.

——. "Water in Dramatic Art." *Gentleman's Magazine* (June 1887), 262:540-53.

Lewisohn, Ludwig. "On Sentimental Comedy and Melodrama." *The Drama and the Stage*, pp. 29-34. New York: Harcourt, Brace, 1922.

Lima, Robert. "Melodramas for Puppets and Playlets for Silhouettes: Four Stageworks by Valle-Inclán." *Modern Drama* (February 1971), 13:374-81.

Lioure, Michel. "Le Mélodrame." *Le Drame*, pp. 34-9. New York: McGraw-Hill—Armand Colin, 1963.

Lockert, Lacy. "The Greatest of Elizabethan Melodramas." In Hardin Craig, ed., *Essays in Dramatic Literature: The Parrott Presentation Volume*, pp. 103-26. 1935. Reprinted. New York: Russell & Russell, 1967.

Lunacharsky, Anatolii. "Voskreschaya melodrama" [Melodrama Revived]. *Teatr i Iskusstvo* (3 May 1915), 18:304-6.

MacDonald, Cordelia Howard. "Memoirs of the Original Little Eva." *Educational Theatre Journal* (December 1956), 8(4):267-82.

McCormick, John. "Joseph Bouchardy: A Melodramatist and His Public." In David Bradby, Louis James, and Bernard Sharratt, eds., *Performance and Politics in Popular Drama: Aspects of Popular Entertainment in Theatre, Film, and Television, 1800-1976*, pp. 33-48. Cambridge: Cambridge University Press, 1980.

McNeill, W. E. "Beginning of Melodrama." *Queen's Quarterly* (October-December 1916), 24:215-27.

Magarshack, David. "Melodrama: A Stanislavsky Improvisation." *Stanislavsky on the Art of the Stage*, pp. 297-304. New York: Hill & Wang, 1961.

Mancardi, Henri. "Dennis D'Inèz vous parle . . ." *Nos Spectacles: Revue technique d'expression* (June–July 1966), no. 118, pp. 3-4.

Marsan, Jules. "Le Mélodrame et Guilbert de Pixérécourt." *Revue d'histoire littéraire de la France* (15 April 1900), 7:196-220.

Marshal, J. "Non-Stop Show: *The Drunkard*." *Colliers* (27 December 1941), 108:28.

"Master of Melodrama: The Centenary of Thomas Dibdin from Gothic to the Crime Play." *Times Literary Supplement*, 20 September 1920, p. 470.

Matthews, Brander. "Tragedies with Happy Endings." *North American Review* (March 1920), 211:355-65.

Mayer, David. "The Music of Melodrama." In David Bradby, Louis James, and Bernard Sharratt, eds., *Performance and Politics in Popular Drama: Aspects of Popular Entertainment in Theatre, Film, and Television, 1800-1976*, pp. 49-64. Cambridge: Cambridge University Press, 1980.

Meisel, Martin, "Melodrama." *Shaw and the Nineteenth-Century Theatre*, pp. 184-223. Princeton: Princeton University Press, 1963.

Mersand, J. "Melodrama: Theatre Vs. Nazism." *Advocate* (1 July 1938), 94:3.

Meserve, Walter J. "An Age of Melodrama: Sensation and Sententia 1850-1912." In Travis Bogard, Richard Moody, and Walter J. Meserve, *American Drama*, vol. 8 of *The Revels History of Drama in English*, pp. 194-202. London: Methune, 1977.

———. "Drama: A Utilitarian Weapon with a Melodramatic Twist." *An Emerging Entertainment: The Drama of the American People to 1828*, pp. 193-200. Bloomington: University of Indiana Press, 1977.

———. "Moralities, Melodramas, and Farces." *An Emerging Entertainment: The Drama of the American People to 1828*, pp. 263-68. Bloomington: University of Indiana Press, 1977.

Moses, Montrose J. "Considering a Certain Type of Melodrama: The 10, 20, 30." *The American Dramatist*, pp. 292-308. Boston: Little, Brown, 1925.

Motherwell, Hiram. "In Defense of Melodrama." *Theatre Guild Magazine* (January 1931), 8:21.

Nannes, Caspar H. "Politics, Melodrama, and the Nineties." *Politics in the American Drama*, pp. 15-24. Washington: Catholic University Press, 1960.

Nathan, George Jean. "Melodrama as Mirror of Contemporary American Life." *American Mercury* (February 1928), 13:249-50.

Nicoll, Allardyce. "Domestic and Social Drama." *A History of English Drama 1600-1900*. Vol. 5, *Late Nineteenth-Century Drama 1850-1900*, pp. 82-103. Cambridge: Cambridge University Press, 1962.

———. "From Tragedy to Melodrama." *World Drama from Aeschylus to Anouilh*, pp. 342-69. 2d ed. Evanston, Ill.: Harper & Row, 1976.

———. "The Melodrama." *English Drama 1900-1930: The Beginnings of the Modern Period*, pp. 179-214. Cambridge: Cambridge University Press, 1973.

———. "Melodrama." *A History of English Drama 1600-1900*. Vol. 4, *Early Nineteenth-Century Drama 1800-1850*, pp. 100-120. Cambridge: Cambridge University Press, 1966.

Nodier, Charles. Introduction to *Théâtre Choisi de Guilbert de Pixérécourt*. Vol. 1, pp. i-xvi. Paris: Tresse, 1841-43.

Nolan, Paul T. " 'New' Old Melodramas." *Players Magazine* (November 1961), 38(2):53.

O'Hara, Frank H., and Margueritte Bro. "Melodrama." *Handbook of Drama*, pp. 28-34. New York and Chicago: Willett Clark, 1938.

O'Hara, Frank H. "Melodrama with a Meaning." *Today in American Drama*, pp. 142-89. Chicago: University of Chicago Press, 1939; London: Cambridge University Press, 1940.

Otten, Terry. "*Woyzeck* and *Othello:* The Dimensions of Melodrama." *Comparative Drama* (Summer 1978), 12(2):123-36.

Paston, George. "Apostle of Melodrama." *Fortnightly Review* (November 1913), 100:962-75.

Peacock, James L. "Jokes in Melodrama as Symbolic Classifiers." *Rites of Modernization: Symbolic and Social Aspects of Indonesian Proletarian Drama*, pp. 151-66. Chicago: University of Chicago Press, 1968.

——. "Melodramatic Form." *Rites of Modernization: Symbolic and Social Aspects of Indonesian Proletarian Drama*, pp. 126-38. Chicago: University of Chicago Press, 1968.

——. "Melodramatic Stories as Conceptions of Social Action." *Rites of Modernization: Symbolic and Social Aspects of Indonesian Proletarian Drama*, pp. 104-25. Chicago: University of Chicago Press, 1968.

——. "Mobility, Romance, and Melodrama." *Rites of Modernization: Symbolic and Social Aspects of Indonesian Proletarian Drama*, pp. 139-50. Chicago: University of Chicago Press, 1968.

Pilcher, Velona. "Elephant and Castle Melodrama." *Theatre Arts* (June 1925), 9:383-92.

Pitou, Alexis. "Les Origines du mélodrame français à la fin du XVIIIème siècle." *Revue d'histoire littéraire de la France* (June 1911), 18:256-96.

Pixérécourt, Guilbert de. "Dernières réflexions de l'auteur sur le mélodrame." *Théâtre Choisi*, 4:493-99. Paris: Tresse, 1841-43.

——. "Le Mélodrame." *Paris ou le livres des Cent-et-un* (1832), 6:319-52.

Pritchett, V. S. "Blood and Thunder." *New Statesman* (10 December 1965), 70:934.

Quinn, Arthur Hobson. "From Tragedy to Melodrama." *A History of the American Drama from the Beginnings to the Civil War*, pp. 199-219. 2d ed. New York: Appleton-Century-Crofts, 1923.

——. "The Height of Melodrama." *A History of the American Drama from the Civil War to the Present Day*, pp. 100-12. Rev. ed. New York: Appleton-Century-Crofts, 1936.

——. "In Defense of Melodrama." *Bookman* (June 1925), 61:513-17.

Rabault, René. "Eloge du mélodrame et d'un certain théâtre de patronage: Souvenirs de Louis Allard." *Nos Spectacles: Revue technique d'expression* (June-July 1966), no. 118, pp. 17-23.

Rahill, Frank. "America's Number One Hit; It Started a War, and It's Still Making Money." *Theatre Arts* (October 1952), 36(10):18-24.

——. "History of Melodrama." *Theatre Arts* (April 1932), 16:285-94.

——. "The Murder Mystery Melodrama: An Inquest." *Theatre Arts* (March 1941), 25(3):233-42.

——. "When Heaven Protected the Working Girl." *Theatre Arts* (October 1954), 38(10):78.

Raleigh, John Henry. "Eugene O'Neill and the Escape from the Chateau d'If." In John Gassner, ed., *O'Neill: A Collection of Critical Essays*, pp. 7-22. Englewood Cliffs, N.J.: Prentice-Hall, 1964.

Reboul, Pierre. "*Peuple Enfant, Peuple Roi* ou Nodier, mélodrame et révolution." *Revue des sciences humaines* (April-June 1976), no. 162, pp. 247-56.

Reynolds, Ernest. "Tragedy and Melodrama." *Early Victorian Drama: 1830-1870*, pp. 94-137. New York: Benjamin Blom, 1965.

Rhodes, Raymond. "The Early Nineteenth-century Drama." *Library*

(June 1935), 26(1):91-112; (September 1935), 26(2):210-31.

Ritchie, Harry M. "The Influence of Melodrama on the Early Plays of Sean O'Casey." *Modern Drama* (September 1967), 5(2):164-73.

Rolland, Romain. "Quelques genres de théâtre populaire:—Le Mélodrame." *Le Théâtre du peuple: Essai d'esthétique d'un théâtre nouveau*, pp. 130-36. 2d ed. Paris: Albin Michel, n. d.

Rosenberg, James. "Melodrama." In Robert W. Corrigan and James L. Rosenberg, eds., *The Context and Craft of Drama*, pp. 168-85. San Francisco: Chandler, 1964.

Rougemont, Martine de. "Le Mélodrame classique: exercice de poétique rétrospective." *Revue des sciences humaines* (April–June 1976), no. 162, pp. 163-70.

Rowell, George. "The New Drama." *The Victorian Theatre: A Survey*, pp. 31-74. London: Oxford University Press, 1956.

Royer, Alphonse. "Le Mélodrame et ses transformations." *Histoire universelle du théâtre*. Vol. 5, *Histoire du théâtre contemporain en France et à l'etranger depuis 1800 jusqu'à 1875*, pp. 350-431. Paris: Paul Ollendorff, 1878.

Scott, Clement. "Black-Eyed Susan, T. P. Cooke, and Genviève Ward." *The Drama of Yesterday and Today*, 2:142-63. London: Macmillan, 1899.

Sedgewick, Ruth W. "Those Dear Dead Days of Melodrama." *Stage* (August 1935), 12(11):38-41.

Shank, Theodore J. "Theatre for the Majority: Its Influence on a Nineteenth-Century American Theatre." *Educational Theatre Journal* (October 1959), 11(3):188-99.

Shipman, S. "All Life is Melodrama." *Theatre* (April 1919), 29:198.

Smiley, Sam. "Manifestoes in Melodrama." *The Drama of Attack: Didactic Plays of the American Depression*, pp. 91-114. Columbia, Mo.: University of Missouri Press, 1972.

Smith, Harry James. "Melodrama." *Atlantic Monthly* (March 1907), 99:322-28.

Smith, James L. "Introduction." In James L. Smith, ed., *Victorian Melodramas: Seven English, French, and American Melodramas*, pp. vii-xxii. London: Dent, 1976.

Sprague, A. C. "Shakespeare and Melodrama." *Essays and Studies* (1965), 18:1-12.

Stoakes, J. P. "English Melodrama: Forerunner of Modern Social Drama." *Florida State University Studies* (1951), 3:53-62.

Stockbridge, Frank P. "The Most Popular American Drama." *Green Book Magazine* (January 1913), 9:80-87.

Stout, Wesley Wynans. "Little Eva is Seventy-Five." *The Saturday Evening Post* (8 October 1927), 200(15):10.

Strong, C. "Passing of Melodrama." *Green Book Magazine* (September 1912), 8:435-39.

Stuart, Donald Clive. "French Melodrama. French Romantic Drama."

The Development of Dramatic Art, pp. 485-513. D. Appleton, 1928. Reprinted. New York: Dover, 1960.

"Successful Melodrama." *World To-day* (April 1911), 20:412.

Sypher, Wylie. "Aesthetic of Revolution: The Marxist Melodrama." *Kenyon Review* (1948), 10:431-44.

Thackeray, W. M. "French Dramas and Melodramas." *Works.* Vol. 22, *The Paris Sketch Book* (1840), pp. 283-304. London, 1910-11. Reprinted. New York: AMS Press, 1968.

Thomas, Michèle. "Les Personnages types du théâtre française: IV. Du Mélodrame au drame de situations ou d'aventures." *Nos Spectacles: Revue technique d'expression* (June-July 1966), no. 118, pp. 8-12.

Thomasseau, Jean-Marie. "Le Mélodrame et la censure sous le Premier Empire et la Restauration." *Revue des sciences humaines* (April-June 1976), no. 162, pp. 171-82.

Thompson, Alan R. "Melodrama and Tragedy." *PMLA* (1928), 43:810-35.

Tomashevsky, Boris. "Frantsuzkaya Melodrama nachala XIX veka" [French Melodrama of the Beginning of the Nineteenth Century]. *Poetika* (1927), 3:55-82. Reprinted. Munich: Wilhelm Fink, 1970.

Travers, S. "The Melodrama Satirized in Theatrical Parody." *Modern Language Notes* (May 1946), 61:299-305.

Trussler, Simon. "A Chronology of Early Melodrama." *Theatre Quarterly* (October–December 1971), 1(4):19-21.

Tung, Constantine. "The Hidden Enemy as Villain in Communist Chinese Drama." *Educational Theatre Journal* (October 1973), 25(3):335-43.

Tyrell, Henry. "Drama and Yellow Drama." *Theatre* (1904), 4:192.

Ubersfeld, Anne. "Les Bons et le méchant." *Revue des sciences humaines* (April–June 1976), no. 162, pp. 193-203.

Van Tieghem, Philippe. "Littérature et société: le mélodrame 1790-1820." *Littérature, Rhythme, Enseignement: Netherlands Verenining tot Bevordering van de Studie van het Frans*, pp. 7-17. La Haye: Vn Goor Zonen, 1966.

Watson, Ernest Bradlee. "Acting of Melodrama." *Sheridan to Robertson: A Study of the Nineteenth-Century London Stage*, pp. 349-79. Cambridge, Mass.: Harvard University Press, 1926.

Wegefarth, W. D. "Decline of the Lurid Melodrama." *Lippincott's Magazine* (September 1911), 88:427-28.

Whitfield, George J. N. "Sentiment and Melodrama." *Introduction to Drama*, pp. 99-131. 2d ed. New York: Oxford University Press, 1963.

Williams, Raymond. "Social Environment and Theatrical Environment: The Case of English Naturalism." In Marie Axton and Raymond Williams, eds., *English Drama: Forms and Development. Essays in Honor of Muriel Clara Bradbrook*, pp. 203-23. Cambridge: Cambridge University Press, 1977.

Woodbridge, Homer E. "Beyond Melodrama." In Oscar Cargill, N. Bryllion Fagin, and William J. Fisher, eds., *O'Neill and His Plays*, pp.
307-20. New York: New York University Press, 1961.
Woods, A. H. "Producing Spine-thrillers." *Literary Digest* (10 August
1912), 45:222-23.

2. Melodrama and the Novel

Axton, William. "Melodramatic Narrative." *Circle of Fire: Dickens' Vis-
ion & Style & The Popular Victorian Theatre*, pp. 219-61. Lexing-
ton, Ky.: University of Kentucky Press, 1966.
Barzun, Jacques. "Henry James the Melodramatist." *The Energies of
Art*, pp. 230-47. New York: Vintage, 1962.
Bogel, Fredric V. "Fables of Knowing: Melodrama and Related Forms."
Genre II (1978), 11(1):83-108.
Brooks, Peter. *The Melodramatic Imagination: Balzac, Henry James,
Melodrama, and the Mode of Excess*. New Haven: Yale University
Press, 1976.
———. "The Melodramatic Imagination: The Example of Balzac and
James." In David Thorburn and Geoffrey Hartman, eds., *Romanti-
cism: Vistas, Instances, Continuities*, pp. 198-220. Ithaca, N.Y.:
Cornell University Press, 1973.
Cawelti, John G. "The Best-Selling Social Drama." *Adventure, Mystery,
and Romance: Formula Stories as Art and Popular Culture*, pp. 260-
95. Chicago: University of Chicago Press, 1973.
———. "Melodrama." *Adventure, Mystery, and Romance: Formula Stor-
ies as Art and Popular Culture*, pp. 44-47. Chicago: University of
Chicago Press, 1973.
Chase, Richard Volney. "A Note on Melodrama." *The American Novel
and Its Traditions*, pp. 37-41. Garden City, N.Y.: Doubleday, 1957.
Coolidge, Archibald. "Dickens and the Philosophic Bases of Melodrama."
Victorian Newsletter (Fall 1961), no. 20, pp. 1-6.
Davis, Earle. "Tears and Terror: The Technique of Sentiment and Sensa-
tion." *The Flint and the Flame: The Artistry of Charles Dickens*,
pp. 75-91. Columbia: University of Missouri Press, 1963.
Eliot, T. S. "Wilkie Collins and Dickens." *Selected Essays, 1917-1932*,
pp. 409-10. New York: Harcourt, Brace, 1950.
Frye, Northrop. "Dickens and the Comedy of Humors." In Ian Watt,
ed., *The Victorian Novel*, pp. 47-69. London: Oxford University
Press, 1971.
James, Louis. "The Urban Mentality: Literature and the Life of the
Towns." *Fiction for the Working Man, 1830-1850*, pp. 146-70.
London: Oxford University Press, 1963.
Lary, N. M. "The Idiot: Melodrama and Ideal." *Dostoevsky and Dick-
ens: A Study of Literary Influence*, pp. 51-84. London: Routledge
& Kegan Paul, 1973.

Levy, Leo. *Versions of Melodrama: A Study of the Fiction and Drama of Henry James.* Berkeley: University of California Press, 1957.

Morley, Malcolm. "Dickens's Contribution to *Sweeney Todd.*" *Dickensian* (Spring 1962), 58:92-95.

Perry, John O. "The Popular Tradition of Melodrama in Dickens." *Carleton Miscellany* (Spring 1962), pp. 105-10.

Prendergast, Christopher. *Balzac: Fiction and Melodrama.* London: Edward Arnold, 1978.

Purton, Valerie. "Dickens and 'Cheap Melodrama.'" *Etudes Anglaises* (1975), 28:22-26.

Sucksmith, Harvey Peter. "Melodrama, Sensation, and Suspense." *The Narrative Art of Charles Dickens*, pp. 289-301. Oxford: The Clarendon Press, 1970.

Thro, A. Brooker. "An Approach to Melodramatic Fiction: Goodness and Energy in the Novels of Dickens, Collins, and Reade." *Genre II* (Fall 1978), 11(3):359-74.

Tortel, Jean. "Le Roman populaire." In Noel Arnaud, Francis Lacassin, and Jean Tortel, eds., *Entretiens sur la paralittérature*, pp. 53-117. Paris: Plon, 1970.

3. TV and Film

Arlen, Michael J. "On Giving the Devil His Due." *New Yorker*, 12 March 1979, p. 126.

Belton, John. "Souls Made Great by Love and Adversity: Frank Borzage." *Monogram* (1971), 3(4):20-24.

Beylie, Claude, and Max Tessier. "Mélo, mon beau souci." *Cinéma 71* (Paris), (December 1971), no. 161, pp. 41-59.

Cahiers de la Cinémathèque. "Pour une histoire du mélodrame du cinéma." no. 28, (1979).

Colina, E., and D. D. Torrez. "Ideología del melodrama en el viejo cine Latino-americano." *Cine Cubano* (1972), nos. 73-75, pp. 14-26.

Dona, H. "Pe locul initii: melodrama de ce?" *Cinema* (Romania), (November 1975), 13:9.

Durgnat, R. E. "Ways of Melodrama." *Sight and Sound* (August-September 1951), 21(1):34-40.

Elsaesser, Thomas. "Tales of Sound and Fury." *Monogram* (1971), 3(4): 2-16.

Fassbinder, Rainer Werner. "Imitation of Life: Uber die Filme von Douglas Sirk." *Fernsehen + Film* (February 1971), 9(2):8-13.

Fell, John. "Dissolves by Gaslight." *Film and the Narrative Tradition*, pp. 12-36. Norman: University of Oklahoma Press, 1974.

Henry, M. "Le Fra Angelico du mélodrame." *Positif* (July-August 1976), nos. 183-84, pp. 13-19.

Kleinhans, Chuck. "Notes on Melodrama and the Family under Capitalism." *Film Reader* (February 1978), 3.

Limmer, Wolfgang. "Das Leid der gefallen Götter: Über die hermetische Welt des Melodramas." *Fernsehen + Film* (February 1971), 9(2):13-15.

Legrand, G. "Du 'boulevard du crime' à 'cinecitta' (Mélodrame et film à costumes dans le cinéma italien)." *Positif* (February 1977), no. 190, pp. 42-50.

Lloyd, Peter. "Some Affairs to Remember." *Monogram* (1971), 3(4): 17-19.

McConnell, Frank. "The World of Melodrama: Pawns." *Storytelling and Mythmaking Images from Film and Literature*, pp. 138-99. New York: Oxford University Press, 1979.

Michałek, B. "Blaski i nędze melodramatu." *Kino* (May 1975), 10:46-53.

———. "Melodramat jako zaklęcie." *Kino* (March 1977), 12:58-9.

Morse, David. "Aspects of Melodrama." *Monogram* (1972), 4:16-17.

———. "Every Article on the Cinema Ought to Talk about Griffith." *Monogram* (1971), 3(4):16-17.

Nichols, Bill. "Revolution and Melodrama: A Marxist View of Some Recent Films." *Cinema* (1970), 6(1):42-7.

Oldenburg, J. "Kosmorama Essay: Melodramaets stor foelelsner." *Kosmorama* (February 1974), 20:134-42.

Piotrovsky, Adrian. "K Teorii Kino-zhanrov" [Theory of Cinema Genres]. In B. M. Eichenbaum, ed., *Poetika Kino*, pp. 143-70. Moscow-Leningrad: Kinopechat', 1927.

Poix, Georges. "Le Mélodrame." *La Cinématographie Française* (7 December 1963), no. 2042, pp. 20-1.

Pollock, Griselda, Geoffrey Nowell-Smith, and Stephen Heath. "Dossier on Melodrama." *Screen* (Summer 1977), 18(2):105-19.

Torrez, D. D., and E. Colina. "El melodrama en la obra de Luis Buñuel." *Cine Cubano* (1973), pp. 156-64.

Vardac, A. Nicholas. "The Melodrama: Cinematic Conceptions and Screen Techniques." *Stage to Screen: Theatrical Method from Garrick to Griffith*, pp. 20-67. New York: Benjamin Blom, 1968.

———. "Melodrama: The Photoplay." *Stage to Screen: Theatrical Method from Garrick to Griffith*, pp. 180-98. New York: Benjamin Blom, 1968.

Vesselo, Arthur. "Villains, Heroes, and Hobgoblins." *Sight and Sound* (Spring 1938), 7(25):14-16.

Wide Angle. Special issue on melodrama forthcoming in 1980.

(The bibliography was prepared by David Nicholson and Daniel Gerould.)

About the Authors

ALBERT BERMEL teaches theater and cinema at Lehman College and the Graduate Center of City University of New York. He is author of *Contradictory Characters, Artaud's Theatre of Cruelty, One-Act Comedies of Molière, Three Popular French Comedies*, and *The Plays of Courteline.*

CHRISTOPHER BOND is an actor, playwright, and director who has worked in British regional theater for a number of years in Liverpool and with Peter Cheeseman at the Victoria Theatre at Stoke-on-Trent, where he created and acted in his modern version of *Sweeney Todd.* His play about women in the Paris Commune, *Scum* (written in collaboration with his wife Claire Luckham) was performed by the radical feminist group The Monstrous Regiment in 1976 which toured throughout Britain. During the 1979 season he directed Bill Morrison's *Flying Blind* at the Harold Clurman Theatre in New York.

PETER BROOKS is the author of *The Novel of Worldliness* and *The Melodramatic Imagination* as well as a number of articles on the practice and theory of narrative in the nineteenth century. He serves on the editorial boards of *Partisan Review* and *Yale French Studies.* He is Chester D. Tripp Professor of Humanities and director of the Division of the Humanities at Yale University.

DANIEL S. BURT was until recently a graduate student in English at New York University where he completed a dissertation entitled "Melodrama, Sensation, and Suspense in the Victorian Novel." He is currently at work on a number of articles on Victorian fiction.

PIERRE-HENRI CAMI (1884–1958), a popular French humorist, writer, and graphic artist was author of some sixty volumes. A specialist in black humor dealing with funerals, undertakers, and corpses and a master of puns and pure nonsense, Cami was admired by the surrealists. Several of his best known sketches, such as *Sons of the Three Musketeers* and *Nights in the Tour de Nesle*, parody Alexandre Dumas père and the conventions of melodrama.

NOËL CARROLL is a professor of film at New York University and a co-editor of *Millennium Film Journal.*

COZETTE DE CHARMOY is a graphic artist and author of numerous books, including *Fatrada* and *Fatrada 2*, *The True Life of Sweeney Todd*, *The Colossal Lie*, *Voyages*, *Nose*, and *François et le Dodo*. A native of London, she has exhibited in Montreal, Ottawa, Geneva, Milan, Paris, Venice, as well as in England.

ALEXANDRE DUMAS père (1802–1870) was a prolific author of novels and plays, writing (either alone or in collaboration) more than 100 comedies and dramas. Dumas was the first important French writer of black heritage. His father, a general in Napoleon's army, was the son of a marquis and a Haitian slave. *The Tour de Nesle*, which played for a record-breaking 800 performances at its premiere in 1832, was Dumas's reworking of a play by Frédéric Gaillardet, with whom he eventually fought a duel over the question of authorship.

JOHN L. FELL is the author of *Film and the Narrative Tradition*, *Film an Introduction*, and *A History of Films*, as well as a variety of articles about film, theater, literature, and jazz music. He is a member of the *Film Quarterly* editorial board, an associate editor of *Cinema Journal*, and a professor at San Francisco State University.

DANIEL GEROULD is a playwright, translator, and writer on modern drama who teaches theater and comparative literature at the Graduate Center of the City University of New York. He has published three volumes of translations of Stanisław Ignacy Witkiewicz as well as a critical study of the Polish author. His dramatic fable, *Candaules, Commissioner*, was played at the Chelsea Theatre and elsewhere in the United States and abroad. He has translated Eugène Ionesco's *Variations on the Same Theme: Journeys Among the Dead* for the recent production at the Guggenheim Museum, and his modern version of the Gothic melodrama, *The Castle Specter*, is to be premiered in Baltimore in April 1981.

MEL GORDON is a professor of drama at New York University and associate editor of *The Drama Review*.

STANLEY KAUFFMANN teaches at the Yale School of Drama and the City University of New York Graduate Center. The film critic of *The New Republic* and theater critic of *Saturday Review*, he is author of *Before My Eyes: Film Criticism and Comment* and *Albums of Early Life*.

MICHAEL KIRBY has written and directed *Eight People, Revolutionary Dance, Photoanalysis, Identity Control, Double Gothic*, and *Incidents in Renaissance Venice* for the Structuralist Workshop, an off-off-Broadway theater. He is also the author of *Happenings, The Art of Time*, and *Futurist Performance;* has exhibited sculpture and other visual works involving photographs in the United States, Europe, and South America; is the editor of *The Drama Review*, and a professor in the graduate drama department, School of the Arts, New York University.

ALMA H. LAW is a resident scholar at the Russian Institute of Columbia University in New York City. She has published numerous articles and translations in the field of Russian theater and drama and has lectured at many universities and research institutes.

JAMES LEVERETT, a theater critic, has contributed regularly to the *Soho Weekly News* and *Other Stages*. His articles have appeared in *Theater*, the *Theatre Journal*, and *Performing Arts Journal* for which he is a contributing editor. At present, he is director of Literary Services at Theatre Communications Group and editor of "Plays in Process," TCG's new script distribution project.

ANDRÉ DE LORDE (1871-1942) was the most successful and celebrated writer for the Grand Guignol theater during its golden period in the first two decades of the twentieth century. De Lorde published more than a dozen collections of horror plays, such as *The Theatre of Fear*, *The Theatre of Death*, and *The Theatre of Madness* and frequently collaborated with the noted psychologist Alfred Binet on pseudoscientific thrillers set in clinics and hospitals.

MARTIN MEISEL is the author of *Shaw and the Nineteenth-Century Theater;* essays on Dickens, Scott, the Pre-Raphaelites, and British and American drama; and *Realizations*, a book on narrative and picture in nineteenth-century fiction, painting, and the theater. He has held Guggenheim, ACLS, and Huntington Library fellowships and an appointment to the Institute for Advanced Study in the Humanities, University of Edinburgh. He is past chairman of the doctoral program in theater and film at Columbia University and is currently chairman of the department of English and comparative literature.

ZDZISŁAW NAJDER is one of the editors of the Polish literary magazine *Twórczość* and a literary historian and critic who writes about twentieth-century fiction. He has taught and lectured at several American universities. His work on Joseph Conrad includes *Conrad's Polish Background* and a forthcoming biography of the novelist. He is also the editor of a complete edition of Conrad's works in Polish translation.

DAVID NICHOLSON has taught and produced plays at The Riverdale Country School, Bronx, New York, for the past fifteen years and has published several pieces on the teaching of drama and theater. His current project, a Ph. D. dissertation on the fairy tale in modern drama, earned the Milton Brown Dissertation Award in the Arts (1980-81) at the Graduate School of the City University of New York. His article, "Gozzi's *Turandot:* A Tragicomic Fairy Tale," appeared in *Theatre Journal* in December 1979.

RENÉ-CHARLES GUILBERT DE PIXÉRÉCOURT (1773-1844) was the author of comedies, comic operas, vaudevilles, and 120 melodramas. A cultivated and learned playwright, Pixérécourt took the art of melodrama seriously and wrote critical treatises about its principles. It was for educational purposes that the "Prince of Melodrama" chose to compose works for an illiterate mass audience.

JULIA PRZYBOŚ teaches at Lafayette College in Pennsylvania. She wrote her doctoral dissertation at Yale University on early nineteenth-century French melodrama and she has been the recipient of a Mellon Postdoctoral Fellowship to continue her studies of Russian as well as of French melodrama. She also writes about French fiction, most recently about

Villiers de l'Isle-Adam's "Vera" for *The French Review*.

STEPHEN SONDHEIM is a composer-lyricist active in the American musical theater. He has written the lyrics for *West Side Story*, *Gypsy*, and *Do I Hear a Waltz?* and the music and lyrics for *A Funny Thing Happened on the Way to the Forum*, *Anyone Can Whistle*, *Company*, *Follies*, *A Little Night Music*, *The Frogs*, *Pacific Overtures*, and *Sweeney Todd*. He is currently working on a new musical, *Merrily We Roll Along*, based on a play by Kaufman and Hart, with book by George Furth, to be directed and produced by Hal Prince in the Spring, 1981.

WYLIE SYPHER is lecturer on English and coordinator of graduate programs in English at Simmons College. Among his most notable books are *Rococo to Cubism in Art and Literature*, *Four Stages of Renaissance Style*, and *Loss of the Self*; his most recent book is *The Ethic of Time: Structures of Experience in Shakespeare*.

VLADIMIR VOL'KENSHTEIN (1883–1974) was a Soviet playwright (*Spartacus*, *The Death of Lincoln*, and *Pope Joan*) and a major theoretician of drama, author of the influential *Dramaturgy*, first published in 1923 and now in its eighth edition. While retaining his basic structural analyses, Vol'kenshtein soon abandoned the use of formalist terminology and diagrams.

ABOUT THE STAFF

JEANINE PARISIER PLOTTEL spent a sabbatical year as a National Endowment for the Humanities fellow. She teaches French at Hunter College, writes about literature, and publishes the *New York Literary Forum*. Her publications include a book about Paul Valéry and numerous articles on Surrealism, Raymond Roussel, psychoanalysis, autobiography, and poetics.

JANE ROGERS TONERO has a graduate degree from Ohio State University where she was a Scholar. She was an editor at Crowell Collier and Grolier, a manager of research and development at McGraw-Hill, and vice president and editor for Mason/Charter Publishing Company.

CECIL GOLANN received her Ph. D. degree in Greek and Latin from Columbia University and spent a year in Italy on a Fulbright grant. Since then she taught English and the classics at Hunter College, worked as an editorial researcher for NBC-TV, and served on the editorial staff of Macmillan Publishing Company.

DOLLY STADE does free lance copy editing, proofreading, and indexing for many university presses.

ADELE GREEN has a degree in French from Wellesley College and from the Sorbonne University, Paris. She writes book reviews and articles of literary and horticultural interest. Her articles have appeared in various publications, including *The New York Times* and *Horticulture*.

LAWRENCE KRITZMAN teaches French at Rutgers and has written widely about the French Renaissance. He is the guest editor of the *New York Literary Forum* volume on *Fragments: Incompletion and Discontinuity*.

MARGOT VISCUSI has just resettled in New York after many years in Paris where she was a writer and an editor for a number of well-known authors.

ACKNOWLEDGMENT: Grateful acknowledgment is made to Robert Q. Lovett, Ruth O'Donnell, Peter Goslett, and Darko Suvin for their assistance in the preparation of this volume.

Index

Production and Design: Editorial and Graphic Services